Planning

Creative

Literacy Lessons

Also available:

The Primary English Encyclopaedia: The Heart of the Curriculum (2nd edition)
Margaret Mallett
1–84312–372–x

Unlocking Creativity: Teaching across the Curriculum
Robert Fisher and Mary Williams (eds)
1–84312–092–5

The Literate Classroom (2nd edition)
Prue Goodwin (ed.)
1–84312–318–5

Teaching Literacy: Using Texts to Enhance Learning
David Wray
1–85346–717–0

Grammar Survival: A Teacher's Toolkit
Geoff Barton
1–84312–343–6

Other titles in the Informing Teaching series:

Literacy Moves on: Using Popular Culture, New Technologies and Critical Literacy in the Primary Classroom
Janet Evans (ed.)
1–84312–249–9

Literacy through Creativity
Prue Goodwin (ed.)
1–84312–087–9

Creativity in the Primary Curriculum
Russell Jones and Dominic Wyse (eds)
1–85346–871–1

Drama and English at the Heart of the Curriculum: Primary and Middle Years
Joe Winston
1–84312–059–3

Making Connections in Primary Mathematics
Sylvia Turner and Judith McCullouch
1–84312–088–7

Improving Learning in Secondary English
Geoff Dean
1–84312–146–8

Planning Creative Literacy Lessons

 David Fulton Publishers

David Fulton Publishers Ltd
The Chiswick Centre, 414 Chiswick High Road, London W4 5TF

www.fultonpublishers.co.uk

First published in Great Britain in 2005 by David Fulton Publishers.

10 9 8 7 6 5 4 3 2 1

British Library Cataloguing in Publication Data
A catalogue record for this book is available from the British Library.

David Fulton Publishers is a division of Granada Learning, part of ITV plc.

ISBN 1 84312 280 4

Typeset by RefineCatch Ltd, Bungay, Suffolk
Printed and bound in Great Britain

Contents

Notes on contributors

All the contributors are members of the Primary English Team in the Faculty of Education at Canterbury Christ Church University College.

Dr Andrew Lambirth is a Principal Lecturer in Education and is currently Publication Mentor for the Primary Education Department and leader of the Primary English Team. Andrew taught in primary schools in Peckham and Bermondsey, South-east London before going into higher education. He has published widely in the field of primary English teaching and has particular interests in writing, poetry, popular culture and education, and the politics of literacy.

Rebecca Austin is a Senior Lecturer in Education. She is currently Programme Director for the part-time undergraduate degree in Primary Education. Rebecca has taught and co-ordinated a number of the English undergraduate and postgraduate programmes in primary English. For over a decade she taught in a number of primary schools across the three key stages in and around Kent.

Dr Hazel Bryan is Director of the Masters Framework and Programme Director for the MA in Educational Studies at Canterbury Christ Church University College. Her doctoral work explored the impact of the National Literacy Strategy on teacher identity and teacher professionalism.

Justine Earl is a Senior Lecturer in Education. She was a primary school teacher and then an LEA adviser before joining Canterbury Christ Church University College. Justine teaches across the range of Initial Teacher Education courses in literacy and music. She also teaches on Masters programmes and is involved in co-ordinating Modern Foreign Language teaching on postgraduate programmes. Justine is also currently undertaking a number of research and development projects in Kent.

Kathy Goouch is a Senior Lecturer who divides her teaching, research time and publications between early years education and literacy. She is currently pursuing research into the nature of early years professionals and their interactions with children. Recent publications include *Birth to Three Matters: A Review of the Literature*, in collaboration with Tricia David and Sacha Powell, and *Creativity and Writing: Developing Voice and Verve in the Classroom*, with Teresa Grainger and Andrew Lambirth.

Teresa Grainger is a Reader in Education at Canterbury Christ Church University College, where she leads the Masters programme in Language and Literacy. Teresa was President of the United Kingdom Reading Association, now UKLA (2001–2), and Editor of the journal *Reading Literacy and Language* (1998–2003). She has published widely on storytelling, drama, poetry and writing, most recently editing *The RoutledgeFalmer Reader in Language and Literacy* (2004) and co-writing *Creativity and Writing: Developing Voice and Verve in the Classroom* (2005, Routledge) with colleagues Andrew Lambirth and Kathy Goouch.

Sue Hammond is a Senior Lecturer in Primary Education teaching both English and early years education. She has previously taught in a range of primary schools across the Foundation Stage, KS1 and KS2. Her school career spanned a period of 20 years, throughout which she promoted an enthusiasm for literature and for empowering children as writers. She has been involved in several classroom-based research projects related to literacy development and continues to work with children and teachers on a regular basis.

Angela Pickard is a Senior Lecturer in Primary Education where she works on undergraduate, postgraduate and continuing professional development programmes. She lectures in English, Early Years and Physical Education, particularly dance. Her research interests include role-play areas and drama, creative and choreographic processes, physical literacy and dance. She is co-author of *Drama: Reading, Writing and Speaking Our Way Forward* (2004, UKLA)

Carol Precious is a Senior Lecturer in Education. Carol was a head teacher in a Kent infants' school before joining Canterbury Christ Church College. She has been involved in a number of research projects including 'Writing in the Air', with Kent County Council, that studied reception children composing oral stories. Carol has interests in early years and the connection between popular culture and literacy.

Yvonne Stewart is currently a Principal Lecturer in Education. Most of her teaching career has been in primary schools in south London where she had extensive experience as a language co-ordinator before joining the advisory service, specialising in effective primary practice. Her senior management roles in schools included the headship of a vibrant, multicultural school. After living overseas,

Yvonne worked for Hampshire Education Authority as a literacy consultant before moving to Canterbury Christ Church College where, among other responsibilities, she teaches English within the Faculty of Education. Yvonne is committed to promoting inclusive, interactive and experiential learning in English and across the curriculum.

Dr Vivien Wilson is the Head of Partnership at Canterbury Christ Church University College. Although much of her work concerns school-based training for Initial Teacher Education students, she continues to teach on primary English courses, has a special interest in oracy and drama, and started her career in teacher education as a drama lecturer. Prior to working in higher education she was a teacher of English and drama in a secondary school and then became an advisory teacher in drama and creative arts, working mainly in primary schools.

Planning creative literacy lessons

Andrew Lambirth

Planning Creative Literacy Lessons offers teachers and student teachers ideas to help conceptualise and implement an effective planning model and inspire literacy learners. All of the authors in this book have been primary classroom teachers who understand the demands of the curriculum and the needs of the children. They have all experienced the planning and implementation of the National Literacy Strategy (DfEE 1998) and have been providing teachers and student teachers with ideas and strategies for utilising the best elements of the Framework for many years. This book is an opportunity to document this work and establish publicly, effective ways to teach English in what might be described as a 'post-Strategy' teaching world; by which I mean an environment in which there is now greater freedom for teachers in classrooms to plan and implement activities based on their own knowledge of the needs of their children. Each author puts forward his/her own tried and tested ideas for planning creative literacy lessons based on a view of how best to exploit the Units of Work model that is becoming a popular framework for planning.

In this chapter I will introduce the background and the principles to the particular philosophy that underpins the book's approach to the teaching of literacy. I will explain how a need has developed for this book, which re-establishes the creative and more autonomous professional position of the teacher of literacy. The chapter will briefly examine the political background of a changing English curriculum and how teachers are now rekindling a belief in their own individual talents as well as finding ways to encourage the individual creative capabilities in the children they teach. The notion of creativity in schools is evaluated as part of education policy and I explain how planning for creative work through a unit of work model can manifest itself.

Teachers as professionals and people

Since the advent of the National Curriculum (DES 1988) and, more significantly, the introduction of the National Literacy Strategy (DfEE 1998), the activity of

Primary English teachers in their classrooms has changed greatly. There have been many debates among educationalists and politicians as to how successful the recent National Strategies have been. What actually constitutes success is often the sticking point within these debates. Is it the raising of standards as evidenced by government created tests, or is it the less measurable effects on children's attitudes to reading and writing, or an improvement in creative approaches to pedagogy by teachers? Among the more indisputable negative results for teachers have been the sharp increases in workload; greater surveillance by line managers, head teachers and inspectors; and a significant reduction in teacher autonomy. In addition, teachers' 'capacity to shape and popularise curricular practice' (Jones 2003 : 136) has been undermined by a shift from a focus on the *process*, to a *measurable product*, of teaching and learning. 'Much of the emphasis in the NLS training materials has been on subject knowledge and content in the curriculum rather than pedagogy, so that teaching styles have only been superficially addressed' (Mroz *et al.* 2000 : 387).

Arguably, the English curriculum, as conceptualised in the National Literacy Strategy Framework for teaching (DfEE 1998), is to be delivered, regardless of cultural specificity, to 'pupils' as an autonomous package called 'literacy' in an environment of teacher and pupil compliance. The implementation of the Strategy has attempted to dispense with the professional questions about the process of teaching and learning that were alive between teachers in earlier decades, replaced by a standard prescriptive programme. Yet teachers and educationalists have always known that establishing prescribed, 'indisputable' answers to teaching questions will only bring forth more questions.

Within an atmosphere of almost, at times, educationally servile conditions, there is a danger, as a teacher, to feel that there is a need to remove one's personal and individually determined contribution. The role of the teacher might well be construed as just a deliverer of learning, mediated by a strategy document. The personal significance of the individual teacher's background, experience, culture and character might even appear redundant, inappropriate and unwanted. Consequently, there are real dangers that classrooms become sterile – devoid of human character, warmth and the individual personality of the teaching professional. The urgency for pace and the dogged determination to deliver learning objectives, stressed in the Strategy documents (ibid.), mould the nature of literacy lessons away from the encouragement of a sense of community and a sharing of culture and interest, formed by a sustained dialogue between teachers and children.

There is a belief that the place of a teacher's individual character is key in constructing an atmosphere of fruitful teaching and learning. This belief is based on a view that effective teaching must have the 'X factor' of artistic input that can only be supplied by galvanising the creative capacities of individual teachers. The main aim of this book, therefore, is to help rekindle the 'X factor' and to encourage teachers to be artists in their own classrooms (Grainger *et al.* 2005).

Literacy teaching for children in the here and now

The generation of creative activities for the teaching of English forms part of the *process* of teaching and learning. Creativity, therefore, has fallen foul of the ferocious determination by government agencies to ensure that schools produce measurable learning *product* effectively by the use of unquestionable methods. The suppression of creative process models of teaching in schools reflects the vision of contemporary government:

> The role of government in this world of change is to represent a national interest, to create a competitive base of physical infrastructure and human skills. The challenge before our party . . . is not to slow down and so get off the world, but to educate and retrain for the next technologies, to prepare our country for new global competition, and to make our country a competitive base from which to produce the goods and services people want to buy. (Blair 1995 : 20)

The drive to 'prepare' Britain for the world market has clearly impacted upon the educational policies of successive governments over the last 15 years or so. The overall thrust has been to give children and young people the skills they need for the market-place – to be able to compete in changing technological conditions and environments – offering the capacity for interchangeable skills and increased 'labour power'. This is the philosophy of a 'developmental state' (Lee 2001) determined to prepare for 'tomorrow'.

Primary schools are, of course, concerned with preparing children for what will come; but ignoring the present may have an adverse effect upon the future. A method of schooling that puts too much emphasis on what society wants children to become conceptualises children not as 'human beings' existing in the here and now, but more as 'human becomings' (ibid.). The only way to achieve full human being status is by adopting the roles prepared for them by the socialisation processes of society. For New Labour this appears to be a young person's adaptability as workers within the global market and undermines the possibility of individual creative capacities and critical approaches to learning: 'Adulthood and full humanity is the achievement of independence, confidence and certainty through the acquisition of knowledge of one's place in society' (ibid.: 39).

Yet we know that the genuine process of education involves recognition of children as social human beings (Geekie *et al.* 1999), where learning depends upon the negotiation of meanings and where those who lead the learning also follow (Wood 1992). Children will not respond well as learners if they are regarded simply as recipients of supplementation. The ideas in this book aim to involve children in a dialogue that constructs meaning through a social process and where the learning is often a mutual accomplishment (Geekie *et al.* 1999). *Planning Creative Literacy Lessons* celebrates children as capable, creative human beings *now*, whose own experiences are already rich and diverse and worthy of exploration. Children are young human beings who bring a unique perspective to all our understandings of the world. The authors of this book look for ways to encourage this dialogue within a community of learners where an active critical approach to texts, information and events is key.

Creativity

Creativity is back! Indeed, it has been back on the educational agenda since the late 1990s but carrying a significantly different meaning. In the past there have been those who have seen 'creativity' in education as a term that signified 'progressive' teachers' and educators' 'lack of commitment to raising standards and passing on established values' (Jones 2003: 165). Now it seems that creativity, business, the workplace and the 'knowledge economy' can live together. *All Our Futures* (DfEE 1999), the report from the government National Advisory Committee, developed this opinion that creativity was not just important to the arts, but also to science, politics and business. It defines creativity as 'imaginative activity fashioned so as to produce outcomes that are both original and of value' (ibid.: 29).

Recently, teachers have begun to see a sanctioning of the possibilities of encouraging creativity in the classroom as a means of promoting the cause of strengthening the economy. The loosening of constraints upon the activities in literacy lessons provides evidence that the need for adaptability to suit all children has begun to be recognised. Elements of the National Literacy Strategy's Literacy Hour that were initially seen as vital – adherence to the 'clock', for example – are now not stressed by strategy managers and Ofsted inspectors as much as they once were. Teachers are beginning to be encouraged (Frater 2000) to conceptualise the National Literacy Strategy Framework as more of a menu for teaching strategy ideas than as rigid directives and a 'blueprint'.

Excellence and Enjoyment (DfES 2002) added to the creativity boom. Arguably, this document came as a response to the concerns of established members of the creative community and groups of parents who were becoming increasingly alarmed by the creatively arid state of the teaching and learning in classrooms under the current model. Alongside the prescribed condition of state school curricula, private schools continued to offer a wider breadth of curriculum – music, languages and visual arts. This approach was becoming increasingly attractive to middle-class parents who, if necessary, were prepared to create an exodus from state schooling if a richer curriculum was not offered to their children (Ball 2003).

So we have an agenda that includes creativity (for whatever reasons). There are opportunities to be exploited, by offering children creative work in literacy as well as in the rest of the curriculum. Indeed, cross-curricular planning initiatives are becoming a popular means of offering a wider breadth of learning opportunities.

Shallcross (1981, cited in Craft 2000) listed some key characteristics of the creative mind:

- Openness to experience
- Independence
- Self-confidence
- Willingness to take risks
- Sense of humour or playfulness
- Enjoyment of experimentation
- Sensitivity
- Lack of a feeling of being threatened
- Personal courage
- Unconventionality
- Flexibility
- Preference for complexity
- Goal orientation
- Internal control
- Originality
- Self-reliance
- Persistence
- Curiosity
- Vision
- Self-assertion
- Acceptance of disorder
- Motivation
- Inclination to the off-beat.

Of course, all these traits could be applied to the world of work and the economy, but they are also essential ingredients for making a person free, alive and aware of the potential control and manipulation by others. They are also elements that help fashion the artist or the scientist with the power to improve the world and the experience of living.

I hope *Planning Creative Literacy Lessons* will be a welcome addition to arguments for a creative approach to literacy teaching that help to foster the traits of a creative mind. The authors of this book construct activities that reflect children's entitlement to express and build upon their own creativity. This is accomplished by exposure and engagement with quality models of creative work in the form of a rich variety of texts, reflecting a range of cultures and artistic traditions across the ages and up to the present day. There is an implicit belief in all the chapters of this book that this way of teaching is imperative for the healthy condition of a child's inner and outer world, both now and in the future.

A lifetime of literacy and an 'hour of literacy'

This book builds upon the premise that literacy, and the learning about literacy, does not begin and end within an hour. Literacy is not just a label for a lesson in school. The Literacy Hour, as advocated in the National Literacy Strategy (DfEE 1998), is not enough. Indeed, literacy and the multiple events that make up literate behaviour – the use of language for thought, communication and social interaction – never ends. The Literacy Hour, or any literacy sessions, should be seen as simply an opportunity to explore and learn from some of the multicultural artefacts of language. From this perspective and starting point teaching and learning can begin.

Units of work

The chapters in *Planning Creative Literacy Lessons* offer a rationale and ideas for teaching literacy in units of work, based upon the individual author's own view of how best to facilitate this. This way of planning integrates speaking and listening, reading and writing. Each of these modes cannot be successfully taught in isolation; each feeds upon the other. Reading requires knowledge of how language works both semantically and syntactically (Graham and Kelly 1997), acquired through our social interaction with the world and culture. Equally, the ability to write needs the experience of reading to provide models of the function, structure and power of written texts (Vygotsky 1978; Barrs and Cork 2001; Grainger *et al.* 2005). It is for these reasons that literacy, taught through units of work, is such an effective model.

A unit of work is generally seen as a planned period of study of a particular written genre that lasts for two, three, four or more weeks. Drawing on the National Literacy Strategy's list of genres, taught spirally over six years, it integrates speaking and listening, reading and writing in an exciting package that allows children the opportunity to immerse themselves in a range of text-types that leads to writing in these forms. It utilises key aspects of the Literacy Strategy (DfEE 1998) – the Literacy Hour, shared and guided reading, independent time and plenaries. It can work with all types of writing – poetry, non-fiction genres, picture-books, scripts and so on. The Primary Strategy for Literacy supports this way of planning. Indeed, the DfES has published exemplification material (www.standards.dfes.gov.uk) that provides examples of how this can be accomplished across the age range to cover the learning objectives at text, sentence and word level.

Planning Creative Literacy Lessons builds upon the units of work model, offering richer, more varied texts and teaching strategies. The authors have accomplished this by incorporating in each chapter what I have called a 'flavour'. The flavour is the focus of the chapter. It may be the way the author has used particular means to teach about their chosen genre. For example, Teresa Grainger (Chapter 4) uses drama as her 'flavour' to teach about short story forms; Carol Precious (Chapter 7) uses popular culture to teach about myths and legends; and Rebecca Austin (Chapter 5) chooses multi-model representation to teach about non-fiction. Each 'flavour' highlights particular concerns, issues or methods that affect the teaching of the chosen genre. Of course, each can be transferred to a whole range of other text-types, but each of the authors chooses one to demonstrate its effects. It is hoped that practising teachers and student teachers may be able to see the relevance of these particular 'flavours' and allow them to influence their own plans for a whole range of text-types. Many of the 'flavours' are instrumental in encouraging active and creative engagement with the literature.

Planning a unit of work – big objectives first

In planning a unit of work a teacher may wish to follow the following steps.

Step 1 – Choosing the text-type and duration of the unit

Starting with the big objectives first, a decision is made as to which text-types are to be taught over the coming half-term. Once this has been decided, teachers will need to plan how long each text-type unit of work will last. For example, traditional tales may need up to three weeks. There should be no hard-and-fast rule about the duration of a unit. Indeed, there is no reason why a unit could not last four weeks. What is important is that there is adequate time for children to really get to know the genres they are learning about. A week, in most cases, would be too short. The length of the unit will, in turn, determine the next unit of work's duration.

Step 2 – Planning a final piece of work

Still planning the big objectives and not yet needing to look at the strategy's text-, sentence- and word-level objectives, a central piece of work that will close the unit needs to be chosen. Depending upon the genre to be studied, this may be an oral retelling by groups or individuals, a performance of poems, a class anthology of poems for the school library, a subverted traditional tale presented in a class book, a class display, and so on. This sets a good target to aim for and will offer a rich means to assess the children's understanding of the genre as well as a number of other key assessment opportunities.

Step 3 – Collecting and selecting the texts

Again, without the need to examine the small objectives of the National Literacy Strategy, collect the books and other texts that will be required to immerse the children in this text-type. These will be essential to demonstrate quality models of the genre, produced by leading writers in the field of children's literature. They can also be used as a way to promote great books. This is one of the great perks of teaching, to be able to select the texts we love to read and share with children. We are fortunate to be living in a golden age of children's literature. There is a wealth of wonderful writing to choose from – fiction, non-fiction and poetry. In addition, teachers can also draw on popular culture to find examples of generic forms that are part of the curriculum. Recent work (Marsh and Millard 2000; Dyson 1997) has demonstrated how popular culture can motivate children to engage with the curriculum and how popular culture texts often contain classic genres that can be used as 'cool' models. These will include film, televisual texts, computer games, comics, magazines, game cards, and so on. The development of technology also means that stories can now be written using video equipment and animation software as an alternative to pens and pencils. A text can take on many forms, and this can be reflected in the classrooms that are 'in tune' with the modern world.

Step 4 – Smaller objectives

The objectives from the Strategy document can now be examined. It is important to remember that these learning objectives were designed to teach *about* the texts. When the National Literacy Strategy was first introduced, many publishers clamoured to produce schemes of work containing extracts of texts designed to enable teachers to teach the prescribed objectives. These texts were used blandly to teach the objectives – precisely the inverse of what should be happening. The objectives teach *about* whole texts, but the texts are not offered solely to enable the teaching of the objectives. Our aim is to teach about the texts that we are offering as part of a coherent unit of work that studies a particular genre. Published extracts fail to model the reading process and experience that whole texts can offer. Literacy hours using extracts present an inappropriate message about what teachers are trying to achieve with the children. Literacy lessons cannot be only about the covering of learning objectives, and texts are not there just to serve this purpose. The main message must be the joy and immense pleasure that literature can bring. At this stage (Step 4) it is a good time to sort and select the appropriate objectives for the whole texts to be presented – of course, where there is no match, these ill-fitting objectives can be saved until a later date. Indeed, many teachers are now recording the objectives that have been taught retrospectively, i.e. going back over the unit and highlighting where the objectives have been covered. This way offers a refreshing change of emphasis away from lessons controlled by checklists.

Step 5 – Checking the range of creative activities

Now is the time to ensure that, where appropriate, the unit presents opportunities for some of the following creative methods – drama, paired and group discussion, storytelling, play and playful activities. Ensure that there are popular culture artefacts available and ICT, that independent reading and writing form part of the weeks, that shared and guided reading is integrated, that there is time to immerse children in the text-types before writing begins, and that progression is evident as the unit moves on.

Step 6 – Enjoy the teaching and learning process

From reading into writing – shaping the unit

Immersion

Research has shown how the best writing comes from those who have experienced high-quality models of written texts and have had the opportunity to engage with their meanings in various ways (Frater 2000; Barrs and Cork 2001). The unit of work planning model provides time for children to be *immersed* in the text-type being studied. In a three-week unit, the first week (or week and a half) can be spent familiarising the children with the text-type. This can happen in 'shared' and 'guided' reading, story times, discussion with the whole class, small groups or pairs, or drama and role-play activities that encourage children to enter the world of the texts. The 'independent' part of the hour can be tailored to complement shared time by further imaginative activities, but, this time, independent of the teacher. *Planning Creative Literacy Lessons* describes many immersion activities that allow the children to understand the genre of writing that is the focus of the unit. It is during the first part of the unit that teachers will also have the opportunity to discuss the features of these texts and demonstrate their strengths and weaknesses.

Research (Medwell *et al.* 1998) shows how effective literacy teachers highlight meaning when teaching about texts. The immersion period during a unit of work encourages individual meaning-making. Within the classroom-community of learners the individual opinions of readers are always valued. 'Creative reading' occurs when readers feel free to explore texts by drawing on their own knowledge of life, other stories and personal experiences. The community shares their opinions of the characters, situations and events and is then given the opportunity to discuss how the authors have been successful, or not. This will entail analysis of sentence- and word-level features of the text in a way appropriate to the age group of children in the class – but the personally constructed meanings come first. The nature of these discussions makes them perfect for the immersion period of a unit of work.

Tools, advocated in the National Literacy Strategy (DfEE 1998), tried and tested years before the Strategy's advent by skilful teachers (Barrs and Browne 1990), like shared and guided reading, are perfect for immersion activities. No longer

9

restricted by 'the clock' they can provide experiences tailored to the needs of the children and to the creative ideas of the teacher.

'The reader in the writer' – moving on to writing

The work of Barrs and Cork (2001) demonstrated that 'reading and writing are two halves of the same process: that of mastering written language' (p. 42). The unit of work model combines reading and writing in order to provide key experiences for apprentice writers:

> In developing their own resources, an apprentice writer's main assets will therefore be their reading and their growing sense of how experienced writers work, which skilful teaching will help them to develop. As children become aware of themselves as both writers and readers they begin to learn to 'read like writers' and 'write like readers'. (ibid.)

Immersion in a range of texts over extended periods in units of work offers these essential resources. As the unit goes on, the nature of the work in the Literacy Hour and beyond begins to change. The emphasis is moved from 'deconstruction' (discussion and engagement around the texts) to 'construction' of the text-type. Activities begin to be aimed at writing of the focus text-type – experimenting with the emotional engagement, structures, styles, themes and content they have been learning about in the first half of the unit. Teachers start to encourage children to work towards the final piece of work that was planned at the start of the unit.

Shared and guided reading moves on to shared and guided writing. These are superb teaching tools that allow the teacher time to model the different stages of the writing process in a collaborative way. 'Shared' can really *mean* 'shared' as the children are invited to contribute their ideas and knowledge in joint construction of a text. *Planning Creative Literacy Lessons* provides many examples of how these tools can be utilised to establish a workshop of apprentice writers.

Guided writing provides the means to step up the intensity of the collaboration between writers and assist them in becoming more 'confident managers of narrative' (Barrs and Cork 2001 : 211). As well as enabling the teaching of the more technical features of writing by, for example, the collaborative editing of a text. The unit ends with the production of the piece of work that was planned at the beginning of the unit. This may be a class anthology of the children's work, a performance, a display of work, individual books for the class book area, and so on.

Phonics and units of work

The teaching of phonics is still given high priority by the Primary Strategy for Literacy. It is worth, briefly, discussing how phonics teaching might look with a unit of work. There is no time here to debate the wisdom of maintaining the unique high status that policy-makers give to this area of language knowledge, but phonics, as an essential skill, does need to be learned. The question remains: 'how is this best done?' Research has shown (Medwell *et al.* 1998) that effective teachers of literacy embed the teaching of phonics within the context of real texts. For example, exposure to poetry implicitly teaches children about correspondence of letter to sound (Bryant and Bradley 1985). In addition, teachers will often take the opportunity that good literature brings to highlight this correspondence while reading and discussing it. The units of work model offers exciting opportunities for incorporating phonics within the context of the texts that are being taught. Enjoying a book and sharing meanings will lead on to an examination of how authors have been so successful – studying words, their sounds, spelling and their impact will become a vital part of the teaching.

The National Primary Strategy for Literacy, however, advocates a playful, but decontextualised, approach to the teaching of phonics. *Progression in Phonics* (DfEE 2000) provides games that teach key objectives from the Framework (DfEE 1998) at word level. Originally, these games were to be played at the beginning of literacy hours in Foundation and Key Stage 1 classrooms. The debate as to the effectiveness of this form of teaching will continue. In the meantime, using the National Literacy Strategy's methods will not undermine the prospect of rich and motivating literacy hours. Any decontexualised work that is deemed to be worthwhile can be carried out relatively quickly at the beginning of a literacy hour before the fun begins. It is even possible to teach phonics in this way outside the Literacy Hour at another part of the day in order not to waste valuable time. Word-level work can then be woven into shared and guided reading times to complement and enrich the exploration of the texts that are being taught.

The book

Planning Creative Literacy Lessons has sanctioned the authors to present a model of planning that has been tried and tested in primary classrooms. The authors approach their chapters individually, drawing on their own personal passions and interests. With the exception of Chapter 2 on the learning environment, each author offers a unit, or units of work, that incorporates immersion in their chosen genre and the opportunities for the children to author their own texts based upon the structures, themes and creative potential that the text-type provides. The authors have deliberately included some genres that have been neglected by books about literacy until now; for example playscripts, science fiction, short stories, novels and multi-model texts. They have also included unusual ways of teaching more familiar genres, such as poetry, traditional tales and myths and legends. The units include ways for teachers to flourish creatively by allowing them the space to model key aspects of aesthetic activity. Many of the authors use drama, role-play and storytelling as devices to entice creative language work. Teachers demonstrating the power of deep creative play is a very powerful component of the units that are offered in this book.

The individual chapters pinpoint particular year groups or key stages within the Primary phase of education, but we hope that teachers can adapt the ideas to suit the children and age group for whom they are responsible. The authors have deliberately set out *not* to be prescriptive, but model examples of activities that demonstrate the rich potential of operating within units of work. The different approaches that the authors take reflect the principles behind the book – the liberation of the professional teacher to make decisions that will promote creative excellence tailored to the children in the class.

Places and spaces: the right environment for literacy

Kathy Goouch continues the introduction to the book that this chapter began by establishing the kind of environment needed for effective literacy teaching and learning to take place. Kathy describes and justifies the essential environment – both physically and psychologically – for fruitful literacy activity to occur. She argues passionately for an environment that offers opportunities for the genuine creative potential of children to be released. This is an essential opening chapter as it describes research that forms the backbone around which the ideas in this book rest. It shows the context within which children can thrive as creative meaning-makers in school.

From ludic to lyrical language

Poetry as a means of liberating creativity in Early Years classrooms is the focus of Sue Hammond's contribution (Chapter 3). Here the chapter is flavoured by a concentration on work with very young children. What is most striking about the activities Sue describes is the prevalence of spontaneity and the way she allows her children to lead her in their adventures with poetry that they all clearly enjoyed. Sue also contributes to the debate around the teaching of phonics with young children and assesses the importance of poetry to word-level work.

Planning with short stories

Teresa Grainger (Chapter 4) provides a dynamic unit of work on short stories. Teresa is well known for her work with drama and storytelling, and for this chapter she adds the flavour of drama to short stories. This genre, officially, is not studied until Key Stage 3, but short stories are, of course, a central part of much of the story writing that children are asked to do in the primary school. This chapter combines wonderfully rich ideas with sound justification for the activities that are offered.

'You have been personally selected . . .': navigating non-fiction, negotiating modes: a critical response to real life

In Chapter 5, Rebecca Austin introduces us to the 'flavour' of utilising texts that combine written language with sound, music and images as means to teach about non-fiction texts. Rebecca uses multi-model texts with Key Stage 1 children in a school in the Medway area of Kent. Drawing on the research in the field of textual multimodality, Rebecca works alongside teachers to develop ways to teach about non-fiction texts while exploiting the children's already wide knowledge of these forms of texts.

Less is more: working with playscripts in Key Stage 2

Viv Wilson discusses the teaching of playscripts in Chapter 6. She highlights the potential and the pitfalls of working with this special form of text. Often when I talk to teachers about teaching English, it is playscripts that often cause them the most concern. Finding good resources and ideas for working with them is often the problem. Viv flavours her chapter with performance and process drama techniques, borrowing her methods from exciting theatrical playwriting traditions like collaborative improvisation-led writing.

The Greek times? Revisiting Greek mythology in relation to children's popular culture

Chapter 7 concentrates on myths and legends. Carol Precious utilises children's interests in popular culture to motivate interest by drawing on children's love of the themes and events that occur in modern texts and asking children to mix ancient with modern in the form of a magazine. The utilisation of children's affinity with playful subversion through popular culture flavours Carol's chapter.

Using novels in the classroom – the whole story

Yvonne Stewart (Chapter 8) concentrates on the teaching of novels, flavouring her work with the principle of using whole texts as a means of drawing children into the worlds that books offer and the introduction of 'literature circles'. The immersion of children in novels is a constant factor throughout her unit of work, which embeds the listening and the reading of whole novels as a class or in small groups.

The supremacy of story: traditional tales and storytelling

In Chapter 9, Angela Pickard demonstrates the power of traditional tales, flavoured by the use of storytelling for Key Stages 1 and 2. Angela makes a persuasive argument for the natural combining of the teaching of traditional tales with storytelling and offers a powerful model for a unit of work.

Using picture-books with older readers

Justine Earl is passionate about picture-books (Chapter 10). She flavours her contribution by making a robust argument for their use throughout the primary school years, into Years 5 and 6 and beyond. Justine provides many examples of exciting work in this genre and highlights the potential for children's intellectual engagement through the exciting ideas she offers.

Long ago, in a galaxy far away . . .

The book concludes with an exciting introduction to science fiction in the primary classroom. Hazel Bryan (Chapter 11) enthusiastically takes her readers on a journey of discovery of the origins of the science fiction genre and the importance of its themes. Flavouring her contribution with a cross-curricular approach, Hazel plays with the use of light and shadow and the magic of cinema to attempt to induce awe and wonder over our place in the universe.

References

Ball, S. J. (2003) *Class Strategies and the Education Market: The Middle Classes and Social Advantage.* London: RoutledgeFalmer.

Barrs, M. and Browne, A. (eds) (1990) *The Reading Book.* London: Centre for Literacy in Primary Education (CLPE).

Barrs, M. and Cork, V. (2001) *The Reader in the Writer: The Links Between the Study of Literature and Writing Development at Key Stage 2.* London: Centre for Literacy in Primary Education (CLPE).

Blair, T. (1995) 'The power of the message'. *New Statesman,* 29 September.

Bryant, P. and Bradley, L. (1985) *Children's Reading Problems.* Oxford: Basil Blackwell.

Craft, A. (2000) *Creativity across the Primary Curriculum: Framing and Developing Practice.* London: RoutledgeFalmer.

Department for Education and Employment (DfEE) (1998) *The National Literacy Strategy, Framework for Teaching.* London: DfEE.

Department for Education and Employment (1999) *All Our Futures: Creativity, Culture and Education.* Report of the National Advisory Committee on Creative and Cultural Education. London: The Stationery Office.

Department for Education and Employment (DfEE) (2000) *Progression in Phonics: Materials for Whole Class Teaching.* London: DfEE.

Department for Education and Skills (2002) *Excellence and Enjoyment.* London: DfES.

Department of Education and Science (DES) (1988) *English in the National Curriculum Key Stage 1 & 2.* London: HMSO.

Dyson, A. Haas (1997) *Writing Superheroes: Contemporary Childhood, Popular Culture and Classroom Literacy.* New York: Teachers' College Press.

Frater, G. (2000) 'Observed in practice, English in the National Literacy Strategy: some reflections'. *Reading,* 34(3), November, 107–12.

Frater, G. (2001) *A Survey of Effective Practice in Writing at Key Stage 2: Essential Extras.* London: Basic Skills Agency.

Geekie, P., Cambourne, B. and Fitzsimmons, P. (1999) *Understanding Literacy Development.* Stoke on Trent: Trentham Books.

Graham, J. and Kelly, A. (eds) (1997) *Reading Under Control: Teaching Reading in the Primary School.* London: David Fulton.

Grainger, T., Goouch, K. and Lambirth, A. (2005) *Voice and Verve: Children's Creativity in Writing.* London: Routledge.

Jones, K. (2003) *Education in Britain: 1944 to the Present Day.* Cambridge: Polity Press.

Lee, N. (2001) *Childhood and Society: Growing Up in an Age of Uncertainty.* Birmingham: Open University Press.

Marsh, J. and Millard, E. (2000) *Literacy and Popular Culture: Using Children's Culture in the Classroom.* London: Paul Chapman Publishing.

Medwell, J., Wray, D., Poulson, L. and Fox, R. (1998) *Effective Teaching of Literacy*. University of Exeter.

Mercer, N. (2000) *Words and Minds: How We Use Language to Think Together*. London: Routledge.

Mroz, M., Smith, F. and Hardman, F. (2000) 'The discourse of the Literacy Hour'. *Cambridge Journal of Education*, 30(3), 379–90.

Shallcross, D. J. (1981) *Teaching Creative Behaviour: How to Teach Creativity to Children of All Ages*. Englewood Cliffs, NJ: Prentice-Hall.

Vygotsky, L. (1978) *Mind in Society: The Development of Higher Psychological Processes*. Cambridge, MA: Harvard University Press.

Wood, D. (1992) 'Teaching talk', in Norman, K. (ed.) *Thinking Voices: The Work of the National Oracy Project*. London: Hodder & Stoughton.

Places and spaces: the right environment for literacy

Kathy Goouch

This chapter is divided into three sections. The first argues that the physical spaces and places for learning, while often seen to be a key influence on the pedagogical choices of teachers, have significant historical and cultural origins and may be used to define the nature of learning that takes place within their structures. The second section discusses some theoretical notions that underpin pedagogical choices in relation to literacy environments. The final argument looks at ideas relating to the professionalism of educators and the material environment that makes and shapes learning in individual classrooms.

Landscapes for learning

The organisation of schools and classrooms represents the physical and intellectual conditions where children's learning potential may be met. It is the responsibility of those who are accountable for children's education to design and construct contexts to inspire, nourish and sustain learning. Traditionally, learning was thought to occur through the straightforward transmission of knowledge from adult to child, and the environment represented this understanding in the austere design of schools. The nature of knowledge to be passed from generation to generation was not in question and schools were sites dealing in certainties: the certainty of how children should behave; the certainty of relationships between educator and child and the certainty of what was to be learned and how it was to be taught. At the beginning of the century, Dewey tells a story of how material evidence denotes the purposes to which schools were put by society:

> Some few years ago I was looking about the school supply stores in the city, trying to find desks and chairs which seemed thoroughly suitable from all points of view – artistic, hygienic, and educational – to the needs of the children. We had a great deal of difficulty in finding what we needed, and finally one dealer, more intelligent than the rest, made this remark: 'I am afraid we have not what you want. You want something at which the children may work; these are all for listening.' That tells the story of traditional education . . . We put before the mind's eye the ordinary schoolroom, with its

rows of ugly desks placed in geometrical order, crowded together so that there shall be as little moving room as possible, desks almost all of the same size, with just space enough to hold books, pencils, and paper, and add a table, some chairs, the bare walls, and possibly a few pictures, we can reconstruct the only educational activity that can possibly go on in such a place. It is all made 'for listening'. (Dewey 1915 : 31)

Some classrooms remain housed in schools of Victorian design (Figure 2.1), the age when children were expected to listen, to learn from instruction, by rote and without distraction from the outside world. The austerity of such architecture, representing a construction of childhood from another age, continues to influence some pedagogies in the twenty-first century. During the 1960s and 1970s new primary school buildings took on a radically different design. Single-storey blocks, often built around a central hall space and containing open-plan classrooms, were created to be used flexibly in an era immediately before and after Plowden (CACE 1967), when new pedagogical and curriculum challenges were presented to teachers. The influences on pedagogy and the constructions of effective contexts for learning are, however, considerably more complex than the bricks and mortar of the school building. Despite decades of reforms in education, it is still often possible, decades later, to see how some teachers' use of the physical classroom space indicates that they are using the classroom in 'ways consistent with the traditional image of teaching embedded in the classroom design' (Bissell 2004 : 29). Our understandings of the concept of 'classroom' remains locked inside the architecture, or the memory of the architecture, of buildings in which we ourselves, as teachers or policy-makers, were once educated. There appears to be an almost romantic association made to very traditional school classrooms, with the smells and the sounds of chalk dust, paint and ink interconnected with sentimental notions of childhood.

Figure 2.1

Consequently, this traditional and somewhat conventional use of space, with the tools of the 'instructor', now often including whiteboards rather than blackboards, and a teacher's desk positioned at the front of a gathering of desks, suggests an idea of school where the 'transmission of worlds through words' (Lankshear and Knobel 1997 : 135) is still the prime function. And the 'worlds' to be transmitted to the waiting children are those selected, often abbreviated and interpreted by the teacher. Such landscapes have been confirmed and compounded in recent years by the introduction of the National Literacy and Numeracy Strategies (DfEE 1998) and the enforced compliance to this national pedagogical reform where whole-class instruction and whole-class response and performance are the central components. And yet many have documented the need for schooling to keep pace with new worlds, new ideas and new ways of thinking (Kress 1997; Bearne and Kress 2001; Lankshear 1997) rather than revert to the simple transmission of existing and fixed understandings.

Of course, how we as a society conceive childhood and children will always be evidenced by the provision we make for them:

> Understandings or 'constructions' of childhood have been reflected in our treatment of children in society, and the assumptions on which the dominant constructions of child-hood are founded are nowhere more obviously exposed than in a country's preschools and schools. (David *et al.* 2000 : 18)

and if we look closely at the world of education observed by Dewey, quoted earlier, there are discernible traces to be found, still, in current provision. Indeed Pring's debate in relation to 'the place of learning' creates a distinction between a view of school as 'monastery or market place' (Pring 2004). He argues that education has become 'big business' and that 'the personal needs of the learner give way to the imperatives of ensuring certain outcomes' (ibid.: 69). Hence, as the dominant discourse currently used is that of audits and commerce (Nutbrown 1998) then:

> teaching becomes the delivery of a curriculum, no longer an engagement with other minds; that curriculum becomes a commodity to be bought and sold, not a range of activities that are differently engaged in by pupils with their distinctive agendas. (Pring 2004 : 68)

The language used, dominant constructions of childhood and the dominant discourse of the time become visible in the material provision in educational spaces and places. How we view children and what is to be taught clearly influence pedagogical choices and thus what we put in place for children to experience.

Questions being asked about pedagogy now, at the beginning of this new century, are neither new nor innovative but are still, as in Dewey's text conceived more than a hundred years ago, primarily centred upon the nature and content of what is to be learned as well as the ways in which learning can effectively take place. The catalyst for the current quest for change, however, appears to be focused upon the apparent dearth of creativity and creative practices in primary classrooms; a cause for concern ranging across 'monastries and market places' as the need for innovation, energy, excitement, individuality and imagination is required in every branch of society as the means for change and progress.

What are we looking for, then, in 'classrooms', in classroom practice, in the choices and preferences made in relation to spaces allocated for literacy learning? Do we want children to have ideas, to dream, to imagine, to play, to create, to symbolise, to taste possibilities, to be tantalised by stories, to delight in words and worlds, to make choices, to tumble around in other authors' and poets' creative spaces and to shape creative places and spaces for themselves? Do we want children also to have control of language and its use, to make appropriate choices in relation to language, to craft and shape language for both functional and creative uses? Above all, do we want children to be *interested* in language and literacy, *motivated* to read, write, talk and listen and *excited* by the idea of sharing ideas? If these are core aims for children today, then creating appropriate land-scapes within which this is all possible must be the central responsibility of all teachers, and geometrically ordered 'ugly desks' made for listening simply will not do.

The planned environment, then, reflects the educational ideologies of those controlling education. One possibility for using the built environments for education is to create a space for learning that prepares and shapes children for the next stage, the adult world; but another, perhaps more attractive, possibility is that of providing spaces and places within which children can shape and construct their own worlds and thereby develop a sense of self as a creator, with control over their environments, rather than being controlled *by* the environment. The danger of the first possibility is that of preparing children for worlds already known, the world of today or, sadly, sometimes, yesterday. The excitement of the second is that children have access to and belong to new worlds, new possibilities and potentials, and new ways of thinking and working which must be nourished and encouraged if it is to be sustained. One of the challenges embedded within this is also that power relations inevitably change, with the emphasis on learners and processes of learning rather than on teachers and what can be transmitted, and accompanying political and social implications need to be overtly considered.

Influences from research on pedagogy

A literate environment for children of all ages requires knowledge and under-standing of the ways in which children develop and learn. Of course, all children do not learn in the same way. Nevertheless, there are key environmental elements that require careful thought and planning. For example, the choice between arranging desks in serried rows facing the front of a classroom or in groups where children face each other represents an understanding of how children most effec-tively think and learn. It would be naïve to believe that schools or classrooms or arrangements of learning spaces are in any sense neutral or devoid of cultural or philosophical influences. How desks are arranged, or whether or not to have desks at all, or how many desks to have, are all decisions that are influenced by cultural and professional cross-disciplinary decisions. Sociologists might argue that:

> What something is, what it does, one's evaluation of it – all this is not naturally preordained. It is socially constructed. This is the case even when we talk about the institutions that organize a good deal of our lives. Take schools, for example . . . (Apple 2004 : 180)

Combined with such views, developmental psychologists argue that knowledge itself is socially constructed and that children actively, and in the company of others, construct their knowledge of the world which is 'shaped by their dialogues with the people around them' (Mercer 2004 : 11). The work of Vygotsky (1978) and, later, Bruner (1986) provides support for the idea that knowledge is con-structed by children 'rather than acquired by a process of accretion' (David *et al.* 2003) and that learners map together new knowledge with existing knowledge to make sense of their worlds. Both also emphasise the effect that other learners and supporting adults have in helping children to learn, and they depict learning as being most effective as a social act rather than as a lone investigation. This model of learning indicates the necessity of designing and managing learning contexts with social groups in mind rather than individual recipients of fragments of knowledge. It also requires opportunities for active learning which, again, has enormous implications for space and organisation that reflect this need.

As well as the social nature of learning, much research currently reflects the significance of culture in learning. Before school age, young children are inducted into literacy practices that have cultural significance in the home. It is within the social contexts of homes that young children's literacy development emerges and grows, and Kress discusses the ways in which 'as children are drawn into culture, "what is to hand", becomes more and more that which the culture values and there-fore makes readily available' (Kress 1997 : 13). Consequently, in cultures and com-munities where print has great significance, children soon become encultured into sign-making acts. In homes where families 'live with the litter of literacy' (Harste *et al.* 1984 : 140) children quickly become accustomed to using this 'cultural tool kit' (ibid.: 15) for purposes of expression. In families, the affective nature of literacy experiences and their everyday contextual occurrence engage children naturally in the use of appropriate materials and space for the activity. So, before school, for many children, literacy acts are often emotionally positive experiences, supported by appropriate resources, scaffolded by parents, carers or siblings, part of a social and cultural experience and therefore both engaging and self-perpetuating. At home then, 'literacy and literate outcomes [are] processes to be experienced, to be placed in relation to other literacy events and practices rather than seen as unchanging objects of study or unquestioning reverence' (Bearne 1995 : 4).

Recreating such a context within a classroom community may not be realistic. However, constructing and contriving opportunities for children to engage in reasonably authentic literacy practices, in the company of others and guided and supported by educators, is a real possibility. This requires a creative and committed view of the potential learning spaces provided in schools, combined with a clear view of the theories and principles that underpin such planning. The choices seem to be between a rather arid and narrow construction of the purposes of education and schooling, i.e. to confer the knowledge we (as educators) own to the next generation *or* rather more expansive notions of teaching and learning, relating to processes rather than performance and with a broader view of the nature of knowledge and the function of schools in society.

Great emphasis is currently placed upon the work of neuroscientists which has come to the attention of the popular press as well as professionals in the field of education. The work of, for example, Susan Greenfield has been particularly influential in debates about when and how the brain develops, critical periods of learning and, specifically, the effect of environments on brain development:

> If you put a rat in an enriched environment where there's [sic] things to play with, then even in adult rats you can see there is far more branching of the brain cells than in a control group. That's because even in adults, the more you stimulate the brain, the more it develops the potential for making connections . . . Its worth pointing out that an under-stimulating environment for children, given what we know about the human brain, would be ethically questionable. (Greenfield 2002 : 21)

Sadly, however, this argument has been used to promote 'hot housing' of very young children. A more measured response has been to understand the research in terms of explaining the difference between 'normal' and 'deprived' environments, rather than implying that 'special enriching experiences . . . beyond those that they experience in everyday life' are necessary for brain development (Blakemore 2002 : 29). Blakemore's interpretation is that 'there is a threshold of environmental richness below which a deprived environment could harm a [baby's] brain' (ibid.). The key evidence from neuroscience that is particularly useful to educators in planning appropriate environments for learning seems to be that:

- the cells that constitute the brain will proliferate at the staggering rate of 250,000 per minute;
- young brains are exceptionally 'plastic' so they are shaped by experience; and
- stimulation for the brain is provided by conversations, experiences and encounters, irrespective of material wherewithal.

(adapted from Greenfield 2000 and David *et al.* 2003)

There is much to learn from the messages and implications from the combined disciplines of sociology, developmental psychology and neuroscience in relation to environments for literacy learning. Evidence across the research now appears to suggest that knowledge is socially constructed; culturally significant literacy practices engage children; effective learning practices are social in nature; and a rich environment, encounters, interactions and experiences have positive effects on developing brains.

The field of education also carries a weight of research evidence to support the construction of effective literacy environments, and over recent years there has been a wealth of significant research studies carried out in education environments that need to be carefully reviewed by practitioners when considering appropriate spaces for children as they learn to be literate. Among these are those researchers debating the significance of talk environments in literacy learning (e.g. Wells 1986, 2003; Cordon 2000; Mercer 2000); the impact of drama upon literacy learning and development (e.g. Grainger 2002; Grainger and Cremin 2001) and the importance of play in emerging and developing literacy (e.g. David 1999; David et al. 2000; Whitehead 1997, 1999) – all of which must influence how educators define and shape the learning environment. Two recent and highly significant research studies make very strong recommendations in relation to literacy environments. The work of Medwell et al. (1998) in Effective Teachers of Literacy was a project funded by the TTA and carried out as a rigorously researched study of the nature of effectiveness and the influences upon those teachers so defined. In the section of the report relating directly to 'classroom literacy environments', attention was drawn to the appropriateness and range of literacy resources; the definition and labelling of key areas for learning; the functional nature of displays, items and resources; the existence of dramatic play areas combined with effective support materials; and, finally, the organisation, management and everyday use of the environment in children's learning. A significant overall conclusion drawn from the study was that 'the classrooms of the effective teachers were distinguished by the heavy emphasis on literacy on the environments which had been created' (ibid.: 78). Alongside these very specific and visual elements of the classroom environment, another significant, but perhaps rather more ephemeral, finding of the research was in the emphasis that the 'effective teachers' of literacy placed upon the creation and recreation of meaning. These teachers were found to place literacy learning in an appropriate context for the learners and to make real and explicit connections for them. The authors described this as a 'functionalist approach' and defined it as the most significant finding of the research. Clear connections may be made between these findings and the work of others cited earlier who argue for a culturally related curriculum and for the provision of authentic, affective and meaning-based opportunities for learning.

The second research project was based around the connectedness of reading and writing – The Reader in the Writer (Barrs and Cork 2001). This was a year-long study mapping and assessing children's writing development from activities centred upon the study of literature and focusing particularly on the use of two core texts. The importance of the findings from this project become clear as the researchers report 'the activities in school, detailed empirical observations of classroom contexts and project activities, teachers' pedagogies and, particularly, children's reading of quality literature' (Meek Spencer 2001 : 20). The quality of the material resources, and the literature used in this research, are particularly worth noting here. Meek Spencer, in her preface, discusses the work of competent authors as 'making worlds for [children] to enter and explore, where they meet the deep matters of meaning making; being and becoming, love and loss, doubt and despair, the psychological realities presented as people and events' (ibid.: 15). Currently, as most teachers are aware, books written and illustrated for children are numerous, and vast numbers are of a very high quality in relation to the criteria expressed above. World-making, childhood events, children's perceptions of the world, children's dreams and fantasies can become part of the literacy environment made and shaped for and with children through the use of literature and the uses to which literature is put in the context of learning. Barrs and Cork (2001) in this project describe activities where children are enabled to enter the worlds of the stories, take on role, experience difference and different worlds, problem-solve and read and write in role. While the built environments of the city schools in which this work and research takes place may not have been originally intended for such activities, the imagination and creative practices of the educators observed ensured a commitment to wide-ranging conceptual spaces for learning, with the support of powerful and effective literature as a material resource.

Research projects such as these are tentative steps in pointing the way forward to new approaches when working with children, to nourish and sustain them as learners. They indicate the potential for constructing and co-constructing meanings and worlds and rearrange, in part, the power structures often embedded in classroom practices to allow the learner to develop some levels of responsibility for learning and to take control of some of the processes involved. In order for this reordering of both physical and conceptual spaces for learning to be effective, educators themselves need to evaluate their roles and intentions in classrooms.

Professionals, pedagogy and the material environment

Creating effective spaces for learning requires both time and commitment. Time is essential for innovation, reflection, documentation, understanding and communication. Although designers, architects and policy-makers are all too often involved in constructing built education environments, it is the educators themselves who shape the space, with commitment to innovative and effective practice. In her Californian study of the ways in which teachers constructed space and place, Bissell found that 82 per cent of her sample constructed and used their classrooms 'in ways consistent with the traditional image of teaching embedded in the schools' architectural designs' with a minority 'deviating from this pattern, either placing the students' desks in a circle or eliminating the desks altogether' or preferring to use alternative spaces (Bissell 2004 : 28). She pointed out the constraints upon teachers made by the physical environment but also described the level of teachers' commitment when they dedicated time and effort to modifying the built environment to better suit the purposes of effective teaching and learning. It is worth restating here that classroom environments and material provision are not neutral; ideological choices are continually being made, and the decisions that are made, and whatever work and functions are carried out in that space, are based upon a perspective or 'judgements of value' (Dahlburg *et al.* 1999 : 119). Indeed, one of the findings of the Effective Teachers of Literacy project was that 'effective teachers had a coherent belief system about literacy and its teaching and these were generally consistent with the ways they chose to teach' (Medwell *et al.* 1998 : 81). The implication is, then, that teachers create and shape environments for learning, often in spite of constraints of building and design or other influences.

The challenge for teachers and educators is to provide the physical space that is required for literacy learning so that children can easily converse, co-construct meanings, negotiate and work in pairs or groups. In addition, there needs to be space for role-play and drama and performance poetry; resources for material explorations to facilitate the construction of narratives such as storytelling props, and in early years settings, small world and other physical resources, for example sand, dough and blocks. A challenge equal to that of providing physical space is that of creating conceptual space for children to explore ideas, to take risks, to experiment, to problem-solve and to share time and ideas with others. All of this is dependent upon teachers' and educators' knowledge of how children emerge and develop in literacy and what is needed to support and scaffold their progress.

A pervading literacy climate and a safe ethos for learning has to be established if young learners are to be inspired and nourished successfully. An environment that includes meaningful environmental print to support, direct and affect children's directions, as well as appropriate resources that reflect and sustain their interests and their worlds, will be visible. An ethos that encourages children to push boundaries in their learning, to investigate new possibilities and to be fearless in their creations will be less immediately evident but will be clearly demonstrated in the variety and innovative nature of children's performances and playful approaches. Spaces for play and playfulness are both essential elements in any learning space to support literacy. In play contexts, children are able to construct, share and shape worlds that may reflect, or distract from, their own. In play, they are also able to make choices, make decisions, solve problems, take the initiative, act independently or in the company of others and, importantly, develop a sense of their own voice. The value of play in literacy learning has been well documented (e.g. Smidt 2002; David *et al.* 2000; Whitehead 1997; Hall and Robinson 1995). However, play cannot occur independently of time and space being created for it and it being accorded value and status. Play is the work of young children and freedom to play is both an entitlement and an appropriate pedagogical choice for those who teach them. Space for play may challenge the need for desks, chairs, teachers' desks, blackboards/whiteboards and will require educators to make clear ideologically informed decisions. Play is not merely the domain of the youngest children in schools; opportunities for play and playfulness, for role-play and drama, for explorations and investigations exist across ages and stages of education and are essential for children to effectively engage with literature and literacy opportunities with interest and motivation (Grainger *et al.* 2005).

In spite of compelling evidence to the contrary, some policy-makers and educators still believe that the 'legacies of nineteenth century elementary education' are 'basic to the primary curriculum' (Alexander 2000 : 566). Alexander continues to explain that 'the 3Rs were directed . . . at the working classes alone; and they were devised not to liberate those working classes but to contain them' (ibid.). Such a view is no longer morally acceptable, but still the contrast appears to be between didacticism and play spaces, and playfulness, freedom and choice.

Within effective environments for literacy, the quality of interactions is another encompassing element, whether in play or in other teacher-led activities. In the preschools of Reggio Emilia in Northern Italy, a central feature of their work is the 'pedagogy of relationships', and the respect both within the school communities and between the school and the community of the city enables the children to see themselves, to develop self-esteem as learners and to understand their place as part of a wider world beyond the immediate. To facilitate this, the architecture of newly constructed schools recreates 'piazzas' within the building as well as age-appropriate, structured spaces surrounding this central area, to allow safe and supported explorations as well as opportunities to meet together informally inside the school with siblings, perhaps, or other children of all ages. Mirrors and reflective surfaces are also common features so that children can study and learn about themselves and reflect upon their own images. Studies of light, dark, shadows and reflection are also frequently observed. This is combined with opportunities to look outside and to capitalise regularly on learning opportunities beyond the school walls and in the community, so that children as learners, their learning and its inspiration become visible to everybody rather than hidden away in secure buildings. Dahlburg discusses how, from Sweden, Reggio was seen to have:

> constructed a new and different pedagogical space . . . a relational space where making connections is a primary concern . . . exploring new relations with art, design, architecture, science, philosophy . . . the school becomes an environment rich in information, where not only the written word is valued, but where images and the senses add meaning to the learning experience. (Dahlburg 2004 : 22)

While this work is related to children in the early years of education (in this case up to the age of 6), there are important principles from which educators of children of all ages can learn. These include the ideas of active learning, of persistence in learning, of pursuing interests, of the social nature of learning, of the importance of encounters and interactions and the overriding, and 'optimistic', notion of the child as gifted, resourceful, independent and with 'an extraordinary potential' (Malaguzzi 2004 : 13). Malaguzzi also believed that children needed 'gifted teachers' and that these were not to be found but could be shaped by working with children and other adults. A key finding of a number of research projects (Dahlburg *et al.* 1999; Wells 1994; Medwell *et al.* 1998, Grainger *et al.* 2005) is that where teachers are enabled to come together for the purposes of 'dialogic exchange' then the underpinning reflective act influences practice and supports professional development. The creation of such reflective spaces based upon the documentation of practice is a core element of the Reggio Emilia approach which has become influential internationally and has also affected new projects relating to the design and construction of new educational buildings, extensions and modifications as well as to the recreation of effective pedagogies here in the UK (Brice Heath and Wolf 2004).

Of course, the physical built environment for learning may change over time and, hopefully, for those who inhabit dark and dingy or inappropriately small spaces, it will. What teachers do with the space, where teachers locate themselves, notions of power and control of the space, the learning and material resources, and the interactions that occur within the space are all within the control of individual professionals. In her fascinating study of teachers' use of space, McGregor (2004) discusses how, 'in the same physical configuration of room, with the same students, lessons with different teachers produce very different patterns of movement, interaction and learning activities'. She continues to quote from a study where the movement patterns of one child were followed. She refers to how a 'seductive pedagogy of persuasion and collaboration seemed to open up classroom space and encourage movement', compared with a second, 'more reductive, masculinist pedagogy, centred around classroom control and order which reduced movement, closed off spaces for learning' (ibid.: 15). Such professional decisions in relation to pedagogy and use of space may be influenced in a number of ways. It may be argued that individual values prompt decisions, our own cultural constructs of childhood, education and schooling, and thus, individual professionals' visions are being represented in classrooms. It may be that there is a broader context for influence, for example from National Strategies, local initiatives or school curricula. Or it may be that without any 'guiding philosophy', a 'cut and paste' model is applied with artificial connections to a range of influencing pedagogies (Goouch and Bryan, forthcoming). At this point in the history of education in the UK, with the range of information and research currently available from across professional disciplines, it may now be timely for professionals in primary practice to engage in dialogic exchange and to forge strong principled practices relating to pedagogy, learning spaces and places, and professional decisions, particularly as government agencies are now debating 'classrooms of the future' (DfES 2003). In relation to literacy environments a key question for teachers and educators to ask may be 'whose vision is being represented in this learning space and in the choice of these material resources?' The ability to articulate *what* should be used to support emerging and developing literacy and to ask *how* and *why* it should be used seems to be critical to professional development and, ultimately, to the literacy developments and performances of children as literacy learners.

In conclusion, it seems that spaces and places for learning should refer to both physical and conceptual space. These will be most effectively created, recreated, constructed and reconstructed by those educators who are aware of children's needs and desires and of underpinning research to support their decisions, by children who may sometimes have intrinsically felt urges to work and play in particular ways, and by educators and children working together to imagine and create, progress and learn together.

References

Alexander, R. (2000) *Culture and Pedagogy: International Comparisons in Primary Education*. Oxford: Blackwell.

Apple, M. W. (2004) 'Culture, politics and the text', in Ball S. J. (ed.) *The RoutledgeFalmer Reader in Sociology of Education*. London: RoutledgeFalmer.

Barrs, M. and Cork, V. (2001) *The Reader in the Writer: The Links between the Study of Literature and Writing Development at Key Stage 2*. London: CLPE.

Bearne, E. (1995) 'Greater expectations: reflections of difference', in Bearne, E. (ed.) *Greater Expectations*. London: Cassell.

Bearne, E. and Kress, G. (2001) 'Editorial'. *Reading, Literacy and Language*, **25**(3), November, 89–93.

Bissell, J. (2004) 'Teachers' construction of space and place: the method in the madness'. *Forum*, **46**(1), 28–32, Spring.

Blakemore, S. J. (2002) 'More questions than answers? Research report'. *Interplay*, Summer, 24–30.

Brice Heath, S. and Wolf, S. (2004) *With an Eye on Design: The Power of Presentation*. London: Creative Partnerships.

Bruner, J. S. (1986) *Actual Minds, Possible Worlds*. Cambridge, MA: Harvard University Press.

Central Advisory Council for Education (England) (CACE) (1967) *Children and Their Primary Schools*. London: Department of Education and Science/HMSO.

Corden, R. (2000) *Literacy and Learning through Talk*. Buckingham: Open University Press.

Dahlburg, G. (2004) 'Making connections'. *Children in Europe: Celebrating 40 Years of Reggio Emilia*, **6**, March, 22–3.

Dahlburg, G., Moss, P. and Pence, A. (1999) *Beyond Quality in Early Childhood Education and Care: Postmodern Perspectives*. London: RoutledgeFalmer.

David, T. (ed.) (1999) *Teaching Young Children*. London: PCP/Sage.

David, T., Goouch, K., Powell, S. and Abbott, L. (2003) *Birth to Three Matters: A Review of the Literature*. Research Report 444. London: DfES.

David, T., Raban, B., Ure, C., *et al.* (2000) *Making Sense of Early Literacy: A Practitioner's Perspective*. Stoke-on-Trent: Trentham.

Dewey, J. (1915) *The School and Society*. Chicago, IL: The University of Chicago Press.

DfEE (1998) *The National Literacy Strategy: Framework for Teaching*. London: HMSO.

DfEE (1998) *The National Literacy Strategy*. London: DfEE.

DfEE (1998) *The National Numeracy Strategy*. London: DfEE.

DfES (2003) *Schools of the Future*. London: DfES.

Goouch, K. and Bryan, H. (forthcoming) *Travellers' Tales: Pedagogical Connections, Boundaries and Barriers in European Settings*.

Grainger, T. (2002) 'Drama and writing'. *Secondary English Magazine*, 5(4), 16–22.

Grainger, T. and Cremin, M. (2001) *Resourcing Classroom Drama*. Sheffield: NATE.

Grainger, T., Goouch, K. and Lambirth, A. (2005) *Voice and Verve: Children's Creativity in Writing*. London: Routledge.

Greenfield, S. (2000) *The Private Life of the Brain*. London: Penguin.

Greenfield, S. (2002) 'Interview'. *Interplay*, Summer, 20–3.

Hall, N. and Robinson, A. (1995) *Exploring Writing and Play in the Early Years*. London: David Fulton.

Harste, J. C., Woodward, V. A. and Burke, C. L. (1984) *Language Stories and Literacy Lessons*. New Hampshire: Heinemann.

Kress, G. (1997) *Before Writing: Rethinking the Paths to Literacy*. London: Routledge.

Lankshear, C. (1997) 'Introduction', in Lankshear, C. (with Gee, J. P., Knobel, M. and Searle, C.) *Changing Literacies*. Buckingham: Open University Press.

Lankshear, C. and Knobel, M. (1997) 'Literacies, texts and difference in the electronic age', in *Changing Literacies*. Buckingham: Open University Press.

Malaguzzi, L. (2004) 'Walking on threads of silk: interview by Carlo Barsotti'. *Children in Europe. Celebrating 40 Years of Reggio Emilia*, 6, March, 10–15.

McGregor, J. (2004) 'Space, power and the classroom'. *Forum*, 46(1), 13–18.

Medwell, J., Wray, D., Poulson, L. and Fox, R. (1998) *Effective Teachers of Literacy*. Exeter: University of Exeter.

Meek Spencer, M. (2001) 'Preface' to Barrs, M. and Cork, V. *The Reader in the Writer*. London: CLPE.

Mercer, N. (2000) *Words and Minds*. London: Routledge.

Mercer, N. (2004) 'Development through dialogue', in Grainger, T. (ed.) *The RoutledgeFalmer Reader in Language and Literacy*. London: RoutledgeFalmer.

Nutbrown, C. (1998) *The Lore and Language of Early Education*. Sheffield: USDE.

Pring, R. (2004) *Philosophy of Education, Aims, Theory, Common Sense and Research*. London: Continuum.

Smidt, S. (2002) *A Guide to Early Years Practice* (2nd edn). London: Routledge.

Vygotsky, L. (1978) *Mind in Society*. Cambridge, MA: Harvard University Press.

Wells, G. (1986) *The Meaning Makers: Children Learning Language and Using Language to Learn*. Sevenoaks: Hodder and Stoughton.

Wells, G. (1994) *Constructing Knowledge Together: Classrooms as Centres of Inquiry and Literacy*. Portsmouth, New Hampshire: Heinemann Educational.

Wells, G. (2003) 'Action, talk and text: integrating literacy with other modes of making meaning', in Bearne, E., Dombey, H. and Grainger, T. (eds) 'Interactions', in *Language and Literacy in the Classroom*. Maidenhead: Open University Press.

Whitehead (1997) *Language and Literacy in the Early Years* (2nd ed). London: Paul Chapman.

Whitehead (1999) 'A Literacy Hour in the Nursery? The Big Question Mark'. *Early Years*, 19(2), 38–61.

CHAPTER 3

From ludic to lyrical language

Sue Hammond

What is the role of poetry and language play in young children's learning and, as significantly, in their emotional and social well-being? This chapter draws on research from a wide range of sources, including scientific research, to provide a background to the selection and use of poetic texts with Foundation Stage children. Motivation and engagement will be prime features to be considered, with particular attention given to natural, uninhibited, often creative, play, and drawing on children's intrinsic desire to learn within a social, cultural context. The importance of language play in young children's cognitive development is a continuous and vital thread throughout the chapter. In addition, an important aspect of any planning in our rich, multi-ethnic, diverse society is how to include children from a range of communities, traditions, experiences and achievements, so this will also be focused upon. Practical suggestions are included, based on these pedagogical assumptions.

In every society, in every century, poetry and song have been a fundamental part of human existence: chants and rhythms, rhymes and repetitions, narratives and refrains are all part of the joy and sorrow that make up our lives. There are the Negro spiritual songs of slaves, physically bound and tethered, whose words and music still soared freely; the chants of latter-day holy men and modern-day football supporters; the poignancy of the emotions and images of the war poets; and the laughter of tongue-twisters, riddles and word play that tickle our senses. The barriers between different cultures and societies can be broken down by a willingness to share the language bonds of rhythm and rhyme. On a trip along the Nile, for instance, a group of middle-aged, middle-class, English tourists and Egyptian guides were united and delighted by the elegant Nubian oarsman when he taught a traditional, repetitious chant to the gentle beat of his drum. At that time, in that setting, the poem brought smiles of pleasure and feelings of peace and harmony, but its memory and revival can generate the same emotions in a different place and time.

Poetry evokes a physical and emotional response that taps into something primeval and deep-rooted in our natures. During his acceptance speech for the

Nobel Prize in Literature, Heaney (1995) referred to the compelling power that poetry has over human response: 'The energy released by linguistic fission and fusion, with the buoyancy generated by cadence and tone and rhyme and stanza' (http://nobelprize.org/nobel/nobel-foundation/publications/lesprix.html) (6 December 2004). This energy is so potent that a poem can be responsible for creating gales of laughter or tears of sadness, regret and remorse, through a careful, deliberate juxtaposition of words evoking warmth, mystery, beauty, fear or cruelty.

A poem can encapsulate our own feelings and articulate them even when we are unable to find a voice: for a colleague who had recently suffered the death of his father there was solace in Philip Larkin's elegy to his father, 'And Yet' (*The Times*, 10 August 2004). How often do we unconsciously draw on the language of Shakespeare when our own words are inadequate? According to Bernard Levin (1986):

> If you have knitted your brows, made a virtue of necessity, insisted on fair play, slept not one wink, stood on ceremony, danced attendance (on your lord and master), laughed yourself into stitches, had short shrift, cold comfort or too much of a good thing, if you have seen better days or lived in a fool's paradise – why, be that as it may, the more fool you, for it is a foregone conclusion that you are (as good luck would have it) quoting Shakespeare. (*The Times*, 10 August 2004)

Language play

The genius of Shakespeare has become part of our *lingua franca* and there is no self-consciousness or social class barrier that restricts the use of his currency; it crosses cultural boundaries. The precision and economy of words in other rhymes and couplets, elegies and odes, puns, riddles, chants, and in contemporary newspaper headlines and catchphrases are all part of a vibrant cultural and multi-cultural heritage that permeates the lives of successive generations. They draw us together, they are exciting, fresh and fluid, they connect us with the past as well as celebrating the present, and they forge links between different cultures and traditions. The language play of market traders, whose repertoire includes references to popular television phrases, such as 'Cheaper than Asda', and (even recently) 'Lovely jubbly', have been the source of great amusement during my own travels to countries as diverse as Turkey, Egypt, India and Malaysia. They exemplify the effects of global communications and the common humanity that bubbles to the surface through humour and shared understandings.

Moreover, in the same way that a scent or a piece of music can transport us to another place or time, poetry can be an intoxicating reminder of an almost forgotten experience. The poet Sue Cowling (2002) says that her poem 'Leaves' reflects 'A sound, a feeling and an image' within its few short lines. This resonates with my own joyful memories of the laughter of my two-and-a-half-year-old son when I hear the simple tongue-twister 'Red lorry, yellow lorry'. Although he is now an adult, I can clearly picture him painting the bedroom walls with his bucket of watered-down emulsion, and the pleasure we both took in the language play that grew from a desire to keep him occupied while I gave the ceiling its fresh coat of paint.

This memory has, however, more significance than its ability to help me recapture memories of my son's early years or parental distraction techniques; the shared pleasure of the language play that we engaged in on this and many other occasions contributed to his general literacy acquisition and the development of specific linguistic skills. As an adult, he is a competent wordsmith, able to craft sentences and aware of the power of written language, but also a confident oral language user who can engage and entertain others, or defuse a situation with his quickfire humour and his ability to form unexpected connections between words and images.

Recently, my three-year-old nephew has been just as delighted by the games we play with rhyming stories, particularly those accompanied by an action or incorporating his name, such as Ahlberg's (1989) *Each Peach Pear Plum*, which became: 'Each, peach, pear, plum; I spy Tom's tum'.

Language play of this sort has timeless appeal because it is a continuation of the natural rhythms of language acquisition, the repetitions of early sounds that babies chant, such as 'dad-dah'. While young children learn the sounds and linguistic patterns of their culture instinctively and spontaneously, adults and older children unconsciously and informally contribute through their observed discourse, and by responding to and incorporating baby babble into established words and phrases.

When children's wonder and inventiveness is maintained and nurtured, they become more adventurous and creative in their explorations of language and its images. Crystal (1998 : 180) examined a number of studies in an attempt to discover 'why the playful (or "ludic") function of language is important for our appreciation of language as a whole'. He concluded that:

> Language play, the arguments suggest, will help the development of pronunciation ability through its focus on the properties of sounds and sound contrasts, such as rhyming. Playing with word endings and decoding the syntax of riddles will help the acquisition of grammar. Readiness to play with words and names, to exchange puns and to engage in nonsense talk, promote links with semantic development.

There is a corpus of research evidence, from Goswami and Bryant (1990), Raban (1998) and Pinker (1994) which convinces us that the ludic language of children should be valued and that recognition should be given to the part it plays in literacy development. Although the natural glee of young children when playing with sounds, alliteration and repetition is easily observed – and may be, paradoxically, because of its association with pleasure and fun – the cognitive and creative benefits of such joyous moments are often overlooked. When we analyse the behaviours of many of the most competent readers and writers in our classrooms we find that their sophisticated use of language and confidence to play with its rules are distinctive. They are able to dissect words and reformulate them, to reorganise language and create new sentences that reflect their own ideas, and experiment with their own thoughts and views. Such linguistic competence undoubtedly has long-term benefits and implications for adult life: we have only to consider the popularity of those people who entertain us with their ability to turn images on their heads in their comedy routines, or catchphrases, or persuasive, pervasive advertising jingles and headlines.

Despite this significance and the deeply meaningful human effects of poetry and language play, they often remain a sidelined, undervalued part of our literacy curriculum, and many children do not experience their enrichment. It is widely believed that our emotional lives are an integral part of our intellectual and creative lives, so to limit the diet that is offered can have damaging consequences. However, the nourishment that is derived from poetry does not come through a sterile or formulaic curriculum where its different forms are dissected and analysed.

As widely documented by educationalists such as Grainger (1996) and Lambirth (2002), real learning comes through personal and shared engagement in the images, tempo and timbre of the language, and from the lived experience of performing poems. Therefore, our classrooms need to be places where poems are memorised, recited, appreciated and celebrated on a personal and social level, in individual and group contexts. The focus, when encouraging children to memorise a favourite poem, is not on learning it by rote but on responding to the pictures and feelings it induces, interpreting its linguistic composition and beat.

While the National Literacy Strategy (DfEE 1998) makes suggestions as to the type of poetry that is taught, term-by-term, year-by-year, it is important that we treat these as the guidance they were apparently intended to be rather than as directives determining our choices. Planning should begin with the rhymes and songs that particular and different groups of children know and love, extending and building on the familiar patterns of their childhoods. Immersion in the genre, as argued throughout this book, is essential for reading development and as a basis for the children's compositions because an awareness of the structures and conventions frees them to be adventurous with their own imaginings. So, too, is a physical and mental space in which children feel confident and at liberty to try, as Craft (2001 : 58) states, 'playing with ideas and new possibilities/combinations'. She argues, in a similar vein to Crystal (1998), that it is through play that fresh openings occur, and that 'early opportunities to play and playing are essential for developing creative adults' (ibid.: 9)

The need to observe and respond to young children's play and interests is now extensively accepted as the most effective and natural way to plan for their learning, and the statutory Curriculum Guidance for the Foundation Stage (2000) promotes this view. Observing and building on children's linguistic experimentation and creativity is as valuable, or more so, as assessing their speaking and listening competence. We can use the insights gained to extend the learning, to stimulate and support further investigations and materials.

Of course, this has to be managed sensitively so that we do not kill the inherent motivation that generates it, but Meek (1991) and others, including Lambirth (2002) and Whitehead (2002), have convincingly argued for the integration of language play into our classrooms and demonstrated how worthwhile this can be:

> The metalinguistic awareness that the experts say is the mark of a good early reader and the risk-taking of young writers is born in speech games, the nonsense rhyme, the topsy-turvy of re-inventing the familiar, and all the lore and language and private subversions that children make up with words. (Meek 1991 : 91)

Through many years' experience of teaching four- and five-year-olds in reception classes, and a brief but recent experience of teaching young children in southern India for whom English is a second language, I have become committed to the notion that we need to be responsive in our interactions with children: to 'read' their faces and body language, to identify the confusion or excitement and adapt accordingly. If we continue instead with our own agendas and predetermined, inflexible objectives, our pupils may become disaffected rather than enthused and empowered as learners.

Although objectives are addressed through the plan that follows, they are the servants rather than the masters. I share the concerns of many educationalists that the delivering of an objective can obscure our view and understanding of what the children are actually doing, saying, thinking and learning. There is a danger inherent in making any suggestions for practice that they will be adopted by exhausted, target-weary, bureaucracy-bound teachers and delivered *per se*. Drummond (2004), when talking of her research into the implementation of the Curriculum Guidance for the Foundation Stage, voiced her concern about the effects of the section entitled 'What does the practitioner need to do?' as a 'prescription' for practice, and the interpretation of the Stepping Stones as 'the official version of all there is for four- and five-year-olds to learn' (p. 11). To use the exemplars as a set of teaching procedures is not only reductionist but is to ignore the insights that have been gained into how the human mind works. Developments in learning occur when new experiences make connections with previous experiences, events and accumulated understandings. Research in recent years by neuroscientists such as Gopnik *et al.* (1999) in which brain patterns have been measured and charted demonstrate how neural connections are formed and extended:

> a brain can physically expand and contract and change depending on experience . . . The brain can make a frequently used connection stronger by pruning connections that aren't used. Experience determines which connections will be strengthened and which will be pruned; connections that have been activated most frequently get preserved. (Gopnik *et al.* 1999 : 187)

Teaching that ignores prior knowledge and children's puzzles, fascinations and predilection to play is likely to have only superficial effects on its recipients rather than the deep-rooted learning and commitment that creates independent readers and writers.

Experience of language play and phonological awareness

Even though it would be naïve to make assumptions about all children in our society, there are some threads of experience that are common to many of the children in our schools: they are likely to have been exposed to traditional rhymes (although, in my experience, not all children know whole rhymes from start to finish) and will have grown up in a culture of ditties, word play – through advertising, newspaper headlines and children's television and comedy sketches – and songs that occupy the popular charts or accompany daily activities. These can provide rich and meaningful contexts for nurturing a love and understanding of poetical forms and of language, through which children can be encouraged to create their own rhythms and rhymes, and discover the patterns in words and phrases. As Grainger (1996) states:

> If children are given the chance to play with the tunes of their popular culture and oral traditions they will learn to experiment in their own voices with these rhymes, and will find new cadences and melodies which they can savour and remember. (p. 30)

As well as the personal pleasure that is evoked by such experiences, the role that language play has in learning to read and write has been discussed previously and recognised as a significant one. Of specific relevance here is the research of Goswami and Bryant (1990) in highlighting the importance of phonological awareness and, in particular, of onset and rime in reading accomplishment. (This has been borne out from anecdotal evidence reported by a colleague who has followed the linguistic development of her three-year-old son with fascination and wonder.) There are obvious and numerous implications for using poetry to introduce and develop such knowledge, some of which underpin the suggestions that follow.

In addition, the debate on the role of phonics teaching has become ever more polarised during recent years. Disagreements centre on the relative values of 'synthetic' and 'analytic' phonics teaching and the skills required for blending when reading and segmenting when writing. In some spheres, particularly the popular press, a systematic phonics scheme is viewed as a panacea for all ills, as exemplified by Hepplewhite (2002) of the Reading Reform Foundation in the *Times Educational Supplement*: 'Synthetic phonics is the key to success in literacy in this country. The National Literacy Strategy has got it wrong all these years.'

In a DfES-commissioned report, Brooks (2003) made an analysis of this debate and the research evidence. He argued for caution in introducing formal phonics training to young, pre-Reception-age children, but suggested the importance:

- of reading that is meaningful;
- of writing that enables children to form whole words;
- of the need for differences in the teaching of phonics for reading and phonics for spelling; and
- of phonics schemes that are structured and progress rapidly, and are active, interactive, lively and fun.

All of this is attainable, I believe, through a play-orientated, child-centred, contextualised approach to literacy that can germinate from the cultural rhymes and lyrical texts in which the sounds and patterns of our language are embedded. The wealth of rhymes and rhyming stories available to select from is vast and not only offers a variety of possibilities for structuring phonic and rime and analogy programmes but also for emergent and independent writing, as well as a wide range of cross-curricular work.

Teachers and carers, therefore, have a responsibility to recognise, acknowledge and act according to children's demonstrations of linguistic understandings and interests. The following Unit of Work is, therefore, flexible and open-ended, and based on the belief that effective learning occurs when children are kinaesthetically, emotionally and cognitively engaged through actual experiences. It also works on the premise that in order to compose in any genre, children need to have a wide experience of listening and responding to, and interacting with, good quality writing. It is primarily aimed at teachers working in the Foundation Stage, although poetry traverses age boundaries and many of the ideas can be adapted for use with various age groups.

Rhymes and language play – unit of work for Foundation Stage

> Playing makes room for the agency and energy of performers and calls for both internal and external accommodation to the activity: to play involves a commitment of the mind as well as appropriate behaviour of the body, a fruitful concept for considering the activities of text processing. (Mackey 2003 : 241)

Foundation Stage

Introduction

While the Unit of Work suggested here (Figure 3.1) begins with the NLS range of traditional nursery rhymes and songs, it is assumed that teachers will use their knowledge of the interests, culture, lore and language of the children with whom they are working to inform and extend their specific choices. These will naturally vary according to the context of the school and the literacy histories of the children. From these beginnings, the Unit expands to include related rhyming

Preparation for the unit	Role-play area based on a traditional rhyme; discussion with parents about home rhymes; invite copies of favourites or people to read them to class; arrange to pair with KS2 class for shared readings and recitations.
Related poems and texts	Nursery rhymes: 'Pussy-cat, Pussy-cat, where have you been?' 'The Cat in the Hat', Dr Seuss 'My cat likes to hide in boxes', Eve Sutton 'Nine Lives', Sandy Brownjohn 'Pat and the Magic Hat', Colin and Jacqui Hawkins 'Rumble in the Jungle', Giles Andrae 'The Owl and the Elephant', Brian D'Arcy 'The Owl and the Pussy-Cat', Edward Lear 'Have you seen my cat?', Eric Carle 'Incy-Wincy Moo-Cow', John Cunliffe
Shared reading and writing	Reciting, singing and enacting known rhymes; adding actions, sound effects or music; locating rhymes in big-book anthologies; using puppets, masks, props; playing with alliteration; rhyme and analogy awareness; generating own rimes; composing together.
Guided reading and writing	Adult scribing children's versions.
Independent	Imitating shared activities through free play with materials and props used; role-play; recording rhymes.
Intended outcomes	Flap book, audio tape and computer text of favourite rhymes and new versions.

Figure 3.1

texts and then more contemporary poetry, selected mainly for its potential to actively involve children in creating their own movements and interpretations, as well as their own compositions. Oral compositions are given equal status and recognition as written ones in the conception of the Unit.

Opportunities for shared, guided and independent work are largely embedded within the plan and a formalised, structured Literacy Hour is not promoted, as I consider it inappropriate for young children. The teacher's predisposition to be playful, to encourage 'tongue-tripping' and risk-taking are, however, considered to be essential ingredients. Suggestions are made for recording and using the children's poetry, as their pleasure in their own alternative versions and those of others will add to their repertoire, motivation and learning.

Preparation and planning

Through working closely with the children's main carers, a deeper understanding of pre- and out-of-school language and literacy experiences is developed. From their earliest interactions with adults, many children learn language during fun, active songs, lullabies and rhymes, such as 'Round and round the garden', 'Pat-a-cake', and 'This little piggy went to market'. During informal observations and interviews with parents I have found this to be the case in families from different ethnic origins, although, of course, the sounds and patterns are culturally determined rather than universal. In her book of Afro-Caribbean rhymes, Hallworth (1997) has recorded chants, rhymes and games from her Trinidadian childhood.

Such language play is often nonsensical, but the songs and rhymes are physically and linguistically satisfying and enriching. They form one of the strands that is later woven into the counting, skipping, clapping and ball-playing rhymes of playground games; a tradition comprehensively documented by Iona and Peter Opie during the 1950s and, with regional and contemporary variations, continues in the twenty-first century.

Therefore, communicating with the important adults in children's lives and community is a worthwhile starting point for any unit of work and acts as a springboard for much of the planning.

Immersion

It is vital that children have a wide experience of any genre in order to make it their own and to compose in it. Undoubtedly, the extent to which this applies to nursery rhymes may vary considerably from school to school, class to class and child to child, but it is also true to say that the children's stock of rhymes can be quickly and enjoyably assessed and addressed. In *shared time*, for instance, using the big book enables the teacher to discuss locating a particular rhyme using the contents page and then noting the children's engagement and responses during the recitation or enactment of it (I have found the teaching assistant during these sessions to be of immense value in noting which children are fully familiar with the rhyme and which are less so.) The children will have their personal favourites and many young children are prepared to lead the chanting or the creation of alternative versions.

Shared reading and writing

With one of my Reception classes the seed that rapidly grew into an entire Unit of Work for all six Areas of Development was 'Pussy cat, pussy cat, where have you been?' Its growth was nurtured through the children's preferences, enthusiasms and autonomous decisions, and supported by careful consideration and responsiveness, and a structure that was both organised and organic. It was first sown when some of the class were choosing familiar poems from a book of rhymes using the pictures on the cover as the first stage in the selection process, and I joined them. Nursery rhymes are often narratives that lend themselves perfectly to being acted out and so, when I suggested they show the 'story' to the rest of the class, 'Pussy cat, pussy cat' was soon brought to life and developed a life of its own. This became the basis of our shared reading and writing sessions, during which the emphasis continued to be on playful experimentation and collaborative composition.

When Jack brought his soft toy cat to school there was another incentive to enact the rhyme, with two groups of children providing the questions and answers. The children directed my scribing of the dialogue into large speech bubbles and these were used in their free play to recite the rhyme, accompanied by actions from the cat and a plastic mouse; these were eventually replaced by actors playing the roles of the queen (resplendent in cloak and crown), the cat, the mouse and a bemused onlooker. It is important to be sensitive to individual children, but Jack was immensely proud of the subversion of the rhyme to include his name: 'Jumping Jack, Jumping Jack, where have you been? I've been up to London to bounce for the queen!'

In addition, the role-play area became a palace. Invitations were issued in the children's emergent writing styles to 'visit the queen', and the children's own narratives developed. The play of individuals and groups of children grew from the rhyme and changed as a result of their experiences. A confidence with its words and sound patterns emerged through familiarity and their subsequent playfulness, enabling them to make imaginative connections and inventions.

Contrasting poems about cats added further to our repertoire, range of experi-ence and fun: Sandy Brownjohn's (2002) *Nine Lives*, with its mixture of poignancy and humour; the big cat rhymes in Giles Andrae's (1998) *Rumble in the Jungle* readily lent themselves to sound effects, masks and individual interpretations of animalistic movement; and the images and language of Edward Lear's 'Owl and the Pussycat' and Brian D'Arcy's (2001) version, 'The Owl and the Elephant', prompted much hilarity and playfulness. There are two highly evocative poems from Nigeria in the *Talking Drums* selection by Veronique Tadjo that cry out to be acted and memorised.

My Cat Likes to Hide in Boxes, by Eve Sutton (1973), *Pat and the Magic Hat* by Colin and Jacqui Hawkins (2001) and Dr Seuss's *Cat in the Hat* (1958) were obvious text choices to support the language focus as well as to extend the children's experience of good-quality stories. Such texts are easily accessible to novice readers; they are enjoyable and motivating and use predictable vocabulary and patterned language that is easily remembered. Thomas, at four-and-a-half years old, rapidly mastered the story of *My Cat Likes to Hide in Boxes* using the pic-ture prompts and occasional action clues (such as a sneeze for the cat from Brazil), and *felt* like a reader, an important prerequisite of *becoming* a reader.

Ryan, also 'rising five', had decided to use the magnetic letters to form the word 'box' when he devised his own rhyme in a sing-song voice: 'x . . . x . . . ex . . . exy . . . wexy . . . sexy . . .'. Both children were engaged in meaningful literacy events that were autonomous and self-motivated, enabling them to practise important skills with minimal interaction, and no interference, from an adult.

Phonological work originated from shared, whole-class recitation of the rhyme where we predicted its patterns and tested our voices. Through this we became aware of its sounds and rhythms as well as its structure, characters and narrative.

It became a perfect opportunity to teach about the onset and rime of certain words. The onset of a word is the opening consonant or cluster of consonants of a word or a syllable, and the rime is the vowel sound and any following consonants. In the word 'band', 'b' is the onset and 'and' is the rime. Led by Catherine, who identified 'cat' within her own name, the 'at' rime developed into the preferred focus of our language play, rather than the 'een' of 'been' and 'queen'. Additional links were made to other children's names and the letters c,t,a,p, followed later by h,f,m,r, became familiar through various games. Actual objects were used so that the children had a sense of the relationship between a rime, or an initial phoneme and a name. These activities were not time-consuming or laboured but active, *laughter-filled* sessions where inventing and experimenting with the music of language was paramount.

Shared or guided work can provide models that the children will imitate independently or use as a stimulus for their own creations. My class delighted in playing with the onset and rime cards, incorporating their own teacherly voices, and then made their own versions using the pieces of coloured card and thick marker pens that were freely available. Several children decided to copy the rhyme to form part of their personal collection, or practised writing the names of the 'at' objects on the whiteboards. Using the rhyming vocabulary, a colleague devised a 'wordsearch' that proved very popular, particularly when some copies were enlarged and laminated so that a wipeable pen could be used and risks taken. The children were thrilled by the challenge of an activity they had observed older siblings participate in and that felt new and fun, yet familiar and *seriously* playful.

Another rhyming task that absorbed children physically, orally and cognitively was the 'Rhyme Hunt' referred to by Rowe and Humphries (2001 : 164) as part of the nursery work they do to raise 'children's awareness of the richness of language and how it may be manipulated by them to suit their preferences and imaginations'.

For the purposes of the 'Hunt', pairs of rhyming objects are secreted away within the classroom for groups or individuals to find and match. Items readily available in most Reception classes, such as a cat and hat, can be added to for extending known rimes or vocabulary; for instance, including a wig to be paired with a plastic farmyard pig can create interest and discussion as well as excitement. When children become overtly aware of the possibilities they will spontaneously experiment with the familiar and the unknown, creating new combinations with the nuances and patterns of their enriched vocabularies.

Cross-curricular opportunities

Furthermore, a renewed acknowledgement of the holistic nature of young children's learning has been a liberating force for many teachers and has resulted in enthusiasm for planning that links areas of learning, rather than creating false barriers between *subjects*. The previous view (DfEE 1998), that activities such as drawing, designing or building, somehow detracted from literacy learning and should be the preserve of specific subject areas showed a limited understanding of the inherent value of real experiences. Apart from the discourse between children and/or teacher and child and a closer examination of the text, there are decisions and hypotheses involved, a necessity to attend to detail and to consider the appropriateness of materials that all promote contextualised language. In addition, the finished product is a potential prop for other shared literacy and cross-curricular learning.

Inspired by the Hawkins's and Sutton's cats in our texts, my pupils made their own 'magic' hats that naturally led to improvised drama, storytelling and music; comparative mathematics vocabulary; geographical and historical awareness (Knowledge and Understanding) and a host of other curricular connections that presented themselves. A colleague suggested designing boxes in which to hide treasures as part of our mathematics and design technology (Creative Development) work, but the treasure boxes also afforded opportunities to discuss the thoughts and feelings involved in making choices about the contents (Personal, Social and Emotional Development). With the release of the *Cat in the Hat* film and website, the potential for integrating popular culture into such a plan is exciting.

There are other possibilities that can originate from a rhyme that becomes a theme that grasps the children's imaginations and takes them on linguistic adventures:

- designing 'Wanted' posters offering a reward for the capture of the cat;
- using photographs of the children to make a flap book asking where individual children have been (during class time or family holidays);
- creating storyboards to depict the sequence of occurrences; and
- making mice from sugar icing and producing a series of photographs or instruction cards to accompany the recipe.

In addition, our cat may have decided to travel to other places and the children's holiday experiences combined with Carle's (1973) *Have You Seen My Cat?* would have been ideal vehicles to support this. A diary could have been kept in which his exploits were recorded, in a similar way to the adventures of *Barnaby Bear* (Knowledge and Understanding of the World); he may have liked a non-fiction book written about his care and preferences, or a video made of his life and times.

Construction of texts

Many collections of rhymes are parodies of the original versions, such as *Incy-Wincy Moo-Cow*, by John Cunliffe, and are marvellous for tickling the senses and subverting linguistic conventions. Modifying a familiar nursery rhyme is a simple task for whole-class or group work because there is a prototype in place from which to work. As alluded to earlier, a particularly worthwhile approach to this is to incorporate one of the children's names into the re-formed rhyme. Our given name has tremendous significance to us, our identity and family connections, and is generally the first word a child recognises in print and later begins to write. 'Little Miss Muffet' was the frame for this rhyme about a four-year-old reception child:

> Little Miss Shana sat on a banana
> Eating her Milky Way.
> Along came a tiger
> Who sat down beside her
> And frightened Miss Shana away!

While the aesthetic writing skills required of the teacher are very basic in such a format, there are ample rewards available from shared composition. It is important to have a name and possible rhyme prepared, but children quickly become adept at this way of working and are easily encouraged to supply their own ideas. A variety of possible words can be considered and, as Graves (1983) suggests, the teacher models and scribes the changes and choices the author, or poet in this case, has to make.

Incidentally, the preceding rhyme soon became a favourite for class recitation and often accompanied routine activities, such as tidying up or waiting in the dinner queue, and, almost inevitably, received the children's own amendments. An interactive display area offered another dimension and, in addition to a large copy of the poem, a doll, plastic fruit, chocolate bar wrapper and a tiger mask provided lots of fun and enactments of the drama in its new metamorphosis.

Simple alliterative games using the children's names and nouns, adjectives or verbs are another way of involving our pupils in oral gymnastics and can be used as an adjunct to, or extension of, traditional tongue-twisters such as 'Peter Piper picked a peck of pickled pepper' or popular texts such as *The Tiger Who Came To Tea* (1999) by Judith Kerr and *Winnie in Winter* (1996) by Valerie Thomas and Korky Paul. Initially, the emphasis might be on encouraging the children to pair another word to a classmate's name, as in 'Alex's alien'. This can be extended to 'Alex's alien ate an apple', or play with images so that 'Alex's alien ate an angry apple'. Producing a class dictionary or Powerpoint alphabet are possible outcomes from this type of game play. With a Year 2 class, a verb dictionary was developed from such a theme and required purposeful thesaurus research before the children were satisfied with a final text that included *an ambling animal, a bouncing bear, a caterwauling catastrophic cat* and *a dingling, dangling dandelion*. This drew on language resources and knowledge that were not normally applicable in school writing contexts: the words of comics, cartoons and jingles.

A rhyming text that is marvellous for encouraging children to create their own name phrases is Margaret Chamberlain's (1998) *Pass the Jam, Jim*. With its food topic and ludic language, it is a delight in its own right and an entertaining read for groups or individuals, but it also invites the reader to play with its text. If we momentarily revisit the animal theme, we can see the potential of composing from the pattern Umansky gives us:

'Feed the cat, Matt,
Where's the bear, Claire?
Look out for the snake, Jake!'

Another theme close to children's hearts might be that of toys:

'Here's your doll, Poll.
Mind your car, Akbar!'

Such rhymes can be used with a series of photos to form an attractive display or become the basis of a multimodal text. They provide popular material for an enlarged text that can be used as a class reader, maybe hiding the children's pictures under flaps to add the element of anticipation and predictability that young children enjoy so much (even if the text is a familiar one that has been revisited on numerous occasions). The basic repetition and arrangement of the language can provide a secure blueprint for the children's own inventions.

Playground rhymes and independent text construction

The oral traditions of communities were referred to earlier as part of a continuum of language play from early child–parent interactions to playground games, and then to adult language play. There is evidence (Grugeon 2000) that playground rhymes continue to thrive and can become a cornerstone for involving carers in sharing their own experiences and extending children's, and for a child's own inventiveness with rhyme.

The next rhyme was recently heard intoned by five-year-old Elizabeth and her friends, complemented by enthusiastic actions and facial expressions:

'I'm telling on you!'
'Why?'
'Because you licked my lolly
And you didn't say sorry!'

From this innocent ditty came the children's own parody, a more subversive and daring version:

'I'm telling on you!'
'Why?'
'Because you licked my bum
And you lied to me Mum!'

First, if we return to Elizabeth's original rhyme, it tells us a great deal about the children's awareness of rhythm and content: in a few brief lines, it narrates a story that can be visualised and is familiar; its pattern is exemplified and supported by a kinaesthetic beat; it provides a simple question-and-answer structure that they utilise for their own constructions. In a nutshell, it demonstrates that when children have freely practised an action rhyme they are often motivated to compose their own in a way that no enforced twenty-minute independent writing time can achieve.

Even if their inventions involve only slight adaptations, they meaningfully contribute to an accumulating knowledge of language and an awareness of what it is to be a poet. Furthermore, there are already parodies of traditional rhymes by established poets that are in print and accepted as poems, such as John Cunliffe's 'Little Jack Horner' (1999). This uses the structure and language of the following nonsense rhyme still chanted in school playgrounds:

Early one morning in the middle of the night,
Two dead men got up to fight.
Back to back they faced each other,
Drew their swords and shot each other.

The intention is not to suggest that teachers abrogate responsibility for, or involvement in, children's learning but that we put more trust in children to direct the process. During shared time, the teacher provides a valuable model and a social context for experiencing new texts or developing a closer understanding of known ones. In guided time, she/he can encourage and support the children in the 'sustained shared thinking', that Siraj-Blatchford *et al.* (2002) have found to be an essential part of the teacher's role, as they use the puppets, props or rhyme box to commit the rhyme to memory and play with the linguistic and narrative possibilities. An important part of the adult role in independent time is to create settings and to offer resources that extend the learning. For example, as part of the follow-up to the children's reading of their own anthology of favourite rhymes, there were finger puppets, blocks and other construction materials available for them to enact the rhymes or explore them in their own way. Five-year-old Joshua used the stimulus of a Lego tree to adapt 'Humpty Dumpty' and the teacher scribed it and enabled him to record it onto an audio cassette.

Humpty Dumpty sat on a tree,
Humpty Dumpty banged his knee,
All the king's horses and all the king's men
Couldn't fix Humpty's knee again.

One key implication for planning that seems to emerge from observation of playground games, and underpins the literacy contexts referred to above, is that young children are not designed to listen passively to the images and cadences of poetry. They should be skipping, clapping, bouncing, singing, drumming or swaying in spontaneous, natural response. Indeed, isn't that when true literacy learning and creativity ensues?

Literature referred to in the text

Ahlberg, J. and A. (1989) *Each Peach Pear Plum*. Oliver & Boyd.

Andrae, G. (1998) *Rumble in the Jungle*. Orchard Books.

Brownjohn, S. (2002) 'Nine Lives', in Foster, J. *One Hundred and One Favourite Poems*. HarperCollins.

Carle, E. (1973) *Have You Seen My Cat?* Scholastic.

Chamberlain, M. (1998) (illus. K. Umansky) *Pass the Jam, Jim*. Red Fox.

Cowling, S. (2002) 'Leaves', in Foster, J. *One Hundred and One Favourite Poems*. HarperCollins.

Cunliffe, J. (1999) *Incy-Wincy Moo-Cow*. Macdonald.

D'Arcy, B. (2001) 'The Owl and the Elephant', in Bloom, V. *On a Camel to the Moon*. Belitha Press.

Hallworth, G. (1997) *Down by the River*. Mammoth.

Hawkins, C. and Hawkins, J. (2001) *Pat and the Magic Hat*. Dorling Kindersley.

Kerr, J. (1999) *The Tiger Who Came to Tea*. Collins.

Korky, P. and Thomas, V. (1996) *Winnie in Winter*. Oxford University Press.

Seuss, Dr (1958) *The Cat in the Hat*. Collins.

Sutton, E. (1973) *My Cat Likes to Hide in Boxes*. Puffin Books.

Tadjo, V. (ed.) (2000) *Talking Drums: A Selection of Poems from Africa South of the Sahara*. A & C Black.

References

Alberge, D. (2004) 'Larkin, P. And Yet', *The Times*, 10 August.

Brooks, G. (2003) *Sound Sense: The Phonics Element of the National Literacy Strategy*. A Report to the Department for Education and Skills, University of Sheffield.

Craft, A. (2001) 'Little Creativity', in Craft, A., Jeffrey, B. and Leibling, M. (eds) *Creativity in Education*. London: Continuum.

Crystal, D. (1998) *Language Play*. London: Penguin.

DfEE (1998) *The National Literacy Strategy Framework for Teaching*. London: DfEE.

DfEE (2000) *Curriculum Guidance for the Foundation Stage: The National Curriculum for England and Wales*. London: HMSO.

Drummond, M. J. (2004) 'Blighting early growth', in ATL report, **26**(7), April.

Gopnik, A., Meltzoff, A. and Kuhl, P. (1999) *How Babies Think: The Science of Childhood*. London: Weidenfeld and Nicolson.

Goswami, U. and Bryant, P. E. (1990) *Phonological Skills and Learning to Read*. Hove: Lawrence Erlbaum.

Grainger, T. (1996) 'The rhythm of life is a powerful beat'. *Language Matters*, Language Arts Volume, July, 30–4.

Graves, D. H. (1983) *Writing: Teachers and Children at Work*. Portsmouth, NH: Heinemann Educational.

Grugeon, E. (2000) 'Girls' playground language and lore: what sort of texts are these?', in Bearne, E. and Watson, V. (eds) *Where Texts and Children Meet*. London: Routledge.

Heaney, S. (1995) Le Prix Nobel Crediting Poetry http://nobelprize.org/nobel/nobel-foundation/publications/lesprix.html (accessed 6 December 2004).

Hepplewhite, P. (2002), cited in *The Times Educational Supplement* (Issue no. 7) by Helen Ward, 15 November, p. 9.

Lambirth, A. (2002) *Poetry Matters*. United Kingdom Reading Association.

Levin, B. (1986) 'All euphemisms are lies: lies told for a purpose-to change reality', *The Times*, 10 August, p. 16.

Mackey, M. (2003) 'Playing the text', in Grainger, T. (ed.) *The Reader in Language and Literacy*. London: RoutledgeFalmer.

Meek, M. (1991) *On Being Literate*. London: Bodley Head.

Moyles, J. (2002) *Beginning Teaching, Beginning Learning in Primary Education*. Buckingham: Open University Press.

Opie, I. (1959) *The Lore and Language of Schoolchildren*. Oxford: Oxford University Press.

Pinker, S. (1994) *The Language Instinct*. London: Penguin Books.

Raban, B. (1998) *The Spoken Vocabulary of Five-Year-Old Children*. Reading: University of Reading, Reading and Language Information Centre.

Rowe, S. and Humphries, S. (2001) 'Creating a climate for learning at Coombs Infant and Nursery School', in Craft, A., Jeffrey, B. and Leibling, M. (eds) *Creativity in Education*. London: Continuum.

Siraj-Blatchford, I., Sylva, K., Muttock, S., Gilden, R. and Bell, D. (2002) *Researching Effective Pedagogy in the Early Years*. London: Department for Education and Skills.

Strickland, D. S. (1998) *Teaching Phonics Today: A Primer for Educators*. Newark: International Reading Association.

Whitehead, M. (2002) *Developing Language and Literacy with Young Children* (2nd edn). London: Paul Chapman Publishing.

CHAPTER 4

Planning with short stories

Teresa Grainger

Introduction

Short stories are written in a wide range of genres from 'My brother Adam never liked me ...' to 'Every full moon the Loup Garou hunted for a fresh victim'. They include mystery narratives, multicultural tales, traditional tales, myths and legends, science fiction, humorous tales and contemporary school and football stories, to mention but a few. They also exist in a variety of formats such as picture-books, novel-sized short story collections and illustrated anthologies, some of which are single-author, some translated and others retold by significant children's writers in edited collections.

Short stories have a real appeal to children because of their immediacy and accessibility, particularly in picture-book format (see Chapter 10), which depend for their success on the interaction between words and pictures (Lewis 2001). However, in this format, the construction of the narrative is closely connected to the images, whereas in short story collections containing few pictures, the literary language of the tale has to be sufficiently powerful to carry the narrative on its own. Since children are rarely invited to write novels, and few will experience the challenge of creating complex picture-books, the short story genre is a very valuable resource for offering appropriate models of *writing* stories. Creatively examined and enjoyed, these stories can increase children's awareness of narrative construction, highlight the need for the careful and immediate creation of characters; and demonstrate the role of the chosen setting and the critical importance of significant narrative action. Different styles of short stories can be fruitfully compared to enable children to ascertain the diversity available and to add to their repertoire of possibilities for short story writing. Their very brevity encourages a more exploratory examination and the promotion of a wealth of *speaking and listening* activities as the teacher will not feel pressured to move on, as is often the case with the novel. So the children can afford to dwell in the present and examine a number of short stories to enrich their knowledge and experience of the genre.

In relation to *reading*, short stories proffer worthwhile material in whatever format they are presented. They are particularly useful for guided reading in which the whole narrative can be read at one sitting, ensuring increased satisfaction and pleasure. This is often important for less experienced readers who benefit from experiencing the coherence of the whole story, whether presented as a picture text or a single tale in a short story collection. Once one or two have been sampled and enjoyed, the children may be motivated to read the remaining stories in the collection. In addition, short stories often make excellent read-aloud material in busy timetables and in a unit of work a variety of such stories can be read to the class. It is also possible that the children will be able to supplement the books available in class with examples from home, since edited collections of folk and fairy tales and publishers' collections of children's stories from all corners of the globe sell well as Christmas/birthday gifts, and may be gathering dust on shelves at home. With a couple of packs of good book plates and a clear borrowing system instituted, the resultant new class book box of short stories can become a valuable addition during a unit of work and for the remainder of the term as a resource for independent reading.

Connections to the NLS *Framework for Teaching* (DfEE 1998)

Despite the fact that the National Literacy Strategy *Framework for Teaching* does not set short stories as a separate genre until Key Stage 3, there are plenty of opportunities to weave these into the curriculum, and as noted, there are many advantages in so doing. Financially this is also advantageous, since although class sets are expensive, short story collections often have at least half a dozen narratives in each book, enabling the tales to be variously enjoyed in shared, guided and independent reading contexts. So the purchase of a good selection for each year group is not prohibitive.

As the following summary indicates, short stories can be imaginatively woven into every year in Key Stage 2.

Year 3 – Term 2: Traditional stories, stories with related themes

A wealth of folk and fairy tales, trickster tales and variations/parodies on well-known themes (*The Three Little Pigs, Cinderella, The Frog Princes,* etc.) exist, as well as collections of animal stories or sea tales, and stories with clever heroines which can be explored (see the recommended booklist at the end of the chapter).

Year 4 – Term 3: Stories from a range of cultures

Contemporary and traditional tales from many cultures are available as picturebooks and novel-sized collections, from significant writers such as Geraldine

McCaughrean, Grace Hallworth and Vivian French are suitable in this term. Or in term 1, when poems with common themes are examined, related collections of short school stories examining bullying or friendship can be shared. Such stories could also supplement term 3 when short novels that raise issues are being explored.

Year 5 – Term 1: Novels, stories and poems by significant children's authors

Most significant children's authors write both novels and short stories and it can be interesting to examine their common themes or different approaches in the way they tackle these different genres. High-quality authors who encompass both include: Dick King-Smith, Joan Aiken, Kevin Crossley-Holland, Jan Mark and Phillipa Pearce. In addition, in term 3, when traditional stories, myths, legends and fables from a range of cultures are explored, then once again short stories can come to the fore, with a focus perhaps on Greek, Norse or Celtic myths, or legendary characters such as King Arthur, Joan of Arc and Robin Hood. These are often found in fabulously illustrated collections: Barefoot, Oxford and Orchard publishers specialise in these.

Year 6 – Term 2: Longer established stories and novels from more than one genre

While there are many classic novels to choose from, and accompanying films to support such work, science fiction stories, ghost stories, mystery tales and school stories can be most easily accessed in the short story form. There is a wealth available by such writers as Helen Dunmore, George Layton, Bernard Ashley and Robert Westall.

Using drama to support literacy learning

In this chapter, drama – the art form of social encounters – is used extensively to examine and explore selected short stories within the planned unit of work. Drama as a tool for learning can make a real contribution to language and literacy development both in extended drama time and in the Literacy Hour. It can be used to support the examination of a wide range of literary genres, both fiction and non-fiction (e.g. Grainger and Pickard 2004; Baldwin and Fleming 2003; Bunyan *et al.* 2000) and is also employed elsewhere in other units of work in this book, but here its use is highlighted as a creative pedagogy and it is fleshed out more fully. Drama activities need to be fully embedded within the shared, guided and/or independent elements of literacy time and not used as 'warm up' tasks merely to motivate children. To do so is to severely underestimate the potential of drama to provide imaginary contexts in which reading, writing, and speaking and listening are a natural response.

Educational drama is variously described as 'classroom' (Grainger and Cremin 2000), 'story' (Booth 1994) or 'process' drama (O'Neil 1995), but regardless of any particular nomenclature, such drama involves children in creating imaginary worlds, dwelling in them and returning to the real world to reflect upon connections between them. It provides a link between cognitive and affective modes of learning and also involves children physically, aesthetically and morally. Through the 'prism of fiction' (Toye and Prendeville 2000) children can consider their own values, learn to tolerate uncertainty and ambiguity (Grainger 2003a) and, most importantly, develop their imaginative capacity (Cremin 2003). Drama relies heavily on the imagination and offers real opportunities for its development through the questioning stance adopted and the extensive 'possibility thinking' involved (Craft 2001).

If literature is used as an animating current to drive the drama then the short story selected needs to represent a potent hook to prompt a journey of exploration and investigation. Learning about the story in such contexts occurs through the children's full intellectual and emotional engagement and the opportunities provided to reflect upon the narrative, its characters, themes and consequences. It is essentially improvisational and is likely to encompass the creation of new characters and new scenarios based upon the story in order to create increase insight. Drama enables children to participate more directly in interpreting and reflecting upon literature and, in the context of short stories, enables greater access to the themes, content and features of these texts.

Drama and reading

Drama enriches reading, writing, speaking and listening in various ways; for example, in relation to *reading*, drama can be used to 'speak the silence of stories' (Hendy and Toon 2001 : 76) as it enables young learners to actively interrogate texts, exploring and making meaning as they take on roles and look beyond the words themselves. Children can co-author new and living fictions through drama, and learn about the nature of reading in the process, as they investigate texts in classroom drama sessions (Grainger 1998). The power of prediction is very strong in both reading and drama as gaps in the text are fleshed out (Iser 1978) and, in addition, imagery and connectivity play a significant role in both reading and drama. Through examining short stories in the context of drama intertextual connections in terms of content, form and purpose may well be experienced, observed and discussed.

Drama and writing

The motivating power of drama can also provide meaningful contexts for *writing*, both individually and collaboratively. In-role work, in the context of a narrative, often leads to more empathetic writing from different stances and perspectives.

This can make a real contribution to children's development as writers (e.g. McNaughton 1997; Barrs and Cork 2001; Grainger 2001a, 2001b, 2003a, 2003b). Recent Primary National Strategy research has also shown that drama can make a marked difference to both boys' attitudes and their achievements in writing (Bearne and Grainger 2004; Bearne *et al.* 2004). As children become imaginatively involved in drama, they generate a plethora of ideas for writing and begin to select and refine these through listening to others' views and orally rehearsing and developing their own. Drama supports children's ideational fluency and enables them to form their thoughts and opinions prior to writing, their writing in-role, therefore, often has a strong sense of stance and a clearer-than-usual sense of perspective.

Drama and speaking and listening

In fictional contexts, authentic reasons to communicate both orally and in writing emerge, and children are frequently involved in discussing their ideas, developing possible responses in role, co-operating with others and adapting their speech. The National Curriculum in England (DfES 2000) describes the elements of *speaking and listening* as: speaking, listening, group discussion and interaction, and drama, and all four elements can be encompassed through quality drama provision. In role, as characters from the text, children are involved in experimenting with language styles and registers and finding language and vocabulary appropriate to the imaginary situation (QCA 1999). If they are given the opportunity to reflect upon these choices, this can contribute to their growing awareness of the spoken word and make a real contribution to their emerging confidence. In drama they will also be listening closely as they co-create the narrative through words and actions.

Mining the potential of a short story

Through increasing both the teacher's and the children's involvement in the issue or theme in a short story, drama can help the class dig down into the substrata of the tale. Teachers need to choose moments to expand on the text which can help young people create a richer understanding of it, but in mining a text's potential it is critical to choose wisely and to consider the scenario's suitability as a dramatic prompt. Questions worth considering include:

- Does the class know enough of the characters/story/setting to, for example, project imaginatively forwards or backwards in the text?
- What possible 'off-stage' scenarios might be occurring that could be fruitfully investigated?
- What possible roles or conventions could be employed at this moment and with what specific purpose?

- How much needs to be read aloud immediately before the drama to contextualise the action?

Tension is a crucial element in drama, and its importance in motivating the children's enquiry must not be underestimated, so particularly challenging or conflict-ridden moments need to be selected, which may, for example, focus on misunderstanding, secrets or pressure. These will help trigger more focused improvisation and draw the children imaginatively into the situations in which the characters find themselves. All fiction is full of unresolved conflicts to choose from, and short stories frequently contain accounts of difficult situations and predicaments which the characters have to face. Tension can also be created through examining missing elements and gaps in the text, e.g. nightmares, premonitions, unmentioned conversations, a character's conflicting thoughts on an issue, or earlier problematic events that hint at the challenge to come. Through drama, these 'omissions' can be constructed, investigated and packed with meaning as the layers of the text are both created and revealed.

If the children do not experience a genuine sense of conflict or difficulty through their engagement in role, or in response to the situations they encounter, then there will be no drama. So it is important to dig down into a rich textual seam within the story, selecting or creating a significant moment of tension to investigate further. The potential of the moment is important not only in relation to the drama, but also in relation to text production opportunities, since any written text produced can be used for teaching about word-, sentence- or text-level features in context.

A wide range of *drama conventions* can be employed to aid the comprehension and composition of texts. These are tools for investigating meaning and represent a palette of flexible choices that frame and focus an investigation in the context of the story (Neelands 1998). So, in addition to selecting a potentially rich and tense moment in a text, teachers need to identify appropriate conventions to serve their purpose. Over a whole unit of work many conventions will be harnessed, but in preparation for a particular piece of writing on a given day, specific conventions may be chosen that are in tune with the text-type and enable the children to rehearse the form of the text orally prior to writing.

As the following diagram (Figure 4.1), adapted from Bearne (2003 : 32) indi- cates, many drama activities can be employed at the immersion/familiarisation stage of the unit of work. They will help to generate and capture ideas, which will feed through to the teacher-led whole-class work on constructing a piece of writing within the short story genre. However, there is no need for drama to be utilised at this initial part of the extended model of composition; children benefit from revisiting their role-play or creating a later decision alley, for example, having reflected upon their ideas. Drama can be used throughout the writing process to motivate as well as to shape and support the children's compositions and enrich their comprehension of the story.

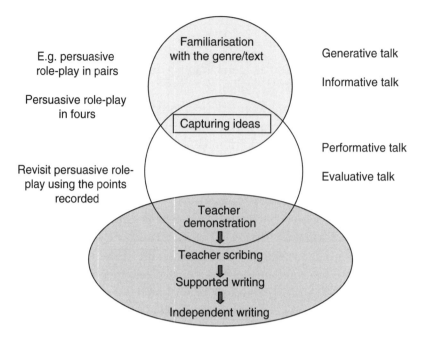

Figure 4.1 The extended process of drama and composition (adapted from Bearne 2003)

Using drama to examine selected short stories

Examples of extended dramas based on short stories and briefer encounters with drama in the context of a unit of work on this genre are detailed here to demonstrate the structured yet responsive nature of drama and to show how easily it can be integrated into literacy planning. In relation to extended drama the three stages of a drama session – namely establishing the drama context; introducing conflicts and tensions; and drawing the drama together, are used in these sessions (Grainger and Cremin 2001).

The activities and approaches described for KS2 learners represent ways to examine the central themes and concerns of the two short stories 'The Rope', by Philippa Pearce (2000), and 'The Golden Gate', by Helen Dunmore (2000). These are found in the short story collections *The Rope and other Stories* (Penguin) and *Aliens Don't Eat Bacon Sandwiches* (Mammoth) respectively. A resumé of the plots of these narratives is useful here to contextualise the work planned. Both narratives focus on boys and their sisters; they deal with relationships in families and examine different aspects of fear. Both are set outside the safe context of home where the boys involved endure difficulties and have to make decisions to overcome their fears.

In 'The Rope', the title story from this collection, we meet Mike who is on holiday at his grandmother's with his sister Shirley. The rope hangs across the local river ready for children to swing across, and fills Mike with dread. He dreams about it, knowing that as part of a ritual, the local kids, with whom he would like

Figure 4.2a, b

to make friends, and indeed his grandmother, expect him to swing across. Mike eventually does seize the rope but he becomes suspended above the river and has to find the courage to drop into the water and swim to the bank. As he does so he is watched by the local children and, in particular, by a boy called Ginger, as well as his mother and grandmother. His sense of shame is profound. At the close of the tale, however, Ginger and Mike find a way to accept their fears and the differences and commonalities between themselves.

In 'The Golden Gate', by Helen Dunmore, David and his family visit Mere Park Funfair for his birthday. He takes his little sister Pearl to queue for the infamous Golden Gate Ride but finds that its strange owner, Bella Damiano, selects Pearl to go on a Golden Mystery Ride without him. Afterwards, he cannot find Pearl and is distraught; his elder brother Rob had been killed two years before in a road accident and now he believes Pearl has also been taken. He hunts for her and loses his worn photo of Rob in the process, but eventually locates her at the top of the Death Slide, part of the Golden Gate Ride. Together, they mysteriously see an image of Rob projected onto the Golden Gate and want to go to him, but eventually turn away and return safely to their parents.

The description of classroom endeavour in the unit of work which follows is not intended to be a detailed account of lessons planned, but seeks to illustrate the many options available when drama is employed as the pre-eminent pedagogy in planning. Teachers could, however, follow this unit of work, selecting from the options and combining their own ideas in response to their children's interests. It is important that while in all such literacy work clear learning intentions are outlined from the outset, the journey actually travelled must be responsive to the children's needs and interests expressed along the way. This enables the critical features of creative learning to be present. These include relevance, autonomy, ownership of knowledge, control of the learning processes and innovation (Jeffrey and Woods 1997; Jeffrey and Woods 2003). So while a relatively detailed account is offered, many intuitive decisions and much of the instruction involved will depend upon the actual exploration. This means that a genuine journey is constructed in consultation with the children, increasing the authenticity of their response, enhancing their engagement and enriching their productivity. The extended process of composition allows time for children to engage fully with a range of motivating activities such as drama, which lead towards purposeful writing, and enable teachers to lead by framing and inspiring, but also by following the children's interests and sensitively shaping the unfolding exploration of the short stories in consultation with them.

The learning intention/long-term outcome of this three-week unit of work is for the children to write their own short stories, making full use of the knowledge about short story writing developed through the three weeks. The specific reading/writing and speaking and listening objectives can be selected from the NLS and QCA banks of objectives in advance of the work, or teachers may prefer to let this unit run its course and retrospectively consider which objectives have been examined through the class's exploration and the opportunities seized for specific teaching. Many teachers in the recent Boys' Achievements in Writing Project undertaken by UKLA for the PNS (Bearne *et al.* 2004) found that this form of planning increased both their freedom and flexibility and they planned to offer such units on a more regular basis to foster increased creativity and to enhance their professional freedom. For the purposes of this chapter, however, the key objectives selected for a close focus orient around narrative action, setting and character. In terms of narrative action, the key events in the two stories are submitted to close examination and the structure of the tales are highlighted in order to help the class identify possible additional or alternative scenarios and appreciate the importance of problematic events and conflicts in short story writing. There are also plenty of opportunities for the children to examine how characters are presented through dialogue and action and to create their own understanding of some of the characters through drama and storytelling. Settings in both the tales are significant and this is additionally highlighted through the use of a film, *Mavis and the Mermaid*, available in the BFI Story Shorts collection (BFI 2001). Throughout, opportunities arise for explicit instruction in context at word- sentence- and text-level, although teachers will need to choose which objectives to follow through in response to the evolving nature of the work and the needs of their specific class of learners. So many planned writing opportunities will be imaginatively framed in support of the long-term goal, although some will be seized as they surface and related objectives explored in context.

Week 1

During this week the children will become better acquainted with the genre of short story writing through extensive read-aloud and through their guided reading groups in which short story collections such as *The Daydreamer*, by Ian McEwan, or *The Fib and Other Stories*, by George Layton, can be enjoyed. Invite the children during this week to bring in any short story collections they possess, whether these are traditional tales or more contemporary narratives. These can then be listed and established as a class book box and borrowed in school for independent reading and for work in this unit. With regard to the particular books to be used for closer examination, it is recommended these are not introduced immediately. Instead you could usefully begin with a focus on personal stories, enabling the children to make connections to their own life stories before turning to the challenge which Mike meets in 'The Rope'. 'The Rope' and 'The Golden Gate', as already noted, are both set within contemporary life, and when the children come to these during the work they will be bringing their knowledge and under-standing of incidents in their own lives. Making connections is a critical aspect of creativity and helping children lean on both life experience and fiction is important in order to support their writing, for as Berlie Doherty (2001) has commented 'fiction is a combination of "I remember and let's pretend" '.

You could commence the unit by telling the children a personal story, if possible one that is set in a holiday context or on a day out somewhere. Track back into your own memory and share this with verve and involvement; this will prompt the class to recall incidents in their lives in the context of holidays and day trips, in settings outside their homes. Ask the children, in pairs, to share their memories of these incidents with one another. Try to avoid limiting their recall by framing your request too tightly. You could help to trigger these reminiscences by showing a photo of yourself on holiday and asking the class to bring in snapshots of their trips to funfairs or holiday snaps which remind them of a story to share.

Whatever your starting point, after pairs have had time to tell their tale, use a musical instrument and set up a story buzz (Grainger *et al.* 2004) or photo-tell session in which the children move around the class telling their tale and listening to their partners before moving on to their next partner in response to the musical sign. In effect, the class move around telling and listening to tales. Through this process they will begin to unconsciously shape their own tale, embellishing certain elements and reducing others. During this time, pause the buzz and ask each pair to decide together on an effective title for their tales; you could read some titles from the two focus books to highlight the economy of words used and to show them that a good title often only hints at what is to come, creating a tempting precursor to the events of the narrative. Examples from these books include: 'The Rope', 'A Close Match', 'A Gap in the Dark', 'Inside Her Head' and 'The Fir Cone'. Their titles can be written on laminated whiteboards and displayed in front of them, so that as the story buzz continues, children are selecting a personal story to hear based on the title.

Towards the end of the session, it would be useful to share some of these titles, to display them and to vote on those that tempt the listeners most. Draw parallels with titles in the short story collections and make the point that as readers we lean heavily on the listed titles in such collections to make our choice, so the impact or otherwise that the title makes is highly significant. Explain to the class that your work together in literacy is going to focus on short stories and that across the three weeks you will be engaging together in a number of activities with the express intention of producing a class anthology of short stories for the parallel year group or their own class to read and share. Explain that you, too, will be working on your own short story and that, if they wish, they will be able to weave their own life experiences or settings just described into these stories, although these will not be autobiographical tales.

On day 2, you could introduce the collection *The Rope and other Stories*, and make any connections to other books by Philippa Pearce that the class may know, such as *The Way to Satin Shore* or *The Battle of Bubble and Squeak*. Draw their attention to the fact that, as an author, Philippa roots many of her narratives in aspects of her life experience. You are seeking to build on day 1 and focus on narrative events which may be mentioned or alluded to within the given title. Remind one another of the key events that were described in yesterday's oral life stories, e.g. losing something precious, getting lost, sibling rivalry, travelling difficulties and so on. Ask groups to create a freeze-frame of one of the displayed titles from the day before, a tableau that shows a critical incident or happening in the narrative. Watch these, and as a class, allocate the titles to them, making connections between the narrative action represented and the titles themselves.

As teacher, you might now ponder aloud about the possible narrative events which could happen in Philippa's story entitled 'The Rope' and inform them that the main character, Mike, even dreams about this rope in the opening paragraph. Where might it hang or lie, to whom could it belong, has someone lost it, what is it wrapped around, is it old and frayed, is it found by Mike? Invite the children in groups of four or five to create a freeze-frame of a key incident described in the story, or of a premonition that Mike has in his dream. Make it clear that no-one dies in the tale, but that their tableau needs to reveal more about the rope, its place and possible purpose, as well as Mike's relationship to it. Voice some thoughts, leaving each one tentative and open and making it clear that while they will not have the same ideas as Philippa Pearce, their thoughts will be valued. In effect, you have created a mystery out of the title through musing upon it and you are leaving this open-ended problem for the groups to solve. When this has been created, move around each group with the children asking questions of each group's freeze-frame or getting the class to tell each other what they think is going on, then encourage the children in the tableau to share their interpretations of the event. Afterwards, in pairs or threes drawn from these groups, ask the children to write the dream or event they have just depicted. Set the work at a pace and try to give them time to share their descriptions with their friends in the freeze-frame group. If possible, read some of these aloud as the class observe the particular freeze-frames again, so their passages complement the physical evocation. Later the same day, read the opening section of the story to the class to page 7 where Mike has to take his turn.

On day 3, re-read the opening section, priming the children to listen carefully to the way in which Philippa Pearce builds up the reader's sense of Mike's fear of the rope through anticipating the events to come and creating an impending sense of doom. Discuss this together, and if you like, copies could be made of pages 4/5 to help prompt the discussion. Then read page 7 and half of 8 to where Shirley, his sister, watches 'his fear, his fear within fear'. Again, you could ponder aloud how Mike is feeling, what images and thoughts are flashing through his mind, and set up the whole class to think out loud in role as Mike. Briefly retell the events leading up to this moment and then think out loud yourself as a model, giving the class space to simultaneously voice their own thoughts in role as Mike. Then create two lines of children facing one another, and with one child in role as Mike, evoke a decision alley. Is Mike going to run away, fake a stomach pain, ask for his sister's help, or is he going to force himself to do this? What does he think of the other kids, his gran and his sister at this time? What conflicting thoughts are racing around his head? As one child in role as Mike walks up the decision alley, the rest of the class voice his thoughts so everyone can hear. When 'Mike' reaches the end of the alley ask this child what they think Mike is going to do and why? What thoughts influenced his final decision? Invite the children to record a diary entry as Mike, written that very night at his gran's. This needs to indicate Mike's sense of dread and reveal what did actually happen and how he felt about it. Share these and reflect upon what they reveal about Mike's emotions and his character. Later that day, read aloud the section which describes his ride on the rope and his descent into the river, to page 12 where Mike feels sick at the thought of going home and strawberries and cream for tea.

On day 4, re-read the same section and invite the children to notice how the author, right up to his climactic fall into the river, continues to reveal Mike's feelings, particularly through the verbs and adverbs which describe his actions of those of others. Invite the children in groups to discuss the ending of the story, and after some time invite these groups to show this in two freeze-frames which depict the significant closing scenes. Read the end of the tale to them and compare and contrast the different versions. Reflect together on the story and invite the class to connect to the tales they told on Monday, were any of these about parallel incidents, when they felt obliged to overcome their fears? Allow the children time to share these and other related incidents with one another, the brother–sister bond may also trigger some life connections and prompt alternative memories.

On day 5, make connections to examples shared on the previous day, and perhaps an example of your own, and consider how different characters perceive the events of any given tale. In relation to 'The Rope', how, for example, does Mum feel about Mike's fall into the river and what might she say to Dad? Create a list with the class of all the key characters and invite the children to select one; then, in pairs, with one in role as this character and their partner in role as Dad or a friend from home, improvise a phone call in which the rope incident is described. You might like to model this with a teaching assistant or a member of the class. As a class, listen to some snippets of these. Stress that acting is not required; this is just a phone conversation; but you are interested in how different characters perceive the events and the various perspectives offered. Discuss these as a class. Does Mike himself feel better for the experience? What has he learnt and what do others think of him now? There is no right answer here, although there is much to infer and deduce from the narrative. Consider together the possible short story themes the children may choose for their own work. Are they thinking of linking in an event from their own lives or inventing a new challenge for their protagonist? Challenge them to reflect upon possibilities for the weekend homework and to bring back some possible thoughts and options. You may want to provide a frame for this, but be wary of not making it too prescriptive, and keep stressing that this is just a short story with only a few characters, one main setting and a limited number of events.

Week 2

This week focuses more upon the second tale, 'The Golden Gate', although you will want to continue to read short stories to the class and in the context of guided reading, making connections and comparisons to the two main tales introduced so far. In this week the children begin to commit their own short story to paper, building on the sharing of oral tales the previous week and their experience of 'The Rope' and other examples from this genre.

On day 1, invite the children to discuss in pairs one major event/narrative action that they think happens in the story. Then provide slips of paper and ask each child to secretly explain what the Golden Gate is and record their expectation of the central narrative action chosen by Helen Dunmore. Only allow ten minutes or so for this and remind the class of 'The Rope' and how the title offered a window of knowledge on the story. Collect their signed slips and seal them in an envelope, stressing they have created possible ideas for a story and are unlikely to have created the same one as Helen since she may have been using her own life or someone else's in the tale.

Read the opening two paragraphs and provide copies for the children. Discuss in pairs and as a whole class the differences and similarities between the two heroes, David from this tale and Mike from 'The Rope'. The children may need to share reminiscences of funfairs and adventure centres they have visited if these did not surface in the personal tales from the previous week. If so, build in time for this to enable them to make personal text-to-life connections about their fears and pleasures in these contexts. Also help the class see how both openings offer hints and premonitions of possible action to come and give the reader a clear sense of the main character's feelings.

Re-read the opening of 'The Rope' and, together as a class, generate a number of titles for a contemporary short story. Then, as shared work, select one title and map out a simple event-based life narrative for it on the whiteboard. A simple story journey will do for this, with a few key words to list the day's events, and in another colour the character's feelings towards the events can be shown. Much will depend upon the title chosen by you and the class. Do not be tempted to prepare a plan beforehand; go with the flow and demonstrate the challenge of mapping out a story based on a significant day in the life of the chosen character. Challenge the children to share their own possible titles and connect these to a significant event for their key character. Supported by the work the previous week – the homework, their life connections and your recent reading of a range of short stories – the children will begin to map out their own story journeys, which can easily be shared due to their brief nature.

On day 2, re-read the opening paragraphs of both stories and model for the class moving from the story journey into the opening paragraph which creates a possible premonition, acts as an effective precursor of what is to come and shares a character's perspective very early on. In your second paragraph, invite the children's suggestions so that the class story is again being co-written between you. Provide time for the class to draft the openings to their own short stories, working as authors to draw their readers in and to capture their interest. Share these in pairs and invite children to read aloud examples of when the writer has successfully hinted at possible future events or revealed the main character's view.

On days 3 to 5 this week, you could continue to read aloud 'The Golden Gate' and examine the events, the characters and the setting, and provide time for the class to work on their own short stories, constantly making parallels between 'The Rope', 'The Golden Gate' and their own tales. For example, at a significant moment of tension in the tale, when David loses Pearl, you could thought-track him by placing a chair in the centre of the class circle and inviting the children to step forward and voice his thoughts in role – does Mum think it's my fault; how can she have gone; I'm not sure I trust Bella Damiano; what can she have done with Pearl; should I ring the police; Rob will never forgive me; he loved Pearl as I do; and so forth. This insight into the mind of the main character at a moment of difficulty could be connected to their work, and time could be set aside for each child to speak out loud as their own character from their narrative. Their challenge is then, as authors, to ensure they convey the feelings and thoughts of their characters in their own stories. Alternatively, you could work on the sense of anticipation in these stories, built up about both the rope 'initiation test' and the intriguing Mystery Ride on the Golden Gate Ride. Highlight for the children how on their story journey plan they could draw a symbol to represent the key focus at several points early in the tale. This can then be woven into the narrative through brief descriptions or, as in these stories, through the boys' sisters' experience of the rope and the ride.

While you will no doubt complete the story of the Golden Gate, allow the children time, working with response partners and in guided writing groups, to discuss their emerging stories with one another and with you, so that the work is redrafted and reshaped during the writing and you can read their developing stories and respond to the needs of the class. For example, if many of them are finding speech punctuation difficult then you could introduce some role-play based on two characters in 'The Golden Gate', and after their pair work you could record a possible written version as shared writing. The improvised conversation will generate ideas with regard to content and provide a valuable context for the teaching of speech punctuation and speech verbs.

Week 3

This week focuses on concluding the stories and publishing these in a class anthology or through reading them aloud to another year group (whatever your intended audience was from the outset). In addition, the short film, *Mavis and the Mermaid*, is introduced to examine a short story represented in another medium. This is not essential, but does provide an opportunity to connect to the children's existing cultural knowledge of film and build on this to develop their understanding of the short story genre. The film is a short story, a traditional tale with four main characters and a seaside setting. It would make a valuable link between this unit of work on short stories and a related and ensuing unit of work on traditional tales, myths and legends.

On day 1 it may be useful to focus on the closing components of 'The Rope' and 'The Golden Gate'. In the former, Mike makes a friend and becomes comfortable with his fears, realising that everyone is afraid of different things. In the latter, David finds his sister and takes her safely home, having finally come to terms with his brother's death. The children, in groups, could show a final freeze-frame from one of the two narratives, which show the relationships between the main characters, or they could as a class create a double group sculpture, one of each of the endings, placed alongside one another. In group sculpture, the children carefully position key characters at a moment in the text and suggest their specific body postures, facial expressions and so forth. Observing these the class could then write speech and thought bubbles to convey Mike's or David's perspective at this point in the tale. If you have a school digital camera, this would help to freeze the image and enable their written captions to be displayed alongside it. Then, in small groups, each child author could explain to their group the closing moment in their tale, and make a group sculpture of this, perhaps even making notes for themselves about this or inviting the group to generate their thoughts or the words between them. This may take some time but will help the young authors sustain a sense of their key character views at the close of their story.

On days 2 and 3, as the children complete their semi-final drafts, it will be important to set time aside for different response partners to read the stories as written and to respond to them as readers, in particular highlighting the coherence, or otherwise, of the narrative, and sharing any parts which are confusing or unclear with the writers. These can then be fine-tuned before the proofreading process begins. Extracts can be read to the class and proofreading partnerships can also be set up and computers used to process the work. Early finishers might collect all the titles and authors and begin to group together the stories for the class collection, a title and front cover for which also need to be conceived. This will involve further examination of the short story collections in the class.

On days 4 and 5, as the final versions are being completed and read to the class and to one another in groups and pairs, the 14-minute film could be screened and used to stimulate discussion about the ways in which the setting, characters and key narrative events shape the tale. Each of these narrative elements interact with one another, and a discussion about how this happens in the film as well as in one of the written stories is possible now that the class know the two narratives well. An apparent mystery surrounds the mermaid tale in the same way that one surrounds the Golden Gate, and a form of resolution is evident insofar as all three stories serve a purpose for the young protagonists who all begin to overcome the difficulties of their situations.

It will be important to celebrate the children's stories and to ensure, for example, that multiple copies of the collection are made available so that other readers can also enjoy their narratives. Some may be read in assembly, others to visitors, or on the school website, and reviews could be encouraged via the school newsletter/magazine or on simple post-it notes. Such feedback to young authors is critical, to ensure they see themselves as genuine writers of literature which is actually read and responded to by a real audience. Their work will represent a culmination of considerable labour and their expanded knowledge of the genre will be reflected in their short stories for all to celebrate and enjoy.

Recommended short story collections

Contemporary short stories

Ahlberg, Allen (1998) *The Mighty Slide*. Viking Kestrel.

Ahlberg, Janet and Allen (1987) *The Clothes Horse and other Stories*. Puffin.

Aiken, Joan (1978) *Tale of One-Way Street* (Pictures by J. Pienkowski). Jonathan Cape.

Aiken, Joan (1981) *A Handful of Gold*. Red Fox.

Aiken, Joan and Jan Pienkowski (1968) *A Necklace of Raindrops*. Penguin.

Alcock, Vivienne (1992) *Ticket to Heaven*. Mammoth, Egmont.

Ashley, Bernard *The Puffin Book of School Stories*. Puffin.

Blackman, Malorie (2000) *Words Last Forever*. Mammoth.

Blishen, Edward (1999) *Science Fiction Stories*. Kingfisher.

Cresswell, Helen (1999) *Puffin Book of Funny Stories*. Puffin.

Cresswell, Helen (2000) *Mystery Stories*. Kingfisher.

Crossley Holland, Kevin (1998) *Short!* Oxford University Press.

Doherty, Berlie (1982) *How Green You Are!* Mammoth.

Dunmore, Helen (2000) *Aliens Don't Eat Bacon Sandwiches*. Mammoth.

French, Vivian (1991) *The Boy Who Walked on Water*. Walker.

Howker, Janni (1984) *Badger on the Barge and other Stories*. Julia Macrae.

Jung, Reindhart (2002) *Bambert's Book of Missing Stories* (trans. by Anthea Bell). Egmont.

McBratney, Sam (1996) *One Grand Sweet Song*. Mammoth.

McCaughrean, Geraldine (1998) *A Pack of Lies*. Penguin.

McEwan, Ian (1994) *The Day Dreamer* (Pictures by A. Browne). Jonathan Cape.

Mark, Jan (1980) *Nothing to Be Afraid of*. Penguin.

Morpurgo, Michael (2000) *From Hereabout Hill*. Mammoth.

Naidoo, Beverly (2001) *Out of Bounds Stories of Conflict and Hope*. Puffin.

Pearce, Phillippa (1997) *The Shadow Cage and other Tales of the Supernatural*. Penguin.

Pearce, Philippa (2000) *The Rope*. Puffin.

Rosen, Michael (1976) *Nasty!* Puffin.

Rosen, Michael (ed.) (2000) *A Century of Children's Ghost Stories: Tales of Dread and Delight*. Oxford University Press.

Rushdie, Salman (1990) *Haroun and the Sea of Stories*. Penguin.

Westall, Robert (1994) *A Walk on the Wild Side*. Mammoth.

Westhall, Robert (ed.) (1998) *The Young Oxford Book of Football Stories*. Oxford University Press.

Traditional tales and stories from other cultures

Coates, Lucy and Anthony Lewis (2002) *Atticus the Storyteller's 100 Greek Myths*. Orion.

Crossley-Holland, Kevin (1992) *Long Tom and the Dead Hand*. Andre Deutsch.

Crossley-Holland, Kevin (2000) *Tales from the Old World*. Dolphin.

Crossley-Holland, Kevin (2000) *Enchantment, Fairy Tales, Ghost Stories and Tales of Wonder*. (Pictures by Emma Chichester Clarke) Orion.

Dickinson, Susan (1996) *The Sea Baby* (Pictures by Peter Bailey) Collins.

Doherty, Berlie (1997) *Tales of Wonder and Magic* (Pictures by Juan Wijingaard) Walker.

Doyle, Malachy (2000) *Tale from Old Ireland*. Barefoot.

French, Vivian (1995) *The Thistle Princess and other Stories*. Walker.

French, Vivian (1999) *Under the Moon and other Stories*. Walker.

Grindley, Sally (1997) *Breaking the Spell: Tales of Enchantment*. Kingfisher.

Hallworth, Grace (1984) *Mouth Open, Story Jump Out*. Magnet.

Hallworth, Grace (1997) *Mermaid and Monster Stories from the Sea*. Mammoth.

Heaney, Marie (2000) *The Thames upon the Harp: Irish Myth and Legend*. Faber and Faber.

Laird, Elizabeth (2000) *When the World Began: Stories Collected in Ethiopia.* Oxford University Press.

Lurie, Alison (1980) *Clever Gretchen and other Forgotten Folktales.* Mammoth.

Medlicott, Mary (1996) *The Big Wide-Mouthed Toad Frog* (Pictures by Sue Williams). Walker.

Rosen, Michael (1992) *South, North, East and West.* Walker.

Williams, Jay (1978) *The Practical Princess and other Liberating Fairy Tales.* Hippo.

References

Baldwin, P. and Fleming, K. (2003) *Teaching Literacy through Drama: Creative Approaches.* London: RoutledgeFalmer.

Barrs, M. and Cork, V. (2001) *The Reader in the Writer: The Influence of Literature upon Writing at KS2.* London: CLPE.

Bearne, E. (2003) *Making Progress in Writing.* London: Routledge.

Bearne, E. and Grainger, T. (2004) 'Raising boys' achievement in writing. *Literacy*, 38(3).

Bearne, E., Grainger, T. and Wolstencroft, H. (2004) *Raising Boys' Achievements in Writing.* Joint Research Project Primary National Strategy and UKLA. London: DfES.

BFI (2001) *Story Shorts: A resource for KS2 Literacy.* London: British Film Institute.

Booth, D. (1994) *Story Drama: Reading, Writing and Role Playing across the Curriculum.* Markham, Ontario: Pembroke.

Bunyan, P., Catron, J., Harrison, L. *et al.* (2000) *Cracking Drama: Progression in Drama within English (5–16).* York: York Publishing Services for NATE.

Cremin, M. (2003) 'The role of the imagination in drama'. Doctoral Thesis, University of Kent.

DfEE (1998) *The National Literacy Strategy Framework for Teaching.* London: DfEE.

Doherty, B. (2001) 'Recognising yourself in what you read'. Keynote address at 'Just Let Me Think': Reflecting on Literacy Learning. United Kingdom Reading Association International Conference, 6–8 July, Canterbury.

Grainger, T. (1998) 'Drama and reading: illuminating their interaction'. *English in Education*, 32(1), 29–36.

Grainger, T. (2001a) 'Drama and writing: imagination on the page'. *The Primary English Magazine*, April, 6–10.

Grainger, T. (2001b) 'Drama and writing: imagination on the page 2'. *The Primary English Magazine*, June, 8–13.

Grainger, T. (2003a) 'Drama: ambiguity and uncertainty', in Bearne, E., Dombey, H. and Grainger, T. (eds) *Classroom Interactions in Literacy.* Milton Keynes: Open University Press.

Grainger, T. (2003b) 'Let drama build bridges between the subjects': *The Primary English Magazine*, 9(1), 8–12.

Grainger, T. and Cremin, M. (2000) *Resourcing Classroom Drama 5–8.* Sheffield: NATE.

Grainger, T. and Pickard, A. (2004) *Drama: Reading, Writing and Talking Our Way Forwards.* Cambridge: UKLA.

Grainger, T., Goouch, K. and Lambirth, A. (2004) *Creative Activities for Plot, Character and Setting 7–9.* Milton Keynes: Scholastic.

Hendy, L. and Toon, L. (2001) *Supporting Drama and Imaginative Play in the Early Years.* Buckingham: Open University Press.

Iser, W. (1978) *The Act of Reading.* Baltimore, MD: John Hopkins University Press.

Jeffrey, B. and Woods, P. (1997) 'The relevance of creative teaching: pupils' views', in Pollard, A., Thiessen, D. and Filer, A. *Children and Their Curriculum: The Perspectives of Primary and Elementary School Children.* London: Falmer Press.

Jeffrey, B. and Woods, P. (2003) *The Creative School: A Framework for Success, Quality and Effectiveness.* London: RoutledgeFalmer.

Lewis, D. (2001) *Reading Contemporary Picture Books: Picturing Text.* London: RoutledgeFalmer.

McNaughton, M. J. (1997) 'Drama and children's writing : a study of the influence of drama on the imaginative writing of primary school children'. *Research in Drama Education,* 2(1), 55–86.

Neelands, J. (1998) *Beginning Drama 11–14.* London: David Fulton.

O'Neill, C. (1995) *Drama Worlds: A Framework for Process Drama.* London: Heinemann.

QCA (1999) *Teaching Speaking and Listening at Key Stages 1 and 2.* Sudbury: QCA Publications.

Toye, N. and Prendeville, F. (2000) *Drama and Traditional Story for the Early Years.* London: RoutledgeFalmer.

CHAPTER 5

'You have been personally selected . . .': navigating non-fiction, negotiating modes: a critical response to real life

Rebecca Austin

This chapter explores ideas for approaching the teaching of non-fiction. The ideas were piloted by a group of hard-working teachers in an infant school in Chatham, Medway. It is 'flavoured' with multimodality – an acknowledgement that print-based texts are just one of the many forms of text with which children engage on a daily basis. Different kinds of texts need to be read in different ways and I suggest how the skills of critical literacy can be developed using texts from a range of different modes. Children in their everyday lives have experience of, and familiarity with, non-fiction texts in a wide range of modes. This chapter considers how literacy teaching in primary schools needs to build on this experience and familiarity. The changing nature of literacy cannot be ignored and I will argue that schools which embrace the changes, working with real texts that are integral to children's lives, will be equipping their pupils to be critically literate in the twenty-first century.

I also provide examples of units of work that are designed for children in Years 1 and 2, suggesting ways in which Early Years and Key Stage 1 teachers can offer creative literacy lessons that develop children's literacy skills in the reading and composition of non-fiction and multimodal texts.

The changing nature of communication

There has been a great deal written about the changing face of technology, the rapidity of the change and the corresponding shift in our understanding of what it means to be 'literate' (Lankshear and Knoebel 2003; Hannon 2000; Kress 2003). Children naturally use what is to hand in order to make and transmit meanings, and the range of tools available is expanding. It is now possible to communicate with others in an enormous variety of modes – ways which require new forms of writing to create new kinds of texts and, inevitably, new kinds of reading to interpret them (Hannon 2000). Children today engage with media texts, visual images, ICT texts and more. They are open to the possibilities these forms of communication offer, and as they develop the skills to create texts in this array of technologies, they are finding new ways to use them.

More than the ability to produce the texts themselves is a need to understand the 'code of practice' that goes with them. What are the 'dos and don'ts of texting, emailing chat rooms and photo-messaging for example? These practices are not fixed and are still evolving as they become embedded within society. E-mail in the workplace can be seen as a burden, stopping people meeting and talking face-to-face, resulting in at least one company banning its use (McClellan 2003) – this was certainly not what was expected. These practices will continue to evolve and teaching must reflect this. Children have an increasingly wide choice of communicative modes, and rather than teaching them the mechanics alone, we have to enable them to make choices about the most appropriate way to get their message across. We cannot teach them literacy 'skills' without acknowledging that those skills are embedded in cultural literate practices. We, as adults, must also acknowledge that those cultural literate practices are not the same as ours.

As adults we have varying degrees of confidence in, competence with, and experience and enjoyment of working with new forms of communication. Some adults have steadfastly refused to keep up with the changes in technology and others have embraced them in both their personal and working lives. These attitudes will inevitably affect the way in which teachers teach, both with and about multimodal texts.

The meaning-making which seems to predominate in primary school classrooms is still print-based. In my experience, while many teachers believe passionately in, and have experienced the joys of, 'reading' and 'writing', there are far fewer at the moment for whom the joys of computer games and texting seem equally exciting and relevant. I believe that teachers need to confront their personal prejudices and fears and accept that the children they teach may find pleasure in reading and composing different kinds of texts from those that they enjoy.

For most adults the starting point in our attempts to understand 'multimodal texts' has been print-based communication and we have used our understanding of the composition and interpretation of print-based texts as our springboard to the understanding of newer forms. For the children in primary schools, this is not necessarily the case. 'Children's familiarity with new forms of representation and communication mean that they are thinking differently from those adults who were brought up in a more print-dominated world' (Bearne 2003 : 98).

If children are thinking differently because of their life experiences within their own family and cultural environments, then it must be the case that teachers have to consider pedagogy to match these differences. Teachers will need to challenge the view that print-based texts should always dominate primary literacy lessons. They will need to challenge this rather narrow view of literacy if children are to engage critically with the texts that matter to them in their literary encounters in their world.

Children's meaning-making

Ben, aged 3, is playing. He holds up a toy car in each hand at about head-height and slowly turns them to and fro. 'You click on one,' he says.

Ellie, aged 5, sits staring intently into a cardboard box which is lying on its side and facing her. She taps her fingers rapidly on an old computer keyboard.

Charlie, aged 6, has drawn a complex series of pictures, one on top of the other, which represent the eight different levels he has so far completed of a Playstation game.

Zara, aged 5, logs onto the internet and using the 'favourites' menu she navigates her way to the CBeebies website.

These children, observed one afternoon in my own home, are demonstrating, by their play, their engagement and commitment to the multimodality of the world of communication in which they live. Kress (2000:96) makes the point that 'Children make meaning in a multiplicity of ways and employ a multiplicity of modes, means and materials in doing so.' Every day, children actively engage with a diverse range of modern modes of communication. Moreover, their engagement can be generally unprompted and uninhibited. While we may marvel that three- and four-year-olds are able to interact with computers, television, video games, mobile phones and more, for them, these are embedded within their everyday interactions with the world. From birth onwards children live with, engage with and use meaningfully a huge range of communicative modes (Kress 2001; Marsh and Millard 2000; Hilton 1996).

For children these are normal communicative activities, they do not confine themselves to any one mode in their play and they are adept at representing their experiences in different modes in order to help them make sense of their experiences. Kress (2000) suggests that we need to practice this art of transforming meanings from one mode to another in order to develop both imagination and cognition. In schools children could be given opportunities to do this through role-playing stories, producing multimedia presentations from internet-based research or using photographs to capture the 'mood' of a poem. If teachers embrace this idea within their teaching (as my units of work attempt to do) they will begin to enable children to broaden their understanding of both representation and communication within the classroom which will start to reflect the practices and opportunities in the outside world. We do not want to confine them to any one mode – be it print or not. The goal is to expand the communicative possibilities within the classroom.

The 'real world' of texts

If children are going to make informed judgements about the world in which they live, literacy teaching in schools must focus on the engagement with and construction of the texts with which they engage in their everyday lives. There is never going to be a question of the increase in technology making print-based communication redundant. However, primary-aged children live now, and will live as adults, in a communicatively multimodal society. We cannot deny them the opportunity to become literate in every mode. I would suggest, for example, that for many children starting school, their familiarity of interacting with televisual texts far exceeds their experience of reading the printed word – yet the interpretation of what 'literacy' means in many schools makes only token gestures towards building on children's visual and aural literacies. Television, despite its prevalence in the vast majority of homes, is frequently restricted in school to 'educational' purposes or an end-of-term treat. In my experience few schools have established media education programmes at primary level. It now seems time for a change: 'the moving image media, film, television, video and an increasing number of websites and computer games are important and valuable parts of our culture. It follows that children have a basic right to learn about these media in school' (British Film Institute Primary Education Working Group 2003 : 1).

These 'multimodal' texts – which contain a combination of oral, visual and 'lettered' elements – make up a large proportion of the texts which children use to make sense of their world. We are discounting the greater part of these children's literate experiences if we confine the teaching of literacy to the reading and writing of conventional texts. It is essential in school that we realise their 'basic right' and provide them with the tools to interpret the huge range of fact, fiction and all that lies between which is offered to them, in whatever mode.

Critical literacy

However you define literacy, it is surely about our day-to-day interactions with the world – how we get by within our social and cultural environments. This may be in our escape from the real world into worlds of fiction, or equally, in our attempts to negotiate our path through the information that bombards us in all its modes. Yet definitions of 'being literate' are not stable and are often contested. For example, adults who by government standards would be considered 'literate', still write to soap-opera characters as if they were real, believe letters which they receive beginning 'You have been personally selected ...' and spend significant amounts of money under the influence of glossy marketing campaigns. Surely, to be literate requires an individual to possess an objective understanding of how different forms of communication function; he/she should be able to look beyond not only the 'words' but also the pictures, gestures, sounds and moving images that each 'text' offers (Freire 1985). Confident readers know that every text has a context, and an author, and every author has a purpose. Experienced readers know that the ways in which texts are constructed reflect the author's intentions. By looking 'beyond the text' competent and critical readers are able not only to protect themselves against powerfully persuasive organisations, but also can gain a deeper appreciation and understanding of the texts they read. Many teachers have aimed to accomplish this in literacy teaching, and for years have invited authors into primary schools to uncover the 'secrets' of their craft, hoping both to demystify the practice and inspire children to try it for themselves. The possibility is there to do this with other forms of texts that employ different or multiple modes of communication. Why not invite photographers, graphic designers and those who compose adverts into schools to talk about their work? Why not make use of the wealth of 'the making of' and commentary materials available instantly on many DVDs? Children deserve to be able to respond in an informed way to the texts they encounter, to recognise and discuss bias or manipulation and also to respect and admire the skilful way in which authors construct their texts, which deepens their enjoyment and understanding. The BFI are clear: 'The media deserve an audience that expect high standards of honesty and accuracy and know how to challenge products that fall below such standards' (British Film Institute Primary Education Working Group 2003 : 6).

The curriculum

If there is to be a national commitment to developing critical literacy across all modes of texts, then it cannot be left to individual teachers and schools alone. Nationally, the emergence of guidelines for primary school practitioners wishing to develop a primary media (or, better yet, multimodal) curriculum has been slow. There is only passing reference to the use of multimodal texts in the National Literacy Strategy (DfEE 1998), but an increasing number of publications from the government have been developed for schools which encourage the use of electronic texts in literacy teaching in the classroom with both small and large groups. Oracy, at the time of writing, has been given a higher profile as a valid mode of communication and learning, surely in recognition of the bias towards reading and writing in the National Literacy Strategy *Framework* (DfEE 1998). Interestingly, concern about learning styles (Lawrence 1993), brain-based learning (Hart 1983) and multiple intelligences (Gardner 1993) seems to be encouraging practitioners to offer children learning opportunities in a wider range of modes and to raise the profile of 'other' forms of communication and learning. This must have a positive impact in classrooms and could pave the way for a deeper understanding of the ways in which literacy in schools could be conceptualised and developed.

However, the most exciting recent development is the production of a National Curriculum for using multimodal texts in the classroom. Developed from research by members of the United Kingdom Literacy Association, and produced in 2004,

More than Words: Multimodal Texts in the Classroom is a huge step forward in the battle to raise the profile of multimodality in literacy and across the curriculum. As yet only for 'information/guidance', it has surely brought the development of a statutory curriculum much closer. The guidance offers case studies in a range of curricular areas and shows how the writing assessment strands can be used to assess children's texts from a range of modes. This is a promising advance in thinking.

Non-fiction texts – looking for truth

Non-fiction is the other area of literacy teaching that this chapter explores. Non-fiction texts offer something different to the reader from their fiction counter-parts. Rosenblatt (1995) suggested that we read 'information texts' in a different way because we are reading for a different purpose. She called this 'efferent' reading, where 'the reader's attention is focused primarily on what will remain as the residue *after* the reading – the information to be acquired, the logical solution to a problem, the actions to be carried out' (p. 23) If this is the case, then the texts we use with children and the reasons we use them must be clearly thought through.

Non-fiction texts are given their own separate section in the National Literacy Strategy Framework planning suggestions (DfEE 1998), the implication being that there is a clear division between fact and fiction. However, a quick look at any classroom bookshelf will reveal a number of texts which lie somewhere in between. Much children's fiction contains verifiable, researched 'facts' – authors such as Beverley Naidoo (1985), in her writing of *Journey to Jo' Burg'*, rely on their own lived-through experiences to offer a story set in a factual past or present. Other texts which might be described as 'faction' deliberately blur the line between fact and fiction – the *Horrible Histories* series (Deary *et al.* 1993–2004) does this through the fictionalisation and 'modernisation' of facts through parody in order to make them more accessible for children. Other texts offer a story alongside facts deliberately embedding them within fictionalised events – 'historical fiction' for example. Taking a more post-modern (Habermas 1978; Lyotard 1979) perspective, one might argue that it is not ever possible to offer a truly 'factual' perspective – that there is no 'truth', just the author's interpretation of the facts. While this might appear to be an extreme view, it is difficult to think of a text which could be said to be truly unbiased, or at least not subject to some kind of 'selection' process – a process in which choices have been made as to which information is relevant to the audience and which is not. Encyclopaedias offer selected 'facts', instructions are often intended for a particular audience, explanations can be used to bolster a particular viewpoint, autobiographies of the rich and famous often gloss over anything that could damage their public persona and persuasive writing clearly sets out to do just that – to persuade.

It is not in the selection of 'unbiased' material that teachers will help children move forward. For, as Mallett (2003 : 116) argues, 'Even the youngest children are entitled to know that there can be more than one viewpoint on issues. Books should be sought which show not only that knowledge is added to and adjusted in the light of new evidence, but also that our attitudes towards it are not static.' With this in mind we can see the need, as was argued for multimodal communication earlier, for children to approach texts critically, making text-to-text and text-to-life connections, and to weigh up the 'truth' for themselves. Outside of the classroom it is clear that children are surrounded by factualised fiction and fictionalised fact. Children are frequently required to make judgements about what is 'real' and what is not – particularly through the medium of film and television. The ability to look critically at all texts and to personally distinguish between 'fact' and 'fiction' is a crucial skill which helps us learn about the world in which we live.

Non-fiction with meaning

Wray and Medwell (1991 : 9) define learning as 'the expansion and modification of existing ways of conceiving the world in the light of alternative ways'. Non-fiction texts can open one's eyes to the phenomena outside of individual lives and experiences as well as consolidating or shifting understanding of what is known and of which there is familiarity. Non-fiction is about real life. The non-fiction texts that I read help me understand and/or function in my world. The non-fiction texts offered to children should be meaningful to them, making explicit links to *their* lives and world. When working with non-fiction texts, opportunities need to be tailored to engage children in 'real life' pleasurable and purposeful activities. Why write letters unless you are in hope of a response? Why write instructions for 'how to . . .' if no-one really needs to follow them? In my experience children are often asked to go through the motions of creating non-fiction texts – using the skills they need to construct them – but are not required to use the completed texts in a meaningful way. Those who embed the teaching of non-fiction in children's real-lives enable them to understand not only the structures of the genre, but the purposes too.

In creating their own non-fiction texts children can begin to understand how authors use a range of means and modes to their advantage in order to offer a particular version of facts, events and information. Non-fiction texts are designed for specific audiences and for clear reasons; they can bring into focus and model the precise ways in which language can be used purposefully for specific audiences to both inform and obfuscate.

> The fact is that all texts are located in a particular set of social practices and understandings. They involve choices. Critical reading involves an explicit examination of these choices and hence the particular social understandings and values underlying texts.
> (Wray and Lewis 1997 : 104)

By coupling the teaching of non-fiction with multimodal texts, opportunities exist to develop children's critical literacy skills within the much wider world of communication in which they live.

The units of work

In this section I have outlined the intended framework and approach for the units and given examples of what this might look like in practice. I offer general ideas and approaches which can be tailored to fit a range of children in a range of classes. It is expected that the units outlined below will be adapted for different topics and audiences – but an open, creative approach to the curriculum will be key. I offer a final outcome to the units and a real audience for the children's texts.

Year 2

Outcome: An interactive, multimodal text, based on children's research about the weather
Aims:

- Children will be able to identify and critique key features of non- fiction texts.
- Children will be able to identify how multimodal texts can be used most effectively to convey the information that they have gathered.

Audience: A parallel class of Year 2 children
Suggested length of unit: 3–4 weeks, depending on children's interest, enthusiasm and ICT skills.

Beginning the unit
As with any topic it is essential to ascertain the children's prior knowledge, under-standing and interest. KWL grids (Ogle 1989; Wray and Lewis 1997) could be used; class, group or individual brainstorms completed; or a class discussion could be recorded on video, tape recorder or paper. The KWL grid takes children through the basic steps of the research process. A KWL grid (Figure 5.1) consists of three columns. The first two columns are concerned with prior reading and prediction. The third is a space for notes.

What do I know?	What do I want to find out?	What did I learn?

Figure 5.1

Questions generated by the children at this stage and throughout the topic could be displayed for reference and answered as and when appropriate. Any specific area of interest or knowledge highlighted by these initial discussions could be incorporated into later plans.

In practice
- In pairs, children discuss what they already know about the weather and decide on key words to write down on individual pieces of paper. They then join up into larger groups and categorise the key words, sticking them down on a large piece of paper as a word web. Two groups then present their word webs to each other – elaborating on the words that have been selected and the reasons for the choice and grouping.
- In groups, the children create a spider diagram. The children use a large piece of paper with the word 'weather' written in the middle. One child chooses two words related to the topic 'weather' and joins them to the word by use of an arrow. The next child chooses two words linked to one of the new words and adds them with arrows, and so on. When the edge of the paper is reached the next child starts again from the word 'weather'.

Immersion
The purpose of this early work is to immerse the children in a variety of text-types, to increase their knowledge and understanding of the topic and to enable them to develop or discover their own areas of interest. It is expected that at the beginning of this unit much of the work would be talk-based and would offer excellent opportunities to develop skills of group discussion (National Curriculum (2000), Key Stage 1 English Speaking and Listening Programme of Study). Shared work would be typically based around reading texts together and looking at new vocabulary and discussing new concepts.

Guided reading of suitable texts including ICT texts could be undertaken. Learning Outcomes for literacy lessons would be focused on reading and understanding and identifying features of non-fiction texts. For example, the children could be given opportunities to browse a range of information texts about the weather. The texts could be video material, written texts, encyclopaedias, fiction and 'faction' texts, pictures, photographs, CD-ROM material and internet pages.

In practice
- In mixed-ability groups the children are given a range of texts containing information about the weather. They read and explore these texts together and discuss what they have found out – adding to KWL grids, word webs or class question bank.
- In shared reading the teacher uses a video clip of the flooding at Boscastle in 2004 (archive material is available from www.bbc.co.uk). The children discuss

whether it is fiction or non-fiction and how they know. They draw up a list of 'facts' and a list of questions to explore further.

- In guided reading the children visit www.wildwildweather.com and navigate to, and read, a page of their choice.

Further development

The next part of the topic will involve the children in more specific discussion about the types of texts that they have been using and their strengths and weaknesses. It is expected that children will have different opinions, which could be explored through class discussion. There are many opportunities at this stage to make comparisons of different text-types and to attempt activities that require the children to move between modes in their representation of information. Children could draw illustrations for print-based texts or compose captions or texts to accompany pictures. This will inevitably lead to a discussion of key features of non-fiction texts in both shared and guided reading sessions and children will develop their vocabulary in their description of the features of non-fiction texts. At this point the focus on multimodal texts such as web pages and interactive CD-ROM material could be emphasised and shared and guided reading might move towards a concentration on these text-types. Children could also be encouraged to discuss their textual preferences and to give reasons for their choice.

In practice

- In a shared reading session the teacher uses the BBC weather page to show an example of a weather forecast for the local area. The children identify the features of this non-fiction text and discuss the use of symbols to stand for different types of weather. In groups, they devise their own symbols for extreme weather.

- Using at least two different web pages about a similar theme, the children discuss the similarities and differences between them and evaluate their usefulness in terms of the information content, layout and usability.

- The children listen to storm sound effects from: www.partnersinrhyme. com/soundfx/Weather.shtml. They watch the 'demo reel' from: www.stormvideo.com. The children discuss the use of audio and video material and how it affects their understanding of 'storms'. How does the use of music on the video affect them? What do they think of the quality of the video? The audio stream? Is it more effective than the printed word? Why?

Preparing to compose

At this stage the children would need to identify a particular area of interest and begin to focus their information gathering. It is now that the teacher could model and discuss note-taking skills and discuss with children the best ways to gather, store and reference the information which they would like to use. This can be accompanied by a discussion of which mode of composition is best suited for each piece of information. The children plan the information they wish to include in their page and the mode in which they wish it to be represented.

This part of the unit will be characterised by the teaching, modelling and sharing of writing with the whole class and working with children in guided writing activities to develop individual work.

In practice

- In a shared writing session the teacher models how to take notes from a web page. The children then work from a different web page on a similar theme and make notes for themselves – they compare and contrast the information they have found with the teachers.

- Children work in groups to decide on the content and mode of the information that they will use for their 'page'. The planning format shown in Figure 5.2 might be used.

Subheading	What form?	Where from?
Tornadoes	Video	http://www.stormvideo.com/tornado.html
The storm of '87	Audio	Interview with grandparents or parents
What is wind?	Written	Weather encyclopaedia
Wind in other countries	Link to website	http://wings.avkids.com/Book/Atmosphere/instructor/wind-01.html
	Cartoon	Microsoft Clipart
What is wind good for?	Written	Wind book
Wind dance	Video	Class video from PE lesson

Figure 5.2

Composition

At this stage the children need to consider how their pages should be put together – what they will look like. As at the previous stage the teacher would need to use shared writing times to model and develop the kinds of resources available for children. Depending on the children's ICT skills and availability of resources, the children could either compose their pages directly or produce a plan for the page which is then 'published' for them by a more skilled adult or child. Here there is potential for older children in the school to act as the producers.

Year 1

Outcome: A promotional video, designed by the children, about there school which will be shown on a loop in the entrance hall.

Aims:

- To enable the children to understand how television texts show bias in their representation of 'factual' information and to appreciate some of the techniques used to persuade the audience.

- To enable children to use this knowledge in the production of their own 'biased' video.

Audience: Visitors to the school

Length of unit: It would be expected that this unit could take 4–6 weeks, depending on availability of resources and technical skill of teachers and pupils.

Beginning the unit

The children's own holiday experiences could be used as a starting point for this topic. Prior to the unit, letters could be sent out to parents asking for examples of holiday videos. Parents could also be asked to come in to talk about how they had set about choosing a holiday destination and the influence of both travel brochures and travel programmes or videos. The parents could also be invited to share any examples of holiday 'disasters' where their expectations had not been met and where the material that they had used to select their holiday had been misleading.

Parents' permission will also need to be sought for video material to be taken of their children for the composition section of this unit.

In practice

- One child's home video from their holiday is used to open up the idea that some material is staged. For example, did parents ask their children to do specific things while they videoed them, or did they just video the action as it happened? What difference does it make?

- A travel agent's role-play area is established and children are encouraged to choose their holiday destinations from a range of brochures, giving reasons for their choices.

Immersion

At the beginning of the unit the children need to see many different examples of holiday programmes. They should begin to develop a technical vocabulary with which they can discuss the video material and through which they could take a critical stance. They need to spend time watching, comparing and discussing a range of videos. The resource *Look Again!* produced by the British Film Institute offers a very useful model of teaching techniques for discussing media texts. Using this as a basis, the teachers can choose to teach the children a limited technical vocabulary so that they can apply these words when it comes to the composition of their section of the video. The literacy lessons in this part of the unit will effectively be 'shared reading' times where the features and forms of the texts are explored and discussed. Holiday brochure material, photographs and postcards could also be used as guided reading texts, with a focus on how the material is presented and the choice of words to 'persuade'. Comparison with other information texts could be developed, where the purpose of the text is to inform rather than to persuade.

At this point in the unit, the children also need opportunities to 'play' with the video camera, to explore and experiment with the functions and techniques that they are beginning to discuss in the literacy sessions and to develop their technical expertise. This is essential so that the later composition section of the unit is not overshadowed by the necessity to teach technical skills. With the help of an adult, the children, in pairs, can be given turns in filming lessons during the school day. Alternatively, the camera could be mounted on a tripod and placed in the middle of a seated circle of the whole class. Activities could then be formulated to allow different members of the class to film the circle. Passing an object round the circle without allowing the camera to see it, stories being told around the circle and circle members stating their opinion on issues are just some examples.

In practice
- Starting with children's holiday photographs or holiday postcards, some simple technical vocabulary is introduced. For example: background, in focus, out of focus, foreground, composition, close-up, long shot. The children begin to evaluate the photographs and discuss what makes a 'good' photograph, adopting the technical vocabulary.

- Children watch one video clip from a holiday programme several times. They identify different aspects each time. For example, looking at the background only, identifying close-ups, concentrating on the soundtrack (music or narration).

- The children watch a video, or talk to a parent or teacher about a holiday 'disaster'. In role, the children complain to the travel agent about their own holiday disaster using phrases such as 'In your brochure it said . . .' or 'In the video everything looked lovely . . .'.

Consolidation
Following the immersion in materials the children need to consolidate their understanding. A few sessions in which children clarify their understanding of key vocabulary and express their perception of how a particular text has been constructed will be essential in preparing them for the creation of their own video text.

In practice
- As a shared writing activity the children produce a leaflet about 'What to look for in a holiday video' which includes a glossary of key terms.

Preparing to compose

The children now need to begin to focus on the topic of their video – their school. At this point the children will need to understand clearly that it is their knowledge and understanding about making media texts that is required, not their knowledge and understanding of holidays.

The children will begin to collect information about their school. They need to consider what they want to include, and what they do not want to include and how they can find out any information that they need to know. This will lead to useful discussion about the good and not-so-good points of the school. The conversations about what not to show and the decision-making process is key at this point in the unit. The children will need to demonstrate the ability to transfer their critical understanding of the techniques used in the holiday material to the composition of a media text involving a different subject. There will be, again, a high level of group discussion at this point, with children being encouraged to offer suggestions along with their explanation of why they think certain things should be included in the video. The children should be encouraged to see this as a process of elimination and various planning stages need to be worked through.

In practice

- The children work in groups around a theme so that crossover is minimised and each group works on its own 'mini-movie', which will then be combined to create the finished product.

- The teacher encourages children to think carefully about the kind of information that they want to capture on video. The children draw on their developing understanding of media texts which they had developed and make decisions such as: Will I stage the action? Will I have a commentary? Will we include interviews?

- Scripts are developed and the action is plotted out. Some children produce simple storyboards (Figure 5.3) with either words or pictures to map out the content of their piece.

The Playground:

Composition

The organisation of this section will be dependent on the availability of resources. The teacher needs to model the composition and work on shared creation of video texts as well as guiding the smaller groups. The work here will probably need to be staggered so that some groups are at the planning stage while other children are filming their section. Some sections will need to be filmed at particular times (for example at playtime). This would also then give opportunity for peer review of the work as it is completed.

	1	2	3	4	5
What will we see?	James standing in the empty playground talking to the camera	Children skipping	Children sitting and talking	James talking to the camera again	A child falling over and being taken inside by a grown up
What will we hear?	James says: 'This is where children at Luton Infants School come to play every day.'	The children playing happily	Playground noise	James says: 'Sometimes children fall over and get hurt, but they are looked after.'	The playground noise
Special information		Film at playtime			Pretend that someone is hurt

Figure 5.3

There is a range of editing software available that is often supplied with video cameras, or it can be bought in high street computer stores. This software enables taped material to be downloaded onto a computer where sequences can be cut and shaped and music and voice-over added. This facilitates another creative dimension to the process of composition.

In order for this unit to be successfully completed the teachers will need to be prepared to be very flexible with the timings and content of the sessions with the children.

Acknowledgements

Thanks to Sue Lythgoe, Angharad Mann, Fran Payne, Jo Starling, Steph Dawkins, Tracey Price, Jo Croney, Liz Gamet, Nicola Cooper, Olive McGinn and Helen Love for their assistance in compiling this chapter.

Useful resources

Books

Carroll, C. (1998) *How Artists See the Weather: Sun, Wind, Snow, Rain.* Abbeville Kids.

Cosgrove, B. (2002) *Weather Eye Witness Guides.* Dorling Kindersley.

Dunlop, S. (2004) *Weather.* Collins.

Evans, L. and Jabar, C. (1997) *Rain Song.* Houghton Mifflin Juvenile Books.

Ganeri, A. (2004) *Horrible Geography Series.* Scholastic.

Hughes, S. (1998) *Out and About.* Walker Paperbacks.

Hunter, R. (2004) *Elmer's Weather.* Anderson Press.

Inkpen, M. (1997) *Kipper's Book of Weather.* Hodder Children's Books.

Meadows, D. (2004) *Rainbow Magic – The Weather Fairies.* Orchard Books.

Rogers, K. (2003) *The Usborne Internet-linked Introduction to Weather and Climate.* Usborne Publishing.

Willis, J. and Ross, T. (1994) *Dr Xargle's Book of Earth Weather.* Red Fox.

Software

Bower, M. and Page, J. (1999) *Weather: CD-ROM Version*. Two-Can Publishing.

Websites

www.bbc.co.uk/weather

www.discoverychannel.co.uk/earth

http://uk.weather.com

www.atschool.co.uk [requires subscription]

www.met-office.gov.uk

www.wildwildweather.com

www.weather.co.uk

www.weatherwizkids.com

www.ukweatherworld.co.uk

Media

DVD/video – *Wild Weather* (2002). BBC.

DVD – *Extreme Weather Experience* (2002). Amazon catalogue no. BDV030.

Television and radio footage of weather forecasts. Weather forecasters from local television channels may be available to visit the school.

Newspaper weather forecasts/reports.

Digital television channels: National Geographic; Discovery Channel.

Teacher resource

Look Again! – A Teaching Guide to Using Film and Television with Three-to Eleven-year-olds. Bfi Education and DfES (available free). E-mail: education@bfi.org.uk

UKLA (2004) *More than Words: Multimodal Texts in the Classroom*. DfES.

References

Bearne, E. (2003) 'Rethinking literacy: communication, representation and text'. *Reading, Literacy and Language*, 37(3).

British Film Institute Primary Education Working Group (2003) *Look Again! A Teaching Guide to Using Film and Television with Three- to Eleven-year olds*. London: DfES and BFI Education.

Deary, T. *et al.* (1993–2004) *Horrible Histories Series*. Leamington Spa: Scholastic Hippo.

DfEE (1998) *The National Literacy Strategy*. London: DfEE.

Freire, P. (1985) 'Reading the world and reading the word: an interview with Paulo Freire'. *Language Arts*, 62(1), January.

Gardner, H. (1993) *Frames of Mind: Theory of Multiple Intelligences*. London: Fontana Press.

Habermas, J. (trans. J. J. Shapiro) (1978) *Knowledge and Human Interest*. London: Heinemann Education.

Hannon, P. (2000) *Reflecting on Literacy in Education*. London: Falmer Press.

Hart, L. (1983) *Human Brain, Human Learning*. London: Longman.

Hilton, M. (1996) *Potent Fictions: Children's Literacy and the Challenge of Popular Culture*. London: Routledge.

Kress, G. (2000) *Before Writing – Rethinking the Paths to Literacy*. London: RoutledgeFalmer.

Kress, G. (2001) *Multimodal Discourse*. London: Arnold.

Kress, G. (2003) *Literacy in the New Media Age*. London: Routledge.

Lankshear, C. and Knoebel, M. (2003) *New Literacies: Changing Knowledge and Classroom Learning*. Buckingham: Open University Press.

Lawrence, G. D. (1993) *People Types and Tiger Stripes*. Gainesville, FL: Centre for Applications of Psychological Type Inc.

Lyotard, T. (1979) *The Post-Modern Condition: A Report on Knowledge*. Manchester: Manchester University Press.

Mallett, M. (2003) *Early Years Non-Fiction: A Guide to Helping Young Researchers Use Information Texts*. London: RoutledgeFalmer.

Marsh, J. and Millard, E. (2000) *Literacy and Popular Culture Using Children's Culture in the Classroom*. London: Paul Chapman Publishing.

McClellan, J. (2003) 'Easing the burden'. *Guardian,* 2 October.

Naidoo, B. (1985) *Journey to Jo'Burg: A South African Story*. Harlow: Longman.

Ogle, D. M. (1989) 'The know, want to know, learn strategy', in Muth, K. D. (ed.) *Children's Comprehension of Text*. Newark, DW: International Reading Association.

Rosenblatt, L. (1995/1938) *Literature as Exploration*. New York: The Modern Language Association of America.

UKLA (2004) *More than Words: Multimodal Texts in the Classroom*. London: DfES.

Wray, D. and Lewis, M. (1997) *Extending Literacy: Children Reading and Writing Non-Fiction*. London: RoutledgeFalmer.

Wray, D. and Medwell, J. (1991) *Literacy and Language in the Primary Years*. London: Routledge.

Less is more: working with playscripts in Key Stage 2

Vivien Wilson

Like all stories, it's a pack of lies that tries to reach out to us and allow us to experience some kind of human truth. Of course it depends on the skills of writers, directors, actors, composers, designers. But it also depends on the creative skills of the audience, those skills of the imagination that allow all of us to leap into other minds and other worlds, skills that are at once quite natural, straight-forward, commonplace and quite, quite amazing. (David Almond 2002 : 93)

Introduction

Of all the literary forms encountered by pupils within the primary school, the playscript is perhaps the most elusive because of its indirect relationship with the reader. This statement may appear contradictory – the reading of a playscript is said to appeal to pupils because of its accessibility: clear layout, short speeches and active collaboration through group reading (DfES 2001). In the case of many playscript texts available to pupils in primary schools this argument is undoubtedly true. However, it can also be argued that these texts are not actually playscripts in the fullest sense of the word; they exemplify features of playscript in terms of layout, but do not always lend themselves to further dramatic interpretation, so that the essential purpose of the written form becomes obscured. The reader engages directly with narrative, poetic and non-fiction texts as an individual, but the playscript is only a partial version of the final text, which will be interpreted by the actor (and/or director) and then presented for further interpretation to the audience. The script is a signpost on the way to the full realisation of the multimodal text, which is the performance.

In what ways, then, can pupils be immersed in playscript, in order to develop their understanding of the form? All too frequently, playscripts are introduced to pupils through group reading activities which remain static, and in which the stage directions become another form of narrative, rather than a bridge to physical action and interpretation. Similarly, writing activities drawing upon the form may become confined to the conversion of dialogue from pre-existing narrative into a short script extract, with an emphasis on the use of adverbs, or even become a reverse operation whereby the script is rewritten as dialogue, focusing on 'verbs of saying', adverbial use and speech punctuation.

While such activities may be of some value in introducing pupils to the differing conventions governing the reproduction of speech in writing, and to the technical conventions of playscript presentation, they provide little or no access to the *purpose* of the playscript as a genre. If the playscript constitutes a signpost for dramatic action, it follows that pupils need to explore the ways in which the words on the page develop the characters and the narrative through that action. This might be through engaging as performers or as audience, and preferably both.

The requirements of the National Curriculum for Speaking and Listening (DfEE 1999) emphasise the role of drama in the Primary English curriculum, and the recent Primary National Strategy publication *Speaking, Listening and Learning: Working with Children in Key Stages 1 and 2* (DfES, 2003) underlines this. The objectives for drama outlined in this publication do not refer solely to scripted performance, of course, but in addition to objectives relating to the use of role-play to support learning in a variety of contexts. There is also an expectation that pupils will engage in performance-related activity.

By the end of Key Stage 1 it is expected that pupils will have had some experience of watching performance and will be able to express opinions about what they liked. In Key Stage 2 this is developed into objectives relating both to elements of performance and to reflection on pupils' own performances and those of others, and to the text-level objectives of the NLS Framework (DfES 2003, *Teaching Objectives*, pp. 18–19).

For pupils in Key Stage 2 there is a challenge in combining an awareness of features of performance in relation to the needs of the audience, with the ability to develop and sustain believable characters and a well-structured plot. For pupils in Years 3 and 4 the focus is on developing understanding of organisational features of playscript, and in beginning to appreciate dramatic effects. These include the ways in which the openings of scenes are structured to engage the interest of the audience, and how scenes are brought to a close in different ways to create different effects.

This understanding is then applied to the writing and the critical reading of playscript in Years 5 and 6. In Year 5, pupils should be able to identify the features of playscript which indicate performance features, with guidance, and to comment on the possible dramatic impact of features of scripts (Bearne 2002). They are beginning to be able to convey information about characters in narrative writing through describing their appearance, actions and reactions rather than using the authorial voice, and this ability may also be reflected in their own playscripts.

Should pupils' experience of playscript begin with the written, the visual or the physical form? Provided that the links between the three are made explicit, each offers its own unique insight into theatrical texts.

From text to action

To introduce pupils to the nature and purpose of script-writing by starting from a good quality text would seem to be a logical approach. The National Literacy (NLS) *Framework* (DfEE 1998) and objectives are based on the premise that pupils' abilities to explore different written forms depend upon familiarity with the genre, developed through reading and analysis of the distinctive features of the text-type.

However, in relation to both playscript reading and writing, there are some difficulties with this approach if adopted too literally, as has been suggested above. The first is the relative lack of good quality playscripts written for primary-age pupils. Of necessity, younger pupils are frequently introduced to the playscript form through texts provided as part of published schemes. While such texts provide an introduction to the presentational features of playscript they do not always offer a high-quality reading experience in terms of the development of character or narrative.

These texts occupy a transitional space between narrative and playscript, precisely because they have been written with group reading, rather than with performance, in mind. In many cases there is a heavy reliance on the 'Narrator', effectively (and sometimes explicitly) identified as a character in the script, to set the scene and to move the action on. This convention further distorts the connection between playscript and the action it represents, and contributes to the difficulties experienced by many primary-age pupils of translating the script on the page into physical action. This overuse of the narrator results from a lack of understanding of the ways in which speech, setting and action can convey information.

Potential misconceptions about the nature of the Narrator's voice in play texts can be addressed through shared and group reading activities, if texts that minimise the role of the Narrator are not available. In playscripts written predominantly for group reading, stage directions are often used to give information about setting, characters' behaviour and appearance. However, the same information can often be provided within the playscript text itself. Shared reading can incorporate 'detective' activities, during which pupils examine playscript to identify elements that indicate details of the set, how characters are dressed and actions they make, in order to appreciate that the Narrator's voice is not always necessary.

Additionally, the role of the narrator is not one with which pupils are familiar from their main experiences of drama as audience: those of watching filmed and televised drama. Thus the experience of the written playscript and the experience of the viewer may have little or no relationship with each other. Later in this chapter the relationship between film and televisual texts and playscripts will be examined in more detail, but activities that involve pupils in watching short films or film extracts to develop an understanding of how character and atmosphere are established can also be drawn upon to illuminate understanding of the nature and purpose of the script as a means towards the end-product, rather than as an end in itself.

Compare:

Scene 1: Jack's cottage. Jack is lying near the door.
Jack (yawning & stretching) What a lovely sunny day!
Jack's mother enters with a basket.
Mother: What are you doing still lying around Jack? Don't you know we have no food left in the house – that straw in your mouth is the only dinner you're going to get if you don't get up and take Daisy the cow to market.
Jack: Oh Mother . . .
Mother: It's no use arguing any more. We have to sell her, whatever you say. We haven't got any money left – we've sold all our furniture except the stools and the table. I'd have sold these curtains but they're already worn to shreds.
Jack: I'm sure something will turn up soon.
Mother: Money doesn't just turn up, Jack. I've been out doing other people's washing until I'm tired through and through and we still don't have enough for a decent meal. Daisy will have to go.

With:

It is a sunny day at Jack's poor cottage. There is very little furniture and the curtains are ragged. Jack is lying lazily by the doorway, sucking on a straw. Jack's mother comes in with a basket of washing. She is tired and hungry.

Where the use of narration is unavoidable, minimise reading stage directions/narrator text aloud – emphasise that this is 'in pupils' heads' (see Practical Suggestion 2, Figure 6.2).

Figure 6.1 Practical suggestion 1: reviewing the role of the narrator

Such activities can also help to counter the second difficulty which can be experienced in attempting to move from reading to writing playscript: the significance of the visual communication of meaning through gesture and action, setting and costume. The publication *Speaking, Listening Learning: Working with Children in Key Stages 1 and 2: Teaching Objectives and Classroom Activities* (DfES 2003) identifies objectives relating to the dramatic features of performance (pp. 18–19). However, in the NLS *Framework* these are sometimes linked to work in different school terms, from those for the text-level objectives for playscript writing. Without a planned approach to working with playscript over the entire year, it is possible that the connections between the construction of text and the performance activities could be lost.

Of course, the most productive approach to developing an understanding of the purpose of playscript as written text is to incorporate dramatic action into the literacy lesson (or alongside it) *throughout* the process of both reading and writing playscripts, so that there is constant reference between the text and action, and the possibility of audience response as part of the learning process, rather than solely to the final performance.

Winston (2004) offers a simple framework for linking dramatic action to shared and group reading of playscript, aimed at lower-primary-age pupils, and the following generic example is based on his outline. As pupils progress through the primary school, the playscripts used need to be carefully selected in order to provide opportunities to examine conventional features of dramatic text beyond the obvious features of layout; for example the use of asides, the use of the mono-logue, and ways in which information is conveyed to the audience without the use of a narrator. In the upper primary years, the NLS *Framework* requires pupils both to be able to write their own playscripts, including production notes, and also to be able to annotate a short section of a script as a preparation for performance and to evaluate the script and the performance for their dramatic interest and impact (Year 5 T1 T.17,18,19). The following outline provides opportunities for these objectives to be met, but can also be used with younger pupils.

Winston (2004) suggests that each group, in turn, might work with an adult to read through their script and develop their ideas one day, rehearse in the 'perform-ance space' the next, and present in the plenary. As the focus of whole-class text-level work progresses, the audience focus shifts accordingly, i.e. beginning with vocal delivery and progressing to gesture, use of space and use of simple props where appropriate. Alternatively, older pupils can cumulatively develop each strand of interpretation and present their rehearsed scripts at the end of the week. In this case, different groups of pupils can be asked to focus on different elements of performance, supported by a writing frame, if necessary, so that all members of the class are engaged throughout.

It would be useful to develop a poster display to show the significant organisa-tional features of playscript and some of the principles of effective scriptwriting. This can then be a reference point for subsequent writing activities (see, for example, NLS exemplification materials: *Plays*).

Where a good quality text is used, time is given for the exploration of how the written text is translated into action, and pupils are actively engaged as an audience, as well as performers, the links between text and purpose will begin to become clear.

From text to writing

The process of writing fiction, whether narrative or playscript, begins with having a story to tell, whether it is our own explicitly autobiographical episode or a narrative within a particular fiction genre. As we, as teachers, are only too aware, finding the story we wish to tell can be a difficult task for many young writers.

Existing narratives can provide the framework for playscript writing, and this is recommended and exemplified within the NLS *Framework*. However, for pupils to be able to engage with *compositional* aspects of writing, we need to minimise the selection of texts or text extracts which are then translated directly into playscript by reworking pre-existing dialogue and narrative, but at the same time support pupils by selecting incidents from known texts.

One useful approach is to identify 'gaps' in the narrative or events that are not fully developed in the text, but which we know must have occurred. Suitable examples would have:

- a small number of protagonists, to enable work on character development;
- a focus on relationships, rather than physical action;
- opportunities to refer backwards and/or forwards in the text to draw on evidence to support the plot and character development; and
- a limited number of settings to enable pupils to focus on plot and character development rather than lengthy stage directions or the need for a narrator.

Select a playscript with relatively few characters (two or three) to use for shared text work; group activities may use the same script, or other suitable examples if available.

Whole-class text-level work
Discuss the text features the class expect to see in a playscript. Using an enlarged text, model the reading of the dialogue to indicate different characters. Read the extract twice, reading the stage directions in a different tone of voice the first time, and then reading dialogue only the second time. Discuss the purpose of stage directions. (It may be necessary to review the pupils' knowledge of the organisational features of playscript at this point, depending on their age and previous experience.) Discuss what the pupils know about the characters from listening to the dialogue – are there any ways the writer helps the reader – i.e. through the use of adverbs or stage directions? Are there ways in which the writer could help the reader more? Annotate the text with further suggestions as necessary.

Group reading activities
Either using more of the same text, or another suitable script, ask pupils to read short sections of dialogue two or three times to gain familiarity with the text and the characters. Encourage them to use the stage directions to assist with use of voice and support discussion about how characters might feel and how they might sound. Either annotate a photocopied version of the text, or use post-its. Annotation can be undertaken with adult support if necessary.

Associated word-level work might focus on adverbs and/or extend vocabulary through developing a word bank of suitable adverbs and adverbial phrases to describe voice tone and gesture, depending on the age group of pupils.

After the initial session spent introducing the text(s) and the principles of annotation, as appropriate to the age group, opportunities for action should be introduced. Either create a working space within the classroom or outside, with adult support available as necessary, and/or provide an opportunity for pupils to work using their scripts in a large enough space for all groups to have room to develop their ideas.

Further whole-class text-level work
In subsequent shared text sessions return to the first script extract to examine aspects of staging, movement and gesture. How can an audience find out how characters feel by seeing how they stand or sit? Ask pupils to demonstrate some of the suggestions made by the class. What movement is necessary for the storyline to be made clear?
For older pupils:
Are there times when it's important for there to be silence or stillness to heighten tension?
How does the writer engage the audience's attention at the beginning of the scene or scenes – through some kind of significant action, through the setting or perhaps a combination of the two?
How do characters enter or leave the stage? For older pupils, introduce terms such as 'stage left', etc.
How do scenes end, and what is the implication for the actors, e.g. everyone has to leave the acting area; everyone stays still for the 'curtain', etc?
In turns, groups apply these ideas to their text through discussion, experimentation and annotation.

Figure 6.2 Practical suggestion 2: reading playscripts with a purpose

Philip Pullman: *The Firework Maker's Daughter*
While Lila undertakes her quest to find the Royal Sulphur, her friend Chulak follows her on Hamlet, the King's precious white elephant, to warn her about the dangers she will face when she meets Razvani the Fire-fiend. After Chulak has helped Lila survive her ordeal he tells her that her father's life is in danger for helping Hamlet the elephant to escape from the King's palace.
'Someone saw and told the King, and now Lalchand has been arrested, and he's going to be executed.'
The text provides brief information about how Lalchand is seen and identified, but no information about Lalchand's arrest or trial are provided. The characters of Lalchand and the King have already been established earlier in the story and can thus form the basis of the playscript.

Possible activities
Discuss and establish a possible sequence of events, e.g.:

King discovers Hamlet is missing
How might this scene be developed? Does the King look out of the window and see Hamlet is missing? Does he send a slave to feed Hamlet, who then returns with the news of his escape? Does the slave who witnessed the escape come to the King and wake him up with the news?

Variations on this scene could be explored through group discussion and storyboarding, or through role-play activities. If the intended outcome is a single playscript created by the class as a whole then the various possibilities will need to be discussed and one version selected, but different versions of this event could equally well be retained and developed by groups as alternative scripts to emphasise the range of dramatic strategies available to the writer.

Slave tells King what he saw and how he followed Lalchand back home
Use evidence from the text to support the slave's story, e.g. how she/he came to see Hamlet's escape, what she/he is hoping for as a reward. How will the King behave? What do we know about him from the text? Will he listen patiently, or is he likely to interrupt, be angry, etc.? Role-play could be used to support this activity.

Lalchand is arrested and brought to the King
Discuss whether it is necessary to portray the actual arrest, or whether moving to the trial is sufficient for an audience to know what has happened.
The trial scene is developed, either as a scene in which Lalchand tries to explain the true situation to the King, or as a more formal trial scene (a more demanding option).
Pupils should draw on their knowledge of Lalchand's feelings for Lila as well as a retelling of events from the text. The character of the King should be sustained from earlier scenes.

In a more formal trial scene the character of the slave would be retained from the previous scene as a witness. Possibly other slaves would be called to testify against Chulak (would they be jealous?). Lila and Lalchand's neighbours might be asked to say what they know about Lalchand (How frightened would they be for themselves?)
Drama strategies such as Teacher in Role (as King) could help to scaffold the development of a formal trial scene.

Figure 6.3 Practical suggestion 3: find the gap

One of the significant challenges for the playscript writer is to make characters identifiable both through the speech they use and the actions or gestures which accompany speech. In the discussion and activities outlined above these elements would need to be explored alongside the development of the plot line. Pupils can be referred back to work undertaken early in Key Stage 2 on different 'voices' in stories, where the ways in which different characters are presented in narrative dialogue are explored.

In the example in Figure 6.3, additional work can be undertaken focusing on the roles of the King, the slave and Lalchand to explore how their different characters can be conveyed to the audience. One possible approach is to provide a 'character frame' which can be used by groups of pupils working independently on developing playscripts throughout Key Stage 2 and which can be adapted to suit the context in which they are working. These questions will be more readily understood by pupils who have also had experience of working with playscripts in the ways suggested in 'Practical Suggestion 3' (Figure 6.2).

These questions could also be used to develop the character collectively through an alternative approach, which is to use a variant of the 'role on the wall' drama strategy. Here, an outline shape is drawn on a large sheet of paper, and words and phrases are added as a collective understanding of the character is developed. This strategy can be utilised for a range of purposes (see, for example, Chaplin 2003) but in this instance the discussion would concentrate on words and phrases which would indicate characters through gesture, position or action and tone of voice. These words and phrases would be added to the outline as work on the playscript progressed through discussion and improvisation.

Similar approaches to working with known texts are provided by Chaplin (2003/4) and Winston (2004). Chaplin's focus is on the development of performance skills in pupils, rather than on the production or written text, but her example of interpreting Belloc's *Mathilda* for performance includes opportunities for pupils to develop and present dialogue through improvisation. These would have the potential to be expanded into short scripts, as suggested in the Speaking and Listening Objectives for Year 4 Term 2 (DfES 2003).

Winston (2004), similarly, uses a whole text, *Blodin the Beast* by Michael Morpurgo, as a source for drama and literacy work. In his suggested outline pupils explore the central themes of the book through the use of a variety of drama

---

How can people find out about the character of the King when they're watching the play?
- Collect any words or ideas from the story that might help you and write a sentence to describe the kind of person you think he is (examples could be provided for further support).
- How does the King walk? What words will you choose to tell the actor how to move like the King? (a word bank could be provided).
- How will we know if the King is pleased or if he is angry when he comes onto the stage?
- Are there movements he can do with his hands or feet to show us how he is feeling? Try out some ideas with the group to see if other people can guess the feeling you are trying to show.
- What kind of voice does the King have? Does he sound the same all the time?
- Are there any special words or phrases the King likes to use when he talks? Which would let you know it was the King, even if you couldn't see him? (For example, the slave might keep saying 'your Majesty' within his/her speeches, or Lalchand might keep worrying aloud about Lila.)
- Will he let other characters finish their speeches, or will he interrupt?
- Where will he be sitting or standing when there are other characters on stage? How can we show how important he is by where he sits or stands?

Figure 6.4 Practical suggestion 4: character frame

strategies and literacy activities, including scriptwriting, with the potential for developing a performance based on their work.

In the examples (Figures 6.3 and 6.4), opportunities were created for pupils to use role-play to support the development of the playscript, based on characters and events deduced from a pre-existing fiction or poetry. Non-fiction texts can also be a stimulus for drama activities which can support playscript writing. The most easily accessible curriculum area is undoubtedly history, again because of the strong narrative element and the wide range of opportunities to develop fictionalised characters based on historical evidence. There are a number of sources for drama activities relating to history: the *Speaking, Listening and Learning* classroom activities provide a video extract and lesson outline focusing on the Roman invasion, using role-play to appreciate the Celtic point of view (DfES 2003); Winston (2004) outlines a sequence of lessons combining work on the Victorians with a citizenship focus; and Readman and Lamont (1994) outline a series of lessons around the Gunpowder Plot. However, these examples using role-play activities would not normally lead to playscript writing, nor is it necessary that they should. Where drama is used to support learning in history, the purpose is usually to support empathy with people from the past and may not develop a narrative that has a clear structure. If we are to support historical learning, and an understanding of playscript as a literary/theatrical form, the event which is dramatised must meet the requirements for playscript potential: a clear plot-line and distinctive characters.

This does not mean that plot development would need to be entirely dependent on historical events, but that where material is drawn from historical sources discussion about the development of events *in terms of how this can be portrayed through a playscript* must take place. Teachers will also need to consider carefully how far the development of playscripts based around historical events represent learning in history as opposed to extended writing in English, as in the example provided in Figure 6.5.

Archaeologists discovered a sealed papyrus scroll containing a letter from Sennefer, the Mayor of Thebes, to his farm steward Baki. In the letter, Baki is ordered to get the farm ready for a visit from Sennefer, and it concludes 'Look out! Get all this work done! I know how lazy you are and that you like to lay around in bed eating.'

The historical record has no further information, but we know the letter was never delivered because the seal on the scroll is intact.

This glimpse of a human relationship from the distant past could provide an opportunity to develop a narrative which explores how the letter failed to be delivered and what happened when Sennefer arrived at his farm. Were his predictions about Baki true and what happened to Baki then? Did Sennefer discover why his letter was not delivered?

While this incident does offer some opportunity to draw on pupils' knowledge of life in Ancient Egypt, its main appeal is the 'human interest' angle which can be explored through group improvisation leading to scriptwriting.

For example:
- A scene where Sennefer writes and seals the letter and gives it to a servant to deliver. The dialogue enables the audience to know what is contained in the letter and how Sennefer feels about Baki.
- A scene depicting how the servant is delayed/loses the letter in some way.
- A scene showing Baki at the farm, during which he is told that Sennefer's boat has been spotted on the Nile. Will he get things ready in time to welcome Sennefer?
- Final scene in which Baki is accused of laziness by Sennefer and threatened with punishment. Sennefer's servant arrives with an explanation of the loss of the letter and Baki is reprieved, this time.

Figure 6.5 Practical suggestion 5: An undelivered letter: a tale of Ancient Egypt. (Source: Woodhouse 2004, Teachers' Book, p. 16)

Drama activities also offer opportunities to explore issues in other curriculum areas and these too might provide legitimate opportunities for the development of playscript (for example, Grainger 2003). Carefully selected news articles can also provide a starting point for exploration through the use of drama and writing activities. Depending on the theme of the article, work undertaken may also contribute to the PSHE and Citizenship curriculum, for instance, with topics such as bullying.

From audience to writer

> Dramatists construct signs, simultaneously using multiple channels of communication, from which audiences deduce the story, much as they do in everyday life. (Simons 2000 : 17)

Within the NLS *Framework* it is not until Year 5 that pupils are expected to make the connection between the playscript, the performance and the audience explicit (Year 5 Term 1: T5, T19, T20). Combining an understanding and appreciation of the variety of factors identified in the *Framework* objectives might appear to require considerable sophistication, compared to the requirements of Year 4, but if prior work has been undertaken with a focus on analysing features of performance, these links can be made effectively.

As with other arts subjects, performance drama needs to incorporate the three elements of making, performing and appreciating. The objectives for *Speaking, Listening and Learning* (DfES 2003) contain the performance appreciation strand from Year 1 onwards, emphasising the fact that previous experience as a critical member of an audience is as important to the writing process for playscript as having had prior experience of reading play texts.

The most common experience pupils will have of playscript, initially, is as members of an audience, rather than as readers of the script itself. In order to develop critical appreciation skills, they need to be supported by structured activities that

> Watch each performance carefully.
> What different ways have been used to show what a character is feeling?
> Think about how they move, how they speak and how they look.
>
> What did you like about how the scene started?
> What did you like about how it finished?
> What did the actors do to make the audience feel interested in their story?
>
> Please choose one piece of advice to give the actors which you think would make their play even better.

Figure 6.6 Practical suggestion 6: Responding to performance

will inform the reading, writing and performing of playscript. Activities might focus on how characters are established and developed through voice, movement and gesture; and how atmosphere is created through setting and sound. Later in Key Stage 2, pupils should be able to identify the significant features of different theatrical styles and genres.

In responding to each other's performances of scripted or improvised drama, pupils should also be asked to use the vocabulary of dramatic effect in their comments. For example, pupils could be given a 'response frame' (Figure 6.6) displayed on a large sheet of paper, OHT or whiteboard.

Where pupils have the opportunity to visit a live performance, or where theatre groups visit the school, questions can also be asked about sets, costume, lighting and other effects.

For the majority of pupils, the audience experience is most likely to be of filmed or televised narrative rather than live theatre, and this may be the easiest and most appropriate starting point for developing pupils' understanding of aspects of performance. The Bfi resource 'Story Shorts' provides a range of short, complete films of between 5 and 15 minutes duration (not extracts) specifically designed for literacy teaching. These complete narratives enable teachers and pupils to consider how the location and scene-setting contribute to the narrative, how characters are introduced and developed though both dialogue and non-verbal communication and how camera position influences meaning. For many pupils, particularly some boys, it appears that exploring these concepts using a visual stimulus has a powerful effect on their understanding, which can then be translated into written work.

A good example of this is the work reported in one of a series of 'Best practice case studies – Case Study 4' (www.standards.dfes.gov.uk/primary) where visual texts were used to support a range of writing objectives with a Year 3 class, including a group of boys who were making insufficient progress in writing. Although the writing objectives did not include the writing of playscripts, part of the work carried out during the project involved pupils watching the opening of the film *Babe – Pig in the City* in order to begin to develop a vocabulary of film (e.g. close-up, wide shot, etc.).

Pupils drew examples of different types of shot and discussed their effect on the viewer. In the case study the class then applied their knowledge of the effects of different types of shot to another film extract and then retold the episode, aiming to recreate the same atmosphere of tension. At the same time, however, these pupils were consolidating their vocabulary of film with the potential to use this understanding in other literacy work involving scriptwriting.

The objectives involving the comparison of written and filmed or televised versions of texts within the Literacy Strategy for Years 5 and 6, for example, will be supported through the development of a film vocabulary, and this in its turn can lead into scriptwriting. An example of this is outlined in Marsh and Millard (2004) based on the print and film versions of *The Lion, the Witch and the Wardrobe*. The pupils first read an episode from the text and then watched the filmed version of the same section of the narrative. They created storyboards for the extract and finally developed their own playscript.

Given the difficulties of accessing a range of examples of quality playscripts for pupils which provide good models of narrative and character development, film and televised media also offer a wealth of opportunities for stimulating discussion and understanding of the construction, and the purpose, of the playscript. Additionally, there are indications that the use of film and televised media as part of literacy teaching can have a powerful effect on children's broader literacy practices (Marsh and Millard 2004). As visual literacy becomes in increasingly important aspect of modern culture, pupils bring their familiarity with visual media to bear on their understanding and use of written language (Browne 1999). Again a response frame can be used to encourage pupils to consider the effect of close-up, medium or long shots in conveying information about characters and creating atmosphere, and how music, setting and special effects provide information.

The increasing availability of digital video makes it possible to consider attempting to produce a short extract from the script, in order to complete the link between writing and performing, and to enable pupils to reflect on the effectiveness of their work. An article describing work undertaken with Year 6 pupils using digital video (Burnett *et al.* 2004) indicates the need for sufficient time to be allowed for such projects to be effective, but also underlines the potential of media work in terms of helping pupils relate to the needs of the audience: 'With film, children can be both readers (viewers) and writers (film makers) at the same time. If they aren't satisfied, they can immediately re-shoot the scene' (p. 24).

The pupils in this project created film scripts based on short extracts from known texts, due to time limitations. In so doing, the authors argue, the text-level *Framework* objectives for Year 6, which ask pupils to compare the print and film versions of a text, are met on a deeper level than would be the case if they had merely watched a filmed version.

The NLS *Framework* objectives for Year 6 in relation to playscript (Year 6 Term 1: T9) require the preparation of a short section of a story as a script, but do not specify that this must be for stage performance as opposed to film. The *Activity Resource Sheet* for this objective, suggests the development of a film or television script as an appropriate task.

http://www.standards.dfes.gov.uk/primary/publications/literacy/nls_framework/485701/year6/term1/ra083.PDF

Another excellent example of the use of film narrative to support playscript writing and response is provided as a case study in Bearne (2002:104–5). Here Gilly McInness worked with her Year 5 class to develop the writing of playscript as a dialogue between actor and playwright, as well as a dialogue between actor and audience. Using a short extract from the popular film *Mulan* as the stimulus, the class extracted the lines of dialogue from the scene and then attempted to add adverbs to indicate tone of voice and stage directions for action. The effectiveness of their writing was then tested in action by being given to another group of pupils who performed the scene adhering strictly to the written script and ignoring what they had seen on the video. In this way, the necessity for the writers to be precise and detailed in their instructions became clear, and scripts were redrafted three times in order to arrive at a finished product.

This approach provided pupils with constructive feedback during the drafting process: 'in every rehearsal the authors discovered omissions in their writing and the actors noted shortcomings in their own scripts' (ibid.: 105).

This process bears a strong similarity to that used by some professional writers, when writing for performance. Here David Almond, the well-known children's author, talks about his experience of writing the play *Wild Girl Wild Boy* and developing it through a workshop approach with the acting company.

> Rewriting was an active and immediate act. If a character's words fell flat we tried out other variations of the words. The half finished script was soon filled with scribbled notes: my own responses, the responses of the directors and actors. (Almond 2002: 89)

The approach also has the potential to provide an insight into the process of dramatic production. Stage directions do not always provide all the information needed to create the final performance, and McInness's pupils were operating not only as playwrights and actors, but also to some extent as directors as they amended and refined their scripts.

McInness's work also enabled pupils to move between the conventions of film and stage. Although her project did not specifically explore similarities and differences between them, this would have been possible.

Conclusion

This chapter has sought to show how the complex concepts underpinning the writing of playscript can be developed in different ways.

Pupils' achievements in playscript writing by the end of Key Stage 2 may not always appear to display the same levels of maturity in characterisation or plot construction that is displayed in some of their other writing activities. This might lead us as teachers to undervalue the range of understanding pupils need to achieve and to display in devising and annotating playscript texts. Much of the knowledge pupils have needed to bring to the creation of the text will only be realised through the theatrical performance, or the production of the short, filmed episode which is the real outcome of this aspect of literacy.

A creative literacy curriculum which supports the development of playscript needs to integrate opportunities for dramatic exploration of text with the critical examination of published playscripts; to link the experience of developing impro-vised performance with the conventions used to represent theatrical action in playscript writing and to develop a vocabulary of critical appreciation to inform subsequent activities in both writing and performance. These opportunities need to be provided systematically throughout Key Stage 2 so that the links between performing, writing and audience appreciation can become explicit to pupils.

References

Almond, D. (2002) *Wild Girl Wild Boy*. London: Hodder Childrens Books.

Bearne, E. (2002) *Making Progress in Writing*. London: RoutledgeFalmer.

Browne, N. (1999) *Young Children's Literacy Development and the Role of Televisual Texts*. London: Falmer.

Burnett, C., Keating, C. and Marchant, G. (2004) 'Shooting the story'. *Primary English Magazine*, 9(5), June, 20–4.

Chaplin, A. (2003/4) 'Performance skills for juniors' (three articles). *Primary English Magazine*, October, December, February.

DfEE (1998) *The National Literacy Strategy Framework for Teaching*. London: DfEE.

DfEE (1999) *The National Curriculum for Key Stages 1 and 2*. London: DfEE.

DfES (2001) *Writing Playscripts: Writing Flier 4*. London: DfES Publications.

DfES (2003) *Speaking, Listening Learning: Working with Children in Key Stages 1 and 2*. London: DfES.

Grainger, T. (2003) 'Let drama build bridges'. *Primary English Magazine*, October, December.

Marsh, J. and Millard, E. (2004) 'Television and film', in Grainger, T. (ed.) *The RoutledgeFalmer Reader in Language and Literacy*. London: RoutledgeFalmer.

Readman, G. and Lamont, G. (1994) *Drama: A Handbook for Primary Teachers*. London: BBC.

Simons, J. (2000) 'Walking in another person's shoes: storytelling and role play', in Nicholson, H. (ed.) *Teaching Drama 11–18*. London: Continuum.

Winston, J. (2004) *Drama and English at the Heart of the Curriculum*. London: David Fulton.

Woodhouse, J. (2004) *The Big Picture: Ancient Egypt* (Teacher's Activity Book, Big Book and E-book). London: BBC.

Best Practice Case Studies – Case Study 4 (www.standards.dfes.gov.uk/primary).

Story Shorts – Using Films to Teach Literacy (www.standards.dfes.gov.uk/literacy).

The Greek times? Revisiting Greek mythology in relation to children's popular culture

Carol Precious

Since the launch of the National Literacy Strategy (DfEE 1998), teachers are now familiar with the guidance and support contained in the *Framework* and it seems that now is an appropriate time to address how to use the Strategy as a springboard for creative, effective literacy learning. A resurgence of interest in creativity is evidenced in the publication of *All Our Futures: Creativity, Culture and Education* (DfEE 1999), *Excellence and Enjoyment* (DfES 2003) and the QCA materials *Creativity: Find It, Promote It* (2000).

This chapter focuses on a variety of ways that children can be introduced to the rich narratives and moral dilemmas contained in Greek mythology and can subvert these in a playful manner in relation to children's popular culture; namely using the wide variety of non-fiction genres contained within children's magazines to encourage children's creativity, humour and enjoyment of writing for a specific purpose and audience. Perhaps it is timely, as this chapter will explore, to avoid condemnation of children's popular culture and seek to find ways in which we can weave together children's interests and motivation to enhance their literacy curriculum. It is envisaged that the final outcome of this unit of work would be the production of a class magazine that could be shared within the school community. Initially this would be hand-produced, including drawings, but to publish a polished, edited magazine in a truly professional format, ICT skills could be utilised, depending upon the children's abilities.

The inspiration for linking myths to popular culture was rooted in my experience with undergraduates in an English session where, when exploring the genre of myths, the students indicated that their knowledge of this area of literature was vague, but they had experienced Disney cartoon versions of the stories. I utilised Marcia Williams's *Greek Myths for Young Children* as a resource, with its cartoon illustrations and using colloquial language in the speech bubbles supported by traditional narrative below each illustration, to refresh and extend their knowledge and understanding of some of the main stories. In order to stimulate their creativity the students were then encouraged to use their knowledge and understanding of non-fiction text-types to cross genres and produce fresh and amusing non-fiction accounts of the characters and stories in a variety of ways linked to their experiences of reading popular culture magazines.

Why the Greek myths today?

The Greek myths are a part of the canon of children's literature and are justifiably included in the National Literacy Strategy's (DfEE 1998) range in Years 3 and 5 in term 2. Dealing as they do with heroism, epic journeys, magic and transformations, these myths are fundamental stories which have involved readers' imaginations and emotions for centuries. However, the storylines are in some ways problematic, as in addressing issues of morality. Bearne (2000) suggests that 'morality may sometimes seem ambiguous or questionable to different cultures' (p. 44). These are tales of greed, broken promises and hearts, treachery, horror and tragedy which we may not consider suitable for children, as indeed they were not the original intended audience. However, these grand, timeless narratives provide a fertile ground to provoke children's imaginative responses as readers and some themes are not at all dissimilar from the plots to be found in many of our current television soaps which are consumed by large audiences at many times every week. For example, Pandora, who had everything that Epimethius could give her, just could not restrain herself from inquisitiveness, and, breaking her promise not to look in the box, unleashes evil upon the Earth. Orpheus and Eurydice is a tale of love lost in which, despite Orpheus's heroic deeds, uncertainty and human emotions result in a tragic ending. Prometheus's punishment by Zeus for giving away the secret of fire would surely compete in terms of pure gore with any contemporary horror tale. Dedalus and Icarus are rewarded for constructing the labyrinth at Crete by virtual imprisonment by King Minas, and when trying to escape with his father, Dedalus, Icarus suffers an untimely death for disobeying his father's instructions not to fly too close to the sun.

The characters have similar characteristics to latter-day popular superheroes in terms of human frailty, tragedy and the performance of incredible tasks fighting evil protagonists. Both Achilles and Superman have vulnerabilities – in the case of Achilles, his heel, and exposure to Kryptonite has drastic effects upon Superman's powers. Spiderman has obvious connections to the fate of Arachne. Similarly, there are the themes of transformation in Greek mythology such as the aforementioned Arachne, Narcissus and Echo which are mirrored in the transformation of Clark Kent into Superman and Peter Parker into his alter ego Spiderman. As Hercules completed his 12 labours, and Theseus slayed the Minotaur, superhero comic characters fight monstrous villains, such a Lex Luther as he plots the downfall of Superman, and Spiderman battles with exotic creations such as Doctor Octopus and the Green Goblin. Through film and comics these are familiar scenarios for the children we currently teach and, as will be discussed later in more detail, influence their imaginative oral and written narratives. This is indeed not a recent phenomenon and as Fox's (1993) study of children's oral narratives indicates, superheroes can be a powerful stimulus:

> Josh and Jimmy had seen superhero films both on TV and the cinema. Josh tells a story in which Superman, Batman and Robin, and the Incredible Hulk are all combined. Strangely enough, though the actions of the story are what we might expect, the telling itself is one of the most literary, in its language style, in the study. (p. 16)

Playful and subversive literacies

One could argue that using myths in relation to popular culture to encourage writing in a subversive manner could be interpreted as 'dumbing down' (Cunningham 1998) the quality and importance of these stories in our cultural heritage. However, I would argue that the practice of comparison with other contemporary texts and playful subversion require high levels of understanding of the original works. From an early age children naturally play with language to subvert meanings (Chukovsky 1963; Grainger and Goouch 1999) and it could be argued that children are only empowered to do so because they have intellectual ownership of the subject matter; that is to say, only when a subject is fully understood can children dissect, reinvent and rework it to suit their own ends. So, far from superficially trivialising stories, subversion demonstrates children's understanding and ability to control the genre. Cathy Pompe's (1996) amusing account of a child's playful connection between the film *Pocahontas* and the once popular *Pogs* illustrates this well: 'Fresh out of the film *Pocahontas*, with *Pogs* still the rage in school, Aisha decided "Cheesy Feet" needed a story called *Pog-a-Hontas*' (p. 112).

Carter (1996) refers to young children's developing ability to tell and understand the language play of jokes as 'playing with patterns of meaning' (p. 163). I suggest that this is something that creative teachers of literacy could capitalise upon to raise the level of children's enjoyment and engagement in their developing abilities as writers. Similarly, Hass Dyson's (2001) research into the effects of popular culture indicates that children are able to stretch, reconfigure and re-articulate their cultural resources, and she argues that these are 'key to literacy learning in contemporary times' (p. 85). Indeed, taking a more extreme viewpoint, Whiteley (1997 : 49), researching how children see television narratives asserts: 'But unless these children can use their media-inspired sources to generate work that fulfils more literary requirements, in the terms within which schools assess their language-based development, they are doomed to failure.'

While children may have not consciously unpicked the grammatical features and language of magazines, as required in more formal school literacy practices, they do indeed have a deep, implicit understanding of the genre through their literacy experiences outside school. An investigation of children's magazines within a unit of work would enable the children to make these understandings explicit within their literacy sessions and form the basis for a critical consideration of the genre.

Research carried out by Barrs and Cork (2001), focusing upon the links between children's knowledge and understanding of literature and writing suggests: 'The significant literary competence that the text teaches the reader is the next step in becoming a writer' (p. 19). It is my belief that, alongside children's natural ability and aptitude to subvert meanings and use humour to gain power over language, certain types of picture-books reinforce and reflect this playfulness.

Subversion: children's picture-books and film

Children with experience of recently published picture-books are no strangers to subversion, particularly with reference to traditional tales. Lewis (2001) writes: 'Being a relatively timeless, closed and immutable genre the fairy-tale attracts subversion and the most active in undermining it have been the makers of picture books' (p. 67).

John Sciezka and illustrator Lane Smith's *The True Story of the Three Little Pigs!* reshapes this traditional tale into a newspaper format in which the wolf describes himself as an innocent victim of journalists seeking sensational stories. The same authors continue the story of the the the Frog Prince who did not live happily ever after and seeks, through a variety of fairy-tale witches and fairy godmothers, to reverse the spell and return to his former frog self. More recently, Lauren Child has delighted a wide audience of children with *Beware the Storybook Wolves* and *Who's Afraid of the Big Bad Book*, where the protagonist, Herb, interacts with well-known characters from familiar traditional tales. In relation to children's responses to reading subversive picture-books, Lewis suggests: 'When children are able to play with language and with texts we can be sure that they are in no danger of mistaking nonsense for sense, have understood the rules and are in possession of a competence that they can apply creatively to their own use of Language' (Lewis 2001 : 79).

Although not published in so great a quantity, there are also post-modern subversions of non-fiction texts such as *How Dogs Really Work* (1993) by Alan Snow, *The Worm Book* (1979) by Allan Ahlberg, illustrated by Janet Ahlberg, and *Mythological Monsters of Ancient Greece* (2004) by Sara Fanelli. While in terms of format and grammatical structures these texts could be regarded as falling within the non-fiction definition of explanatory texts, they are, none the less, fantasy. Reading and analysing these texts could also serve to increase the children's understanding of this type of creativity and they could be used as models for their own ideas. Terry Deary's (1993) immensely popular *Horrible Histories* series is a further example of this genre.

The current climate of playfulness in relation to children's literacy experiences in relation to popular culture is further evidenced by the popularity of subversive treatments of texts to be found in film. The success of *Shrek* (see Chapter 9) and *Shrek 2*, with the director's playful twists of the themes of traditional tales within a larger narrative, and, similarly, *The Incredibles*, debunking the superhero comic genre, are appealing to both child and adult audiences as entertainment in a global context.

Popular culture and magazines

Children's popular culture is often regarded as problematic with teachers. Lambirth (2003) concluded that the teachers he worked with did not value popular culture's potential as a tool for literacy learning while reminiscing affectionately about personal experiences of the genre in their own childhoods. However, there is an undeniable movement and body of research to support the use of popular culture within the literacy curriculum (Whiteley 1996; Hass Dyson 2001; Marsh and Millard 2003).

Marsh and Millard (2003) identify popular culture as integral to children's lives and as such cannot be neglected when considering literacy in its broadest sense. Similarly, Hass Dyson (2001) challenges notions of childhood as currently experienced by children in the USA as opposed to idealised childhoods which have echoes of teachers' affectionate memories relating to their own literacy experiences when young. Is it possible that sentimentality softens, changes and re-creates our memories of childhood, not just into idyllic memories of endless summers but also, as teachers of literacy, memories of classic texts?

The demands of the National Literacy Strategy (DfEE 1998) in terms of curriculum coverage, concerns over the results of Ofsted inspection and assessment, Grainger (2004) argues, are 'challenges to teachers' professionalism, self-confidence and engagement with teaching suggesting that teachers' professionalism has clearly been both reduced and re-described' (p. 4). Perhaps now is the time to reclaim our creativity and plan experiences which will challenge children's imagination, based upon their experiences of enjoyment outside the school regulated curriculum?

Children's magazines form a considerable part of children's reading in the home, something that publishers have been quick to make capital of, and their formats are more sophisticated than comics, using a multimedia approach including photographs, graphics, posters and cartoons.

Figure 7.1 is an analysis of the content of a number of magazines for children currently available in my local newsagents and supermarkets. These have been split into those which, predominantly, are aimed at a boy readership and those obviously aimed at girls, followed by those common to both.

There are common themes, such as letters, puzzles and articles promoting films, but generally, within the analysis above, there are very distinct themes divided in gender terms. These could be considered problematic in terms of the construction of gender identities, in that those published for girls tend to focus on gossip,

Girls' magazines	Boys' magazines
gossip	monsters
pop stars	football stars
fashion	superheroes
make-up	jokes
horoscopes	DVD games
websites	card games
mobile phones	non-fiction factual articles
shopping	things to make
makeovers	cartoon stories
photographic stories	
Articles common to both types of magazine	
puzzles	
advertisements for films	
letters	
quizzes	

Figure 7.1

clothes, fashion accessories and pop stars, while those aimed at boys include scatological humour, features on footballers, superheroes and a variety of monsters connected with popular culture. The free gifts which often form a part of the magazines' attraction for children are similarly stereotypical with 'Scary Kits' for boys and combs, bracelets, rings and make-up for girl readers. The use of colour in the magazines is also worthy of note, with pink predominating for girls and strong primary colours for boys. However, in terms of developing children's critical literacy, these magazines provide a variety of contexts in which to deconstruct and challenge the messages they give to children.

Planning the unit of work

The unit of work will focus explicitly on generating, as the final outcome, a class magazine, presenting the characters and narratives of the Greek myths in a humorous, subversive style, which can be shared throughout the school. However, Figure 7.2 sets out the progression of literacy activities to achieve the final goal.

Immersion

Initially, the children can be introduced to a variety of myths through hearing them read and collaborating in shared, guided and independent reading. The

Immersion in mythical stories, including storytelling, reading and drama

Exploration non-fiction genres in magazines

Compiling lists of text-types
Constructing written texts using shared, guided and independent writing

Using ICT to publish the magazine

Figure 7.2

teacher, as storyteller (using no book), recreating the original oral transmission of the myths, would also be an effective strategy, both to engage the children in the narrative and to encourage the children to retell the stories and familiarise themselves with the settings, characters and plots. However, there are many good versions, published in good quality books.

For inexperienced readers, Marcia Williams's *Greek Myths* has very accessible versions, as the stories are presented in a cartoon form containing both a simple narrative and supported by speech bubbles. For older children, *The Orchard Book of Greek Myths* and *Atticus the Storyteller's Top 100 Greek Myths* are a useful resource. There are also a wide variety of internet website resources.

Which stories to include in the immersion activities should be the choice of the teacher, depending upon the resources available, but the following are suggestions as to some of the more accessible and exciting tales:

- Pandora
- Theseus and the Minotaur
- Prometheus
- Orpheus and Euridyce
- Narcissus
- Daedalus and Icarus
- Perseus and Medusa
- King Midas

- The labours of Herakles
- Arachne

Immersion activities could involve the use of process drama techniques, including hot-seating, freeze-frame and thought tracking (see Chapter 9). These oral activities will enable the children to discuss character, motives and plot, investigating similarities and differences between the main characters and the situations in which they find themselves. It is here that the seeds of change can be developed as children are encouraged to view the narratives through the eyes of different characters. For example, how the minotaur actually felt to be imprisoned within the labyrinth, only to be fed every six years.

The children's oral and dramatic activities can then be translated into print and recorded, and by a variety of means, such as story mapping (drawing a map, by pictures and words of the devlopment of the story) or storyboards (pictorial representations of the story's progression, similar to comic strips), to create a sense of the narrative in the myths selected by the children. Using paired and group talk, characters can be discussed and represented in pictorial form with their various attributes represented as notes surrounding a depiction of the character. These can then be used as a basis for constructing the main body of the magazine.

Exploring non-fiction genres in magazines

- Introduce the topic of magazines.
- Invite the children to bring in and share their favourites.
- In groups, discuss and categorise the different types.
- Use these categories to investigate and explore the content.
- Create lists of common content themes.
- Discuss whether there are any obvious gender divides.
- Analyse the format and presentation of the different features.
- Draw up a list of common features to be included in the class magazine.
- Using the children's knowledge and understanding of non-fiction text-types, make links between these and the articles they have identified.

Using the six non-fiction types identified within the National Literacy Strategy (DfEE 1998) the grid shown in Figure 7.3 identifies possible links with common features in magazines.

Organising the writing

I suggest that this would be best approached through organising the classroom so that the children can work in response pairs using a writer's workshop process.

Recount	Report	Procedural	Explanation	Persuasion	Discussion
news page	Top Ten monsters	horoscopes	letters	advertisements	interviews
diaries		directions to play games	problem page	film posters	editorials
gossip	Top Ten tragedies	recipes		holiday brochures	

Figure 7.3

Response pairs are writing partners, either chosen by the children or the teacher. Their function is to provide mutual, friendly, critical support throughout the writing process. The writer's workshop process would involve:

- individual drafting;
- the child reading this first draft aloud to her/himself;
- reflecting upon the writing and making decisions about any changes; and
- reading the draft to a response partner.

   Ground rules will need to be established as to the nature of the role of the response partner and a general agreement that this is to be a collaborative, supportive activity needs to be stressed.

- The response partner concentrates and listens carefully as the draft is read.
- Positive, supportive comments should be made about what the partner likes about the writing.
- Suggestions can be made as to ways in which the writing may be improved.
- Is the story structure clear?
- Is there anything missed out?
- Could anything be added to enhance the writing?

After making any adjustments to their writing, in accordance with this dialogue with a response partner, the children can then conference with the teacher to share and discuss their writing.

Playing with the texts

The following is an outline suggestion of a unit of work and is by no means presented as prescriptive. The ideas are intended to be merely examples of what might be done and it is envisaged that individual teachers and pupils will select and add their own ideas to the examples. The actual writing tasks could be approached by a variety of methods using shared, guided and independent writing.

The format follows the non-fiction text-types outlined in the National Literacy Strategy (DfEE 1998), identifying objectives and linking these to possible writing outcomes. I should also like to acknowledge the influence of my colleague, Tony Mahon, in the construction of this format.

A recount
Possible forms in relation to magazine articles: diary, news page, readers' letters, biography, e-mail, gossip columns.

Objective
To write as a character from one of the Greek myths a recount in one of the above forms.

The task
- Review the components of a recount text.
- Invite the children to choose a Greek myth that they know well.
- In pairs, the children can talk and think about what happened to that character and how he or she might have felt.
- Allow the children to decide what form of recount they are going to write for the magazine. It might be helpful for them to organise their ideas as a story map, a storyboard, a time-line or a flowchart.
- In pairs, make a first draft of the recount using the appropriate organisation structure, linguistic features and form.
- Revise and edit the accounts and share them with other members of the class.

Suggestions

Myth	Form
Theseus and the Minotaur	News page – 'Monster in the Labyrinth Slain!'
Pandora	Diary – the events leading up to opening the box
The gods	gossip
	e-mail
King Midas	biography

Figure 7.4

Text-type: recount

Purpose	To retell events that actually occurred
Generic organisational structure	• Orientation – scene setting, opening • Events – recount of events as they occurred • Re-orientation – a closing statement
Linguistic features	• Written in the past tense • In chronological order using temporal connectives • Focus on individual or group participants
Forms	Diary, letter, e-mail, newspaper account, biography

Figure 7.5

Instructional texts
Possible forms in relation to magazine: recipes, instructions how to make some-thing, directions.

Objective
To write clear instructions, using link phrases and organisational conventions.

The task
• Review the components of an instructional/procedural text provided.

• Ask the children to think of an object or a type of food from the myths that they know.

• Having made a decision, discuss in pairs the instructional text chosen and the steps involved.

• A time-line or flowchart could be constructed to clarify organisational thinking.

• Complete a first draft using the appropriate organisational structure, linguistic features and form.

• Revise and edit the text and share with other members of the class.

Suggestions

Object	Form
The Trojan Horse	'How to make' instructions
The labyrinth	How to find the minotaur
Prometheus's gift to Zeus	Recipe

Figure 7.6

Text-type: Instructions/procedures

Purpose:	● To describe how something is done through a series of sequenced steps
Generic organisational structure	● Goal – a statement of what is to be achieved
Linguistic features	● Written in the present tense or imperative
Forms	● Recipe, instruction manual, directions

Figure 7.7

A non-chronological report
Possible form in magazine: description of a mythological monster.

Objective
Write a non-chronological report using organisational devices (e.g. numbered lists, headings), generalising details and omitting unimportant details.

The task
● Review the components of a non-chronological report provided.

● Ask the children to select their favourite mythical monster.

● Draw the monster to investigate its special features.

● The children decide which form they are going to use for their writing.

● In pairs, brainstorm the information that is going to go into the report.

● Write a first draft using appropriate organisational structure, linguistic features and form.

● Revise and edit the report.

● Share it with other members of the class.

Suggestions

Myth	Form
Odysseus	A report on the monster Scylla

Figure 7.8

Text-type: non-chronological report

Purpose	To describe things the way they are
Generic organisation and structure	• An opening, general classification, e.g. description of the phenomenon, some or all of its qualities • Parts and their functions • Habits/behaviours or uses
Linguistic features	• Written in the present tense • Non-chronological
Forms	Descriptions of a town, country, factsheet, tourist leaflet, description of a science experiment

Figure 7.9

An explanation

Possible links to magazine: features on characters analysing motives.

Objective

Write an explanation of a process, improving cohesion through paragraphing, linking phrases and organisational devices.

Task

• Review the components of an explanation provided.

• Ask the children to reflect upon why a particular event occurred in a particular myth.

• In groups or pairs, the children brainstorm what might be included in their explanation. Using a flowchart or a word web will help them clarify their thinking.

• Write a first draft using the appropriate organisational structure, linguistic features and form as in the grid provided.

• Revise and edit the explanation and share it with the class.

Suggestions

Myth	Form
Orpheus and Euridyce	Letter from the snake explaining why he bit Euridyce Letter from Orpheus explaining why he looked back

Figure 7.10

Text-type: explanation

Purpose	To explain the processes involved in natural and social phenomena, or to explain how something works
Generic organisational structure	• General statement to introduce the topic • A series of logical steps explaining how or why something occurs • These steps continue until the final state is produced or the explanation is complete
Linguistic features	• Written in the present tense • Uses temporal connectives
Forms	• Description of a scientific process, explanation of why a historical event occurred, flowchart, poster

Figure 7.11

A persuasive text
Possible links to magazine: an advertising poster.

Objective
Design an advertising poster.

Task
- Review the components of a persuasive text provided.
- Ask the children to reflect upon a specific hero from a myth.
- Decide upon which form of persuasive text to write.
- Draft the text using an appropriate organisational structure, linguistic features and form.
- Revise and edit the text and share it with a partner.

Suggestions

Myth	Form
The twelve tasks of Harakles	Film advertisement
Theseus and the Minotaur	Magazine article

Figure 7.12

Text type: Persuasion

Purpose	To attempt to convince the reader
Generic organisational structure	• An opening statement • Arguments – often in the form of points plus elaboration • Reiteration – summary and restatement of the opening position
Linguistic features	• Written in the simple present tense • Focus upon generic participants • Uses mainly logical rather than temporal connectives
Forms	• Advertisement, poster, newspaper editorial, campaign leaflet, brochures, fliers, magazine article

Figure 7.13

A discussion
Possible links to magazine: magazine article or a letter on a controversial issue.

Objective
Draft and write letters expressing a point of view.
Write a commentary on an issue.

Task
● Review the components of a discussion text provided.

● Ask the children to reflect upon an event in a myth which they consider to be a controversial issue.

● Brainstorm which might go into the discussion text. Think about the issue from as many perspectives as possible. It might be useful to record the ideas in a for-and-against grid.

● Draft the text using appropriate organisational structure, linguistic features and form.

● Revise and edit the text and share it with a friend.

Suggestions

Myth	Form
Arachne	Letter: Should Athene have acted as she did?
Echo and Narcissus	Magazine article: Did Narcissus deserve his fate?

Figure 7.14

Text-type: discussion

Purpose	To present arguments and information from differing viewpoints
Generic organisational structure	• Statement of the issue plus a preview of the main arguments • Arguments for, plus supporting evidence • Arguments against, plus supporting evidence (alternatively, argument/counter argument, one point at a time) • Recommendation – summary and conclusion
Linguistic features	• Uses the present tense • Generic human or non-human participants • Logical connectives
Forms	Newspaper/magazine article, balanced report, leaflet on a controversial issue

Figure 7.15

Constructing the magazine

The format of the magazine should be the children's decision based upon their reading experiences of the genre to enable them to establish ownership of the final product. In assembling the various articles there are the following to consider:

● the title;

● an editor's introduction;

● the sequence of the articles in the magazine;

● a numbered contents page;

● inserting the advertisements;

● how ICT could be used.

These considerations will require a considerable amount of talk and negotiation between the members of the class and of course, the children's ICT skills. However, the children's writing could be word-processed to give a polished finish to the final product. The magazine could be constructed by laminating the pages and assembled using a comb binder.

The final product could then be shared with other classes and if laminated should be durable.

Endpiece

Although I have not addressed questions of gender at any great length in this chapter, there are a few points I should like to make with reference to gender issues. Although addressing pupils in Key Stage 3, aged 11/12 and 12/13, Gill Venn's (1996) research into constructions of femininity in relation to the images to which they are exposed identified that in terms of popular culture 'Teen magazines were clearly the favourites across both groups' (Venn 1996 : 134). While the research did not centre solely on magazines, but also upon English teaching in general, she stresses, 'Thus it seems vital that, as teachers, we aim to empower girls from all cultures to resist stereotypical images of femininity as portrayed by popular culture' (p. 147). I also feel that this is important and something that should be critically analysed during classroom discussions in relation to the magazines that the children might bring to school. Earlier in this chapter I made comments upon the clear gender differences in magazines and it would certainly be most appropriate to address these as a part of the children's critical literacy development.

Following on from this gender issue, there is the question of boys' literacy development and the current concerns, in particular, about boys and writing. Smith (2004), researching successful boy readers in a two-year study, focused upon non-fiction reading of boys from the ages of five to seven. She found it noteworthy that all boys in her sample regularly read periodicals, so perhaps we should not always associate popular culture with a possible lack of achievement. Meek (1998) also supports the notion of the attraction of subversion for boys:

> One thing more: boys are intrigued by subversions. J. Scieszka's *The Stinky Cheeseman and other Fairly Stupid Tales* entrusts young readers with post-modern aporia – 'Who is the ISBN Guy?' 'Where is the Lazy Author' – good for showing off what isn't taught in lessons. (p. 122)

Perhaps as teachers we should not make too many adverse reactions and judgements in relation to children's popular culture and seek to find ways in which we can weave together the children's interests and motivation to enhance their literacy curriculum? 'Anarchy and humour are children's best protective and subversive devices with which they upturn the most sacred icons and declare their grasp of what's going on' (Pompe 1996 : 112).

Picture-book bibliography

Allan Ahlberg (1981) *The Worm Book* (illustrated by Janet Ahlberg). Viking.

Lauren Child (2001) *Beware of the Storybook Wolves*. Hodder Children's Books.

Lauren Child (2003) *Who's Afraid of the Big Bad Book?* Hyperion Books for Children.

Lucy Coates and Anthony Lewis (2002) *Atticus the Storyteller's 100 Greek Myths*. Orion Children's Books.

Terry Deary (1993) Horrible Histories series. Scholastic Hippo.

Sarah Fanelli *Mythical Monsters of Ancient Greece.*

Alan Snow (1993) *How Dogs Really Work*. HarperCollins.

Marcia Williams (1994) *Greek Myths for Young Children*. Walker Books.

References

Barrs, M. and Cork, V. (2001) *The Reader in the Writer: The Influence of Literature Upon Writing at KS2*. London: Centre for Literacy in Primary Education.

Bearne, E. (2000) 'Myth, legend, culture and morality', in Bearne, E. and Watson, V. (eds) *Where Texts and Children Meet*. London: Routledge.

Carter, R. (1997) *Exploring Spoken English*. Cambridge: Cambridge University Press.

Chukovskii, K. (1963) *From Two to Five* (trans. M. Morton). Berkeley: University of California.

Cunningham, V. (1998) 'Reading now and then', in Cox, B. (ed.) *Literacy Is Not Enough: Essays on the Importance of Reading*. Manchester: Manchester University Press.

DfEE (1998) *National Literacy Strategy Framework for Teaching*. London: Department for Education and Employment.

DfEE (1999) *All Our Futures: Creativity, Culture and Education*. Sudbury: Department for Education and Employment.

DfES (2003) *Excellence and Enjoyment: A Strategy for Primary Schools*. Nottingham: Department for Education and Skills.

Dyson, A. Hass (2001) 'Where are the childhoods in childhood literacy? An exploration in outer (school) space'. *Journal of Early Childhood Literacy*, **1**(1).

Fox, C. (1993) *At the Very Edge of the Forest: The Influence of Literature on Storytelling by Children*. London: Cassell.

Grainger, T. (ed.) (2004) *The RoutledgeFalmer Reader in Language and Literacy*. London: RoutledgeFalmer.

Grainger, T. and Goouch, K. (1999) 'Young children and playful language', in David, T. (ed.) *Teaching Young Children*. London: Paul Chapman.

Lambirth, A. (2003) '"They get enough of that at home": understanding aversion to popular culture in school'. *Reading, Literacy and Language*, **37**(1), 9–13.

Lewis, D. (2001) *Reading Contemporary Picture Books, Picturing Text*. London: RoutledgeFalmer.

Marsh, T. and Millard, E. (2003) *Literacy and Popular Culture in the Classoom*. National Centre for Language and Literacy, University of Reading.

Meek, M. (1998) 'Important reading lessons', in Cox, B. (ed.) *Literacy Is Not Enough: Essays on the Importance of Reading*. Manchester: Manchester University Press.

Pompe, C. (1996) '"But they're pink!" – "Who cares!": popular culture in the primary years', in Hilton, M. (ed.) *Potent Fictions: Children's Literacy and the Challenge of Popular Culture*. London: Routledge.

Scieszka, J. (1990) *The True Story of the Three Little Pigs by A. Wolf* (illustrated by Lane Smith). London: Viking.

QCA (2000) *Creativity: Find It Promote It*. London: QCA.

Smith, S. (2004) 'The non-fiction reading habits of young successful boy readers: forming connections between masculinity and reading'. *Literacy*, **38**(1), 10–16.

Venn, G. (1996) '"I don't know where I am with myself": the later years of childlhood – constructions of Femininity', in Hilton, M. (ed.) *Potent Fictions: Children's Literacy and the Challenge of Popular Culture*. London: Routledge.

Whiteley, D. (1996) 'Reality in boxes: children's perceptions of television narratives', in Hilton, M. (ed.) *Potent Fictions: Children's Literacy and the Challenge of Popular Culture*. London: Routledge.

Williams, M. (1994) *Greek Myths*. London: Walker Books.

Using novels in the classroom – the whole story

Yvonne Stewart

We 'fall in love' with particular books to precisely the extent to which they correspond to what is potentially inside of us. The love affairs will be more intense if the match is closer, less passionate if the match is only partial. But as with both friends and lovers, we do not simply see ourselves in the mirror of the other; we also learn new things, extend our inner worlds, enrich them, and furnish them with new possibilities. (Crago 1993 : 288–9)

Reading longer texts

Fiction narrative is still the main genre that children are exposed to in the taught English curriculum in primary schools. Yet in some ways the novel has lost centre stage, despite the National Literacy *Framework*'s (DfEE 1998) promotion of literacy, and has been overtaken by extracts: disembodied excerpts amputated from the living text. There is no doubt that a knowledgeable reader will always gain more from a text. However, the purpose of using a whole novel for literacy learning is to develop this knowledge in context, thereby strengthening the reader, as well as driving the writer within. For children to fall in love with, and feel passionately about, a text, they have to experience it in its entirety.

Reading a novel is a high-status activity which enlightens children into the 'cultural capital' (Hammond and Mackin-Horarick 1999) of literature and literate behaviours. This chapter means to harness the power of the novel to generate children's personal and emotional responses, as well as promoting discussion and interaction through literary investigation. This chapter brings together these processes and considers how we, as teachers, can encourage children to fall in love with books; to use novels to capture children's emotions and promote the critical thinking essential for true *interpretive* literacy (Meek 2001 : 12) rather than what Wells calls the 'mechanics of literacy' (1987:148). When we read a novel we engage in a relationship with the characters and their experiences; we are involved emotionally and intellectually. Being able to reflect, discuss and critique deepens this experience. Literate behaviour involves responding and choosing how to take our responses forward. Giving reading and talking about children's literature high priority will not only support children in their literacy development but will also engender confidence, excitement and enjoyment.

A creative approach to literacy teaching through novels capitalises on a high level of child involvement, where children are immersed in one text over a period of time and have power over their own experiences and responses to the books they encounter. Through the process of this deep level of engagement with the text children are able to 'turn language and thought in upon themselves' (Donaldson 1978 : 88); a dynamic process of personal and intellectual growth. Different ways of using whole novel texts to engender this deep level of involvement will be discussed here.

Over the past few years we have seen the promotion of short extracts for literacy teaching. However practical the use of short extracts has been for Literacy Hour teaching, it is essential that children experience the whole novel. Through overuse of extracts we have been giving children a distorted view of what reading is and how narratives work, and are essentially moving away from the author's intent. While extracts are useful in skill development, real reading goes beyond that. Fiction authorship involves the construction of a complete narrative; a complete emotional experience. That is how novels are crafted and constructed, and that is how they are meant to be read. The story within a novel transports the reader to other places, other times and into other ways of being. However skilfully used, this cannot be done to best effect with an extract. Total involvement is key to literacy development and here we discuss the use of the novel to capture the reader. By working through a novel together, children are, with the author's help, able to open the door to literacy in the most meaningful and powerful way.

Children are encultured beings who bring their own lived experiences to the text. They therefore understand texts in their own distinct and unique way. By using children's literature we are able to capture this uniqueness and allow for this diversity as we plan opportunities for their responses to be taken forward. We need to ensure that their experience of literacy goes beyond the limits of the different structures and language features of disembodied texts and offer children the opportunity to explore the purposes and motives in authorship (Partridge 2001), for this is where the true cultural capital of literacy lies. For example, it is important when reading Phillip Pullman's *A Subtle Knife* that we engage in discussion about how Pullman crafts suspense in the first chapter, when Will, one of the main characters, realises that there are intruders in the house and that they are getting closer to where he is hiding:

> And now what could he do? Nothing, for the moment. He crouched in the dimness, heart pounding, listening hard. The two men were in the hall. He heard one of them say quietly, 'Come on. I can hear the milkman down the road.'

> 'It's not here, though,' said the other voice. 'We'll have to look upstairs.'

Using novels in the classroom

'Go on, then. Don't hang about.'

Will braced himself as he heard the quiet creak of the top step. The man was making no noise at all, but he couldn't help the creak if he wasn't expecting it. Then there was a pause. A very thin beam of torchlight swept along the floor outside: Will saw it through the crack. Then the door began to move. (Pullman 1997:6–7)

We would expect to discuss the way he uses his art purposefully to develop tension within the reader here. In contrast, 43 pages later is poetry:

All through the day the witches came, like flakes of black snow on the wings of a storm, filling the skies with the darting flutter of their silk and the swish of air through the needles of cloud-pine branches. Men who hunted in the dripping forests, or fished among melting ice-sloes hear the sky-wide whisper through the fog, and if the sky was clear they would look up to see the witches flying, like scraps of darkness drifting on a secret tide. (ibid.: 50)

Pullman uses poetic language and imagery as velvet to our senses. Some would argue for studying these for linguistic purposes in isolation within the Literacy Hour. However, the power comes when we discuss these within the context of the whole narrative. It is then that we come to understand how these two sections are inextricably interconnected and come from the mind of a literary giant. This is how we make sure that children walk in the company of authors, and come to understand how powerful the author's ability can be in exploiting and manipulating language to the benefit of readers.

Will any book do?

The literature they meet must be alive, must be fiercely alive, or there's no point and they're deprived. (Byatt 1998 : 44)

There are many who say that as long as the children are reading it doesn't matter what they read, and I have a certain amount of sympathy with this view and have always ensured that the reading material in my own classrooms covers a wide variety, from poetry, picture-books, novels and compilations to magazines, comics, newspapers and catalogues. One recognises that there is a place for encounters with different kinds of texts, as we know that 'different texts offer different kinds of reading experiences' (Styles *et al.* 1994 : 44). However, some of these can give pleasure in the short term and may not linger in the mind (Byatt 1998); they may not have the impact that we want for children in the long term. So when choosing texts for deep engagement, for promoting critical literacy in the short and long term, I suggest that we, as discerning professionals, should choose books that have been authored to captivate and promote children, and those which are sure to touch their emotional lives.

The introduction of the National Literacy Strategy (DfEE 1998) spawned a plethora of texts designed and marketed for child consumption. Many are targeted at adults who still, in the main, are responsible for purchasing the books that children read (Meek 2001). The sales of children's books have rocketed over the past few years, and among these are some of the most powerful and challenging texts ever written for the child audience. We are fortunate, therefore, to be able to choose from a wide range of texts. This range is important, and children, as we know, have different tastes and interests which we need to cater for.

In making choices about children's fiction literature, we bring to bear our professional knowledge and take account of the kinds of literary experiences we hope children will engage in. Therefore, one essential element in effective literacy learning and teaching is that we as teachers have read children's books and developed our own knowledge of children's texts in depth.

In so doing we come to recognise that some texts are formulaic in construction, for successful marketing, while others are artistically crafted and the quality stands out in the text; and we come to know that quality texts have children as protagonists, taking centre stage within the narrative, where children themselves are the powerful role models.

A novel like *I Am David*, by Anne Holme, for example, illustrates how an author demonstrates the agency of a child character through the story. David, the main character, is active in determining his own life by the choices he makes. Within the narrative a myriad of human characteristics and emotions are portrayed, from compassion to loathing, from bravery and resilience to weakness and despair. Within the text, children witness the development of human character and values, and are changed by the experience. In experiencing this text children are active participants in the life of David as it unfolds.

The National Literacy Strategy (DfEE 1998) has outlined the range of novel texts that children are expected to encounter in Years 4–6, but we have to decide which texts are good enough for the children we teach; ones that meet the 'emotional investment' of children (Crago 1993).

Learning through interaction – speaking, listening and thinking

> Thought undergoes many changes as it turns into speech. It does not merely find expression in speech; it finds its reality and form. (Vygotsky 1962 : 126)

While it is important in education that children are able to articulate their thinking, we know that speech has dynamic effects on developing the thinking process (Vygotsky 1962; Britton 1970; Wells 1986). This indisputable link between thought and language places speaking and listening as key elements in generating cognitive processes, and as such is central to developing critical thinking and literacy learning. This chapter promotes the view that the literature children read forms the context for talk. All aspects of working with novels covered here are purposively planned to create as many opportunities as possible for oracy development. Planning with interaction and collaboration in mind means that we offer opportunities for dialogue throughout our work with literature.

This approach to literacy allows for spontaneous personal responses, while acknowledging that at other times this will be drawn out and developed more explicitly. It is important also to allow children time to reflect on the effect of the text: offering opportunity to digest the emotional impact of the events that they become involved with through the words of the author; letting them experience the power of words when used by a skilled mind and crafted for maximum impact. Spaces, therefore, are essential elements to the learning process.

Because we are in the false situation of the classroom we have to plan the pauses carefully to ensure that they happen, offering thinking time for the children to absorb the moment. For that is what readers do. This kind of practice helps to develop thoughtful, competent and critical readers (Brabham and Villaume 2000).

Plan creatively for creativity

Knowledge, skills and time are necessary for any creative process. Plans are detailed sketches of these intents; they offer the opportunity to do our thinking away from the classroom, harnessing and utilising our knowledge of the children, of the English curriculum and of children's literature to best effect. Planning helps us to be clear about the learning intentions and about what and where different aspects of the teaching, reading, writing, speaking and listening are going to take place. Our English planning is where we generate the opportunities essential for pupil interaction, creating possibilities for a range of discourses within the context of children's literature. Children enjoy a variety of approaches. Sameness dulls the learning experience and leads to boredom, which is anathema to learning. We want children to 'live the literature' (Graves 1983:75), so we need to plan spaces for this to happen.

There is a broad scope of reading opportunities within the school day (Figure 8.1) and I consider each of these in some detail below, highlighting ways in which novels could be used effectively. None of them is exclusive. One may decide to read to the children as part of shared reading, or run literature circles in independent time. What is important is that our plans capitalise on different approaches to the full. Having literature at the heart of the literacy curriculum is powerful (Barrs and Cork 2001), so planning ways that allow for inspiration and flexibility is essential. Then the true value of working with novels is gained. Time also needs to be planned to move the novel reading forward, allowing as much time as possible for necessary discussion and exploration. Our role as teacher will vary depending on the focus of the work.

We meet children's individual needs by incorporating effective scaffolding and adjusting the challenge to enhance learning. We do this while doing our planning, as we work through the text, adjusting our plans in response to what we find out about the children, their responses to the text and the experiences we have planned. We listen, observe and adjust our plans accordingly, to ensure that the

1	Reading to Children		
2	Shared Reading	Guided Reading	Independent Task
3	Literature circles		
4	Cross-curricular		

Figure 8.1

learners have the time and space for expressing their ideas and for responding to others in thoughtful and probing ways (Brabham and Villaume 2000). We will begin by considering opportunities when reading to children.

Reading to children – immersion in novels

> Good teachers read aloud when they want to engage children with texts they might not choose themselves. (Meek 2001 : 13)

Reading to the whole class may seem common practice, yet I know of at least one local authority which advised, with the introduction of the Literacy Strategy (DfEE 1998), against the need for teachers to read to their classes. I argue here that reading to children is a fundamental way of drawing children into the life of a text. Quite complex texts can be negotiated with a diverse range of readers, scaffolded by the teacher's skill as an experienced and enthusiastic reader.

When reading to the whole class the teacher takes centre stage with the text, and when read well, we are able to bring the text alive, implicitly exploring and negotiating the meaning with the children. The power comes from the texts we choose and how carefully we set the scene. So we close the blinds and light a candle when we read Robert Swindell's *Room 13* or Leon Garfield's *Smith*, ready for the fear. We lose our inhibitions and develop a range of voices so that we can bring different characters alive. What does David Almond's Skellig's voice sound like? These are the decisions we have to make when reading to children, and we need to be consistent when reading a long text, because they remember. We are experienced readers so we know that timing is paramount, that there are times when silence is magic, and we have them there in the palm of our hand, suspended in time, totally engrossed, experiencing literature at its best. When Charlotte dies in White's *Charlotte's Web*, or Sewells' Black Beauty sees his friend Ginger dead in the back of a cart, the emotion is palpable. Children deserve moments like this and we are fortunate to be in the position to make them happen.

By reading to children the teacher is able to support them in the sheer enjoyment of the literary experience; the language, narrative and key features of the text. Intervention at this level is implicit in the experience as a whole. We must be open to showing the children how we feel; we are in this together. So it's alright to laugh at Gran with 'a mouth like a cat's bottom' when reading Roald Dahl's *George's Marvellous Medicine*, or shiver when Stanley and Zero, in Louis Sacher's *Holes*, are covered in lizards. This is part of the experience we share. Reading to children is a highly effective and natural mode of working. It models reading at its best as it draws children into an enjoyable and engaging relationship with the text.

Reading novels in the Literacy Hour

> Sadly, there is still a fairly general assumption that texts which exemplify what reading can be like are the reward for learning to read, rather than the means by which readers are made, right from the beginning. (Meek 1998 : 117)

The use of children's literature should be central in the teaching of reading and writing and should therefore also be central to teaching and learning in the Literacy Hour. Consequently, we need to look carefully at the opportunities we offer children to engage with literature within the framework of literacy teaching. How best to use the frame of the Literacy Hour to support literacy teaching, using the whole novel text, is considered here. While the framework of the Literacy Hour is used, it is used in a flexible way.

To plan a unit of work around a novel we need to get to know the text and plan points for intervention. For example, when working with longer texts, a half-hour slot for shared reading is needed for immersion in text-level work. This longer period is necessary, rather that splitting the whole-class session between text-, word- or sentence-level work. Three to four whole-class sessions a week are envisaged where the focus is the text, i.e. reader response, characterisation, settings, narrative form, cliff-hangers, etc. You cannot work to any depth in 15 minutes, as sufficient time will be required to share the texts, discuss, respond, enjoy, celebrate and identify features of authorship, which the children may or may not have experienced before.

To move the reading forward one must capitalise on independent time within the Literacy Hour, while using guided reading to scaffold the learning. Decide which parts of the novel will be read to the class outside the hour and which read independently at home. The teacher's knowledge of the text, and their planning and preparation for this, are key to the success of a literature-based unit of work.

Shared reading

Key points, or markers, in the narrative should be identified for shared reading at the planning stage. Decide which aspects of the texts will be the narrative markers for the focus of shared reading. Concentrate on 6 to 10 narrative markers within the text as key teaching points over a three-week unit of study. This, of course, will depend on the novel being used. These markers may also be the key focus for writing. Allow extra time at the beginning of the unit for introducing the setting, characters and motivation for the narrative journey. This also ensures that children understand the first events of the story. Usually, the first chapter has critical events that impact upon the remainder of the story (Geist 1999). For example, the first three short chapters of *Holes*, by Louis Sachar, are essential for the first session of working with this novel, for this is where all the clues necessary for the cohesion of the narrative are held. The story is then cleverly woven around them, and revisited in the satisfying conclusion. To ensure that the novel as a whole remains central during each shared reading session it is important that it is itself explicitly referred to and displayed alongside the OHT/PowerPoint slides which are used for shared focus.

As always the effectiveness of these sessions depends on the prepared focus and pace. The readers' response is central to these sessions and as such should be planned as interactive opportunities. The deep level of understanding that one is aiming for when working with longer texts depends on the quality of interaction. In this context it will have direct impact on children's understanding and ultimately on their achievement. To ensure this occurs, the teacher needs to plan and organise in ways that maximise 'discursive space' (Hilton 1996:2). Allow for personal response, discussion and thinking time; capitalise on drama techniques such as freeze-frame, captions and hot-seating (see Chapter 9), where appropriate, to extend, deepen and support understanding.

Independent reading

It is interesting that pure reading opportunities are rarely planned for during the independent literacy session in the Literacy Hour. Yet independent reading is a high-status activity that undoubtedly moves children's reading forward. As such, reading as a consolidation/development activity should be valued. When working through a novel we capitalise on independent time, offering children time to engage independently with the text at their own pace. This also gives us opportunities for focusing on specific children or groups for guided reading. Using this capsule in the hour the children move deeper into their understanding of the text, by scaffolding their learning as we discuss the texts with them. Guided reading is the ideal opportunity for assessment for learning. The information gathered here impacts on our planning and drives the adjustments that we make.

When working with a longer novel for a limited period of time (e.g. in a three-week unit of work), reading to the children, in or outside the Literacy Hour, will enable us to maintain the pace necessary to move the narrative forward and allow the children to engage with the text at different levels (see above). This usually works well and maintains immersion in the text over the length of the unit of study. One can also use established literature circles to embed the class novel during a unit of study in the Literacy Hour.

Literature circles

> During literature conversation, participants can include their own personal insights, their emotional responses, connections they are making to other texts and to the comments of others. (Booth 2001 : 137)

The literature circle context is powerful in engendering authentic responses to literature. They are intended to offer children opportunities to engage in conversations about texts that they have chosen to read. Key processes involved in literature circles are discussion, the element of choice, trust and collaboration, independence and ownership, all motivating features which allow for individual response and creative interpretation. Using quality children's literature is fundamental to this process (Meek 2001). Given the right context, these conversations develop naturally, for children's responses are not uniform. Books become something different for each reader (Martin and Leather 1994 : 39) and children respond to different literature in different ways.

The strength of the circles is that children are placed in the driving seat within flexible groupings, and given key roles and responsibilities around book choice. Emotional and social understanding and development are integral aspects of becoming and being literate; working through a novel of choice together in a literature circle promotes these processes. The context encourages children to verbalise their various interpretations while valuing the insights and understanding that their peers offer (King 2001).

Establishing the literature circle

There are several different ways of organising literature circles. Generally, however, the children are organised into groups of four to six. The groups should be mixed-ability, if the range is not too great, so that the children can support and learn from each other. Once the groupings have been decided each group chooses a book they are interested in reading together. Initially, sets of books used for guided reading are the key resource for this, although once the circles are up and running the children may well be motivated enough to bring in their own texts to study, as adults do in *their* literacy circles. This is usually an indication of true involvement.

Discussion during the circle time is about the section of the text they have identified for that session. Each literature group meets two or three times a week (Booth 2001). This can be in or outside the Literacy Hour, but using independent time in the Literacy Hour for literature circles seems to be an ideal way of utilising available English time to move the children's literacy learning forward. The children themselves are in charge of managing the circle, studying a novel of their choice, and are therefore highly motivated. Time needs to be allowed each week for some individual reading and preparation. This could be as part of the literature circle time, in independent reading time (e.g. ERIC – Everyone Reading in Class) or part of extended writing. It could also form part of homework. With some models for literature circles the organisation stops here and the discussion in the circles is open and unstructured. In other models the children each have identified roles and each child is expected to contribute to the discussion from their role perspective. I will look at this approach in more detail.

The teacher's involvement

The teacher's role is important in setting up the organisation of the literature circles and supporting groups initially in taking on their different roles and responsibilities. Planning time for these sessions to work effectively is important. It may be necessary to spend some time with each group to achieve what may seem, in the short term, a fairly tight and detailed organisation. The teacher may need to model appropriate discussion behaviours at first while developing a more facilitating role once the children become more confident (King 2001). However, the children quickly get used to working within literature circles and our role then is a collaborative one: discussing, listening, observing and interacting. Once the initial setting-up period is over, children are free to manage, organise and sustain the literature circles themselves (ibid.). The opportunities for assessment are evident. Teachers who work with literature circles are surprised at the perspectives and insights that children bring to their response roles.

Children's roles and responsibilities

Different roles are assigned to group members on a rotational basis (Figure 8.2) and, over time, each child contributes to the circle from a different perspective. The roles take account of different learning styles, allow for different strengths and interests and offer the opportunity for moving away from the notion that there is only one predetermined way to respond to a text. The roles are detailed in Figure 8.2.

The children prepare for their circle meetings, according to their various roles. They are enthusiastic about their roles and are keen to contribute from the different perspectives. The children themselves decide how many pages they will read between each session. The children work within a time-frame. A cut-off date needs to be decided for each novel being read. At the end of each literature circle session the children assign the roles for the next literature circle, and also decide how much of the novel they will read before they next meet (Lopez 2004).

There are different ways for children to gather information and evidence of the work they are engaged in. With some, audio-recording is used, while others organise and collect the work they produce in a folder. Others expect the children

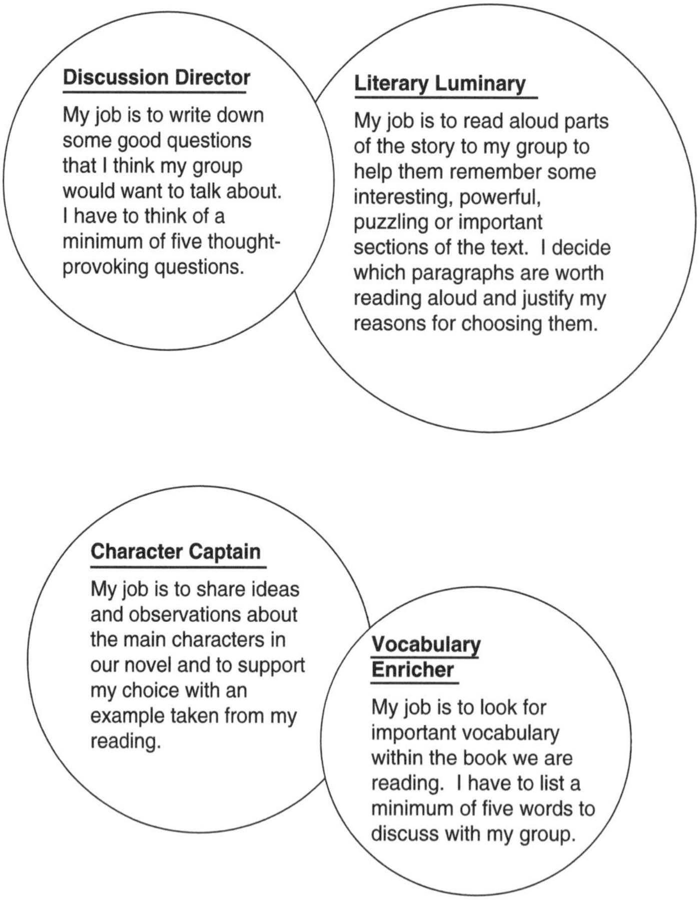

Discussion Director

My job is to write down some good questions that I think my group would want to talk about. I have to think of a minimum of five thought-provoking questions.

Literary Luminary

My job is to read aloud parts of the story to my group to help them remember some interesting, powerful, puzzling or important sections of the text. I decide which paragraphs are worth reading aloud and justify my reasons for choosing them.

Character Captain

My job is to share ideas and observations about the main characters in our novel and to support my choice with an example taken from my reading.

Vocabulary Enricher

My job is to look for important vocabulary within the book we are reading. I have to list a minimum of five words to discuss with my group.

Figure 8.2 Roles adapted from Lopez (2004) by Hermione Stewart and colleagues (Cossey Junior School Norwich).

to record in their journals/reading diaries short reflections on their own and other's contributions to the circle during that session and also consider how the discussion may have changed or reinforced their opinion of the book (Lopez 2004). This would need to be kept brief so that the focus does not move away from discussion to writing, as this could negate the purpose of the literature circle. Any writing is there to support the discussion process.

The choice and variety offered by literature circles frees children to explore ideas with energy and enthusiasm. They approach their responsibilities seriously and negotiate their ideas with their peers. They also have fun and really enjoy the positive responses they receive from their group. The children's responses are pertinent and enlightening. As the circles progress and children's confidence grows they become more deeply engaged with the texts they have chosen and more creative in their responses. They grow in stature as readers.

Cross-curricular

The novel is a valuable resource for a cross-curricular or thematic approach to learning and teaching. It can be used to augment curriculum areas other than English and to enrich and extend children's experience and understanding. For example, in history, children's literature is used to bring the subject to life from the child's perspective. The imagery and emotions portrayed through the characters offer unique historical experiences. Texts such as *Goodnight, Mr Tom* (Michelle Magorian), *Carrie's War* (Nina Bawden) and *The Machine Gunners* (Robert Westall) enhance themes around World War 2. Hetster Burton's *Through the Fire* illustrates the Fire of London with clarity and compassion.

Chosen carefully, a novel can also be the core of the topic. Berlie Doherty's *Street Child*, for example, is one such novel where the work is powerful enough to generate learning across the curriculum, as well as strengthening understandings of the Victorian context in which the story is set. Here we can offer children the opportunity to live the life of Jim Jarvis, a child who, through poverty, experiences the workhouse; Victorian ragged school education and Dr Barnardo's refuge; along with many other aspects of life in Victorian England. History, English, art, music, PHSE and RE can all be developed through this novel.

Writing

While the main theme in this chapter is reading novels and responding through discussion, using writing to support reflection is important. Writing can be used to support and sustain children's oral responses to texts. Most of the objectives for writing in the Literacy Strategy are related to the replication of the taught genre. When writing is inspired by longer narrative texts we need to look beyond the strait-jacket of the replication of different genre structures (Partridge 2001). A variety of forms should be available for children to draw on in order to support their discussions. The writing should be kept to short, manageable pieces that are in note form to feed into discussion. However, in the context of novel reading, other kinds of writing may be appropriate to strengthen and extend their discussions. There may also be other short forms that are written for different audiences and need to be crafted for impact and quality results. All will offer insights into the depth of understanding and engagement:

- reading diary/journal
- synopsis
- vignettes – enhanced by music/illustrations
- action sequences – these could be in words or pictures, i.e. storyboards
- questions for characters – to prepare for hot-seating
- delay and suspense (Mills 1996:120)

- mapping key moments in the storyline
- exploration of pivotal points
- tabulation – for/against, pros/cons, before/after
- prose
- posters
- adverts
- scripts
- video sequence
- letters
- reports
- poetry
- character webs (Brabham and Villaume 2000)
- research related to real-life issues – children in prison, refugees, homelessness
- multimedia texts.

Choice is an important element in the process of writing. If we really understand that children respond differently to the texts they read then they should not all have to write their responses in the same way. Opportunities for collaborative writing and working with response partners are also elements of interactive learning. The repertoire we offer should inspire children to be different.

Conclusion

The materials we use in the classrooms should be chosen to captivate children's imaginations, provoking thinking and, on occasion, intense emotions. Such insights and reflections are essential elements of affective and effective learning. Encouraging discourse around quality children's literature takes them beyond functional literacy and into deep engagement with texts, authors and literary imagination. Children are able to gain understanding and insight into their own lived experiences through the vicarious nature of the experience of being immersed in the imaginary worlds of others.

We need to think beyond the mundane, reaching for new, compelling and imaginative ways of engaging children in order to augment current effective literacy practices with creative approaches to learning and teaching the English curriculum. It is essential that we recognise the active agency of the children we work with. Given space and support, children can be far more creative than we could imagine; we often limit children's capabilities and potential by our own limitations and adult inhibitions. The way we resource learning and trust their capabilities frees them up to be creative. Risk is a process integral to learning and

Martin, T. and Leather, B. (1994) *Readers and Texts in the Primary Years*. Buckingham: Open University Press.

Meek, M. (1998) 'Important reading lessons', in Cox, B. (ed.) *Literacy Is Not Enough*. Manchester: Manchester University Press.

Meek, M. (2001) Preface, in Barrs, M. and Cork, V. *The Reader in the Writer*. London: Centre for Literacy in Primary Education.

Mills, P. (1996) *Writing in Action*. London: Routledge.

Partridge, B. (2001) *Genre and the Language Learning Classroom*. University of Michigan Press.

Styles, M., Bearne, E. and Watson, V. (eds) (1994) *The Prose and the Passion*. London: Cassell.

Vygotsky, L. (1962) *Thought and Language*. Cambridge, MA: MIT Press.

Wells, G. (1986) *The Meaning Makers: Children Learning Language and Using Language to Learn*. London: Hodder and Stoughton.

Websites

Geist, L. (1999) *Literature Circles for Young Readers* (http://www.multiage-education.com/) (accessed 3 January 2005).

Lopez, J. (2004) *Literature Circles* (http://litsite.alaska.edu/). (accessed 3 January 2005).

The supremacy of story: traditional tales and storytelling

Angela Pickard

Every day we swim in a sea of stories. In our lives and in our thought patterns stories are pervasive. Our stories make us unique and yet also bind us together as human beings and aid us in identifying and empathising with others. Our 'aspirations, disappointments, joys and fears are rehearsed and replayed in the stories we tell ourselves and the stories we tell others' (Bearne 1994 : 86). We hear stories, see stories and feel stories.

This chapter explores the potential of traditional tales with particular reference to fairy tales. The unit of work is constructed around the ancient art form of storytelling and connects the language modes of speaking, listening, reading and writing. It encourages both teachers and children to explore and play with tones of voice, the rhythms and rhymes of words and phrases, figurative language and aspects of character, plot, setting and sequence through sharing and engaging with a range of tales. This will lead to children experimenting with their own versions of tales and developing a variety of storytelling techniques, culminating in a storytelling festival and celebration.

Ideally, a regular commitment to reading, analysing, evaluating, telling and retelling traditional tales from a variety of cultures, in spoken and written form (Howe and Johnson 1992) is needed, in order to understand the features and organisation of the language and truly establish a storytelling ethos.

Traditional tales

Narrative in all its forms creates an avenue for children to explore the texts, language and culture of their worlds. It is therefore both a mode of reasoning and representation (Bettelheim 1991). Tales that belonged to the oral tradition of storytelling were handed down by word of mouth through successive generations and across different cultures and are now known as traditional tales. This term refers to myths and legends (see Chapter 7), fables, folk tales and fairy tales. There are fine differences between them, but all reflect ways of making sense of human experience. Therefore, traditional tales and fairy tales invite a rich range of explorations, interpretations and investigations.

Meek (1988, 1991) and others have argued that fairy tales make a significant contribution to children's emotional development. Children can easily make life-to-text and text-to-life connections in their reading and can interweave elements of their own lives into their written versions (Bearne 1994).

> Listening to a fairy tale and taking in the images it presents may be compared to the scattering of seeds, only some of which will be implanted in the mind of the child. Some of these will be working in his conscious mind right away; others will stimulate processes in his unconscious. Still others will need to rest for a long time until the child's mind has reached a state suitable for their germination, and many will never take root at all. But those seeds which have fallen on the right soil will grow into beautiful flowers and sturdy trees – that is, give validity to important feelings, promote insights, nourish hopes, reduce anxieties – and in doing so enrich the child's life.
> (Bettelheim 1991, cited in Grainger 1997:26)

The oral nature of traditional tales certainly entertains, inspires and challenges people but they have also survived because they 'offer alternative worlds which embody imaginative, emotional and spiritual truths about the universe' (ibid.: 23). Through exploring issues, dilemmas and the moral codes of characters in stories, children's own values and understandings are developed through the bridge between fantasy and reality. This enables the listener to use their imagination and develop a greater sense of self.

Folk and fairy tales are memorable and quickly become familiar. They are also full of conflict, ambiguity, challenge or misunderstanding, so can engage the children in deeper discussion and richer response as they build their own under-standing of events, predicaments and moral dilemmas through the 'prism of fiction' (Toye and Prendiville 2000 : 115). In using and applying a whole range of reading processes the children make deductions and imaginative connections, so deeper possibilities are explored (Rosenblatt 1978; Chambers 1993; Meek 1991; Martin and Leather 1994; Barrs and Cork 2001). Martinez *et al.* (2003) found that familiarity with stories was an important aspect to developing preschool chil-dren's responses to text. The children made more comments when responding to stories that they had experienced and the focus of their responses changed over repeated readings. Martinez *et al.* suggest that as the children gained control over particular aspects of stories, they were able to attend to different dimensions.

The nature of traditional tales makes them ideal to be told and retold, enabling children to learn about the word and the world (Friere 1972) and can facilitate sophisticated and challenging examinations:

> the practice of narrating stories, either invented or retold, helps young children to come to know what it is to think through problems, argue cases, see both sides of questions, find

supporting evidence and make hypotheses, comparisons, definitions and generalizations. (Fox (1990), cited in Grainger 1997 : 33)

Features of traditional tales (folk tales, fairy tales and moral tales)

As traditional tales encompass a range of types it may be useful to consider the features and identify them accordingly. Of course, some tales draw on features from a range of stories and therefore overlap.

Folk tales tend to share wisdom, often through trickster tales with quick-witted animals as key characters, either alongside, or instead of, humans, such as Ananse the spider man from Africa. In such stories children meet a range of dilemmas, power struggles, magic, strength and examples of intelligence.

Figure 9.1

Fairy tales are folk narratives that often include elements of magic, kings, queens, magical people or the supernatural. The best-known are those by Hans Christian Andersen and the Brothers Grimm. There are easily identifiable characters and often predictable plots. However, now there are many modern and subverted versions that offer a twist.

Figure 9.2

Very short, overtly moral tales are fables; these; too, often feature animals. The most familiar are those by Aesop, such as *The Ant and the Grasshopper* and *The Hare and the Tortoise*. Key characteristics of particular animals are often a feature. Stories that explain the origins of natural or supernatural phenomena with human and superhuman characteristics are myths. Examples include Greek and Norse myths. These feature highly as part of Hindu and Aboriginal culture and often include dances as a key part of the storytelling process.

Figure 9.3

Themes

Traditional tales deal with powerful and common issues of experience in relation to the human condition. They absorb us in the examination of themes of opposites, such as good and evil, rich and poor, young and old, beauty and ugliness, wise and foolish, weak and strong. Other themes include the nature of the supernatural, the origins of the earth and man, animals that aid people, tests of individual skill and the journey as a symbol of self-discovery. The nature of human qualities and behaviour such as trust, betrayal and disappointment are explored through the predicaments of characters and related complex and challenging issues.

Stereotypes

It is important to note that, of course, traditional tales and fairy tales are not without pitfalls. Many such tales have been criticised due to their stereotyped characters in relation to looks, personality traits and gender roles. Glastonbury

(1982) sees females as portrayed as victims in these stories, whereas Zipes (1983) claims that, originally, in many of these stories, women and girls had more power-ful roles and that the stories have been constantly reworked. However, beginning with a stereotype does not necessarily have to be seen as negative. After all, there are, occasionally, useful truths in stereotypes. However, we can also move beyond and challenge stereotypes to help children see other possibilities. Children need not be passive listeners and readers (Rosenblatt 1978; Meek 1991; Chambers 1993; Martin and Leather 1994; Barrs and Cork 2001) and can often deconstruct texts, write and read 'against' texts and explore a range of possible meanings and gender roles (Moss 1999; Marsh and Millard 2000).

There are now many tales available that do indeed offer a different perspective and challenge stereotypes such as *Princess Smartypants* and *Prince Cinders* by Babette Cole, *The PaperBag Princess* by Robert Munsch and *The Practical Princess and Other Liberating Fairy Tales* by Jay Williams and Rick Schreiter. A balance of the more traditional and modern tales will offer a wealth of material to raise awareness and prompt discussion, developing more reflective, responsive and critical readers.

Structures

Traditional tales often have distinctive, predictable and sequential story patterns and narrative structures since they were originally designed to be sufficiently memorable to the teller and accessible to the listener. Cumulative tales such as *The Great Big Enormous Turnip* and *The Fat Cat* enjoy the addition of elements as the story progresses that encourage the audience to join in with the repetitive phases and chants. Sequential stories such as *The Three Billy Goats Gruff* and *The Three Little Pigs*, involve a repeated single event and the same words being used each time. In order to memorise pattern, in European cultures the numbers 3 and 7 fre-quently occur. Examples include *Snow White and the Seven Dwarfs*, *Goldilocks and the Three Bears* and *Mrs Goat and the Seven Kids*.

Language

The language of many traditional tales is full of rhythm, rhyme and repetition. Other features, such as set openings and endings, symbols, metaphors, imagery, intertextuality and implicit meaning, aid their memorability and potential for creative oral and written retellings. The musical syntax or 'tunes of the tale are twirled on the tongue' (Grainger 1997 : 41). Children can therefore construct, reconstruct and subvert both words and grammatical structures. Paley (1981) observed how children revealed their knowledge about language and story struc-ture through their playful encounters. Such playful experimentation with rhymes and chants enables young children to recognise similarities in sounds and words, and sensitivity to rhyme, rhythms and poetically repetitive sounds in language or phonological awareness has been linked to children's later success in reading (Bryant 1989; Goswami and Bryant 1990).

A wealth of memorable and enduring traditional and altered tale texts exist and it is through the vitality and precision of their writing that authors expose children to word patterns and structures in clever and imaginative interweaving of images, words and viewpoints.

Storytelling

Oral storytelling occurs as part of everyday life in the home, on the street, in the playground or on the phone. Wilkinson *et al.* (1990) remind us of the vast array available to us:

> There are those which retrieve and construct the history of the family, and those which go back beyond it; there are stories which envisage the future – what we will do when ... There are stories of humorous, scurrilous, pathetic incidents, polished by constant retelling. There are garrulous, reiterant, obsessive stories. (p. 30)

Humans are natural and powerful tellers of tales and children can grow in confidence as telling a story is a unique and personal performance (Grugeon and Gardner 2000). Telling stories encourages the development of a range of voices, registers, accents and dialects (Howe and Johnson 1992). The teller captures his audience in the compelling social and interactive process, bonding with them in a display of dramatic competence as the story speaks to the senses. The storyteller's face, voice, body and personality help to convey meaning and mood (Mallan 1991) and the audience engages in being both listener and participant, actively creating each tale in their own imaginations. It has been suggested that, essentially, it is the engagement of the imagination that determines the breadth and depth of an experience and therefore the consequent learning (Goodwin 2004).

> Storytelling is a dramatic improvisation, a symbiosm, where speakers and listeners construct and occupy worlds of their own creation. Through voice and eye and gesture, the listener is drawn into a story, woven into the tale as a participant, to feel anger, fear, despair and joy. Storytelling is interactive: it moves the listener back and forth from spectator to participant. The storyteller achieves this through inflection, emphasis, cadence, pace, pause and register. (Corden 2000 : 147)

Stories exist in every country, and every culture, and entertain, educate and give cultural identity. They can offer an accessible way of sharing information and advice about the world using both the real and imagined, in relation to morals, warnings, consequences, hopes, fears and explanations. 'Stories, like dreams, take us to places we have never seen, activities we have never experienced, events we have not witnessed, and introduce us to people we have not met' (Harrett 2004 : 1).

Tales are created about every conceivable aspect of life, from the past, present and future, and can take many forms such as anecdotes, jokes and songs. As Harold Rosen (1984) remarked, 'they are cheap as dirt, common currency and a popular possession. They are heard, created and relayed as enthusiastic recounts, casual conversations or engaging performances.' Bruner (1986) proposed that narrative is an essential mode of thought through which we construct our world of worlds and that oral story and anecdote constitute the primary way of entertaining 'possible worlds' (ibid.) of abstract thought and language.

Hardy (1977) suggested that 'we dream in narrative, daydream in narrative, remember, anticipate, hope, despair, believe, doubt, plan, revise, criticise, construct, gossip, learn, hate, and love by narrative' (p. 34). Narrative is a 'primary act of mind' (ibid.) and the medium through which we filter all our experience. Through telling and retelling stories we can grapple with, explain and make sense of experiences and events (Hardy 1977; Wells 1987; Harrett 2004). Oral narratives often incorporate linguistic features that display a sophistication that goes beyond the level of conversation (Mallan 1991). Young children can develop narrative competence early, since they hear all sorts of stories in all sorts of different social contexts. As Wilkinson *et al.* (1990) suggest, a family lives by its stories, so as children learn to talk, they also learn to tell stories. We need to learn strategies of narration when we are very young in order to grasp that we can become our own narrators, the storytellers of our lives (Zipes 1995).

Children soon realise that narrative possibilities are endless and will take and make narratives by adapting the storyline, noting that this is acceptable, inevitable and enjoyable. As Whitehead (1997) suggests, the ability to place ourselves right in the centre of a story is a valuable start to becoming a reader and a writer. Stories come from experience – heard, seen or lived. As tales are told and retold they change, become embellished or simplified. 'Stories are not reproduced through rote memorisation, word-for-word, sentence-for-sentence; they are retold and reborn on each occasion with a different audience' (Grainger 1997: 64).

Literary meaning-making involves (among other things) knowing how to move through story worlds or follow the narrative strands of a story. This knowing requires the reader, viewer and listener to realise that characters shape the storyline and are also, in turn, shaped by it. To fill in these gaps children must draw on personal experiences and knowledge about the world, including a host of linguistic and cognitive abilities.

Participating in storytelling helps to develop a storehouse of story structures, characters, settings, dilemmas and resolutions. The richer the background of telling and retelling, the more children will be able to tell their own stories. Through hearing stories and telling tales their awareness of character and plot is gradually expanded into aspects of style (Fox 1993). Children possess an implicit knowledge of grammar, gained through living and communicating in a social world (Corden 2000). As Taylor (1994), in relation to read-aloud argues, teachers are repeatedly exposing and reinforcing patterns of grammar and other formal properties of language. Storytelling builds on the implicit and makes explicit some of the differences between spoken and written language (Corden 2000).

Through their storying, children show their grasp of narrative intent, their openness to layered meanings, their efforts towards character building (Martinez *et al.* 2003) and integrate language structures into their own writing (Kress 1986; Bearne 1994). They display their dexterity with special effects associated with media, like cartoon films and soap opera, as well as literary features linked with written texts. The children will be talking like a book (Fox 1993).

This important link between oral language and writing is explored by Rosen. He suggests that we can celebrate oral language and represent everything we say in the written form:

> noises, grunts, shouts, whispers, slang, rude words, dialect phrasings and the like. Much of this is a highly undervalued, uncherished area of human creativity. It exists as a main carrier of our culture and identity, and yet children in schools get few chances to celebrate it. Writing it does give them that possibility. (Rosen 1998: 23)

Storytelling, then, is another way to value children's lives, their stories and cultural experiences where the tale, the teller and the told can work in harmony (Grainger 2001; Medlicott 1989; Colwell 1980).

This creative way of working enables children to transform original stories into a variety of fresh encounters, situations, dilemmas and developments. The fostering of children's creativity, creative enterprise (Bruner 1962), ability to produce new knowledge (Dacey and Lennon 2000) or possibility thinking (Craft 2000) may help children to identify and establish a range of strategies and a framework for ways of dealing with events, or 'route-find' (Craft 2000; Annarella 1999) in their lives. Weaver (1999) describes this as developing 'an entrepreneurial culture', which he argues is essential in society. We must, therefore, value and promote creativity and use creative approaches wherever possible.

Unit of work: Constructing texts: spoken and written for Key Stages 1 and 2

We live in a society that offers a broad range of texts. 'Children now have available to them many forms of text which include sound, voices, intonation, stance, gesture, movement, as well as print and image' (Styles and Bearne 2003:xvii). Children are immersed in a computer game culture, 'many story lines of fantasy games can be compared to genre of traditional tales of heroes and monsters and good triumphing over bad' (Grugeon and Harding 2004 : 30). Film and television programmes are another way of 'providing children with a rich experience of stories told in different ways to different audiences and an experience of different genres' (Browne 1999 : 107).

This unit of work uses film and book texts. There are activities that are appropriate for both Key Stages 1 and 2. The whole unit encompasses a process of development, and progresses from immersion to modelling to further exploration to extension and final product. It is expected that the teacher will select, adapt and refine suggested activities to suit the children they are working with as some will be more appropriate for a particular age and stage than others. Storytelling can play an enriching role inside and outside literacy time since it fosters the interdependence of the language modes. Specific learning outcomes, as well as continuous, ongoing learning, will be evident through a focus on traditional tales and the creative context of storytelling.

It order to gain the most from the unit, it is important that time and space is given to the children to be absorbed in a culture of traditional tales and storytelling and to thrive in the literature-, play- and talk-rich classroom.

Immersion in traditional tales

The following activities involve the children in investigating typical ingredients that make up traditional tales, particularly fairy tales.

An initial activity can involve the children in sharing what they already know about traditional tales by listing titles of known tales. This activity can be undertaken in groups, pairs or individually and will enable you to gain a more accurate picture of the tales that the children are familiar with. It will also provide a rich repertoire to lean on for future work. The lists can then be sorted and classified further, using cards or post-it notes, in a variety of ways such as genre, theme, tales of three, tales of rescue or heroes, tales of animals, etc.

The children could be involved in identifying traditional beginnings and endings such as:

- Once upon a time . . .
- Long, long ago . . .
- In a land far, far away . . .

- . . . they all lived happily ever after.
- . . . and that was that.
- . . . and they were never seen again.

and displaying these as posters in the book area.

Examining typical characters can be an engaging, worthwhile activity as tales often have memorable, significant characters. An exploration of one or many of those in fairy tales might include:

- wolves
- female characters – Goldilocks, Little Red Riding Hood, Snow White, Cinderella, queens, witches, fairies, mermaids, princesses, stepmother, etc.
- male characters – Prince Charming, Beast, woodcutter, Jack, Puss in Boots, Rumplestiltskin, kings, dwarves, giants, etc.

Features of the character can be analysed and compared. Role on the wall could be used where a child lies on a large piece of paper and an outline of him/her is drawn. This becomes the outline of an important character. It is given prominence in the classroom throughout work on the story. Information and feelings about the character are written into the shape and added to as the children get to know the character better.

Character profiles, passports, 'Wanted' posters, drawings, pictures, images and photographs can be developed. This would be a record of important points to note and information about a character. It will feature personality traits as well as appearance. Stereotypes and notions of heroes and heroines in relation to behaviour and physical appearance can be identified and discussed. Introducing the children to tales that offer stronger and alternative gender roles such as those mentioned earlier – *The Paper Bag Princess* by Robert Munsch, *The Practical Princess and Other Liberating Fairy Tales* by Jay Williams and Rick Schreiter and *Princess Smartypants* by Babette Cole – can be helpful and fuel interesting discussion.

Figure 9.4 Wanted poster

Drama conventions can be used:

- teacher in role
- freeze-frame
- thought tracking
- hot-seating

Such techniques (Figure 9.5) can be used to deepen understanding of character traits and action. By 'empathising with the characters, children develop their ability to take roles, identify with others, solve problems and imagine alternatives' (Grainger and Pickard 2004 : 12). An examination as to why a writer chose a particular character in relation to key themes and plot can also be helpful.

Teacher in role

This technique involves the teacher taking on a role or roles of characters. 'Through these the teacher can support, extend and challenge the children's thinking from inside the drama' (Grainger and Pickard 2004 : 41).

Freeze-frame

The creation of a still image, sculpture, statue or tableau making involves whole-body actions which are held still and silent in order to create and express an image of an idea, theme, emotion or moment.

Thought tracking

Freeze-frames can be brought to life as the teacher touches a child on the shoulder so that they may voice their thoughts or feelings in the form of words, noises or sound effects. Alternatively, the class could speak their thoughts or feelings simultaneously.

Hot-seating

The teacher, individual child or a group of children assume the role of one or more characters and are questioned by their classmates in order to find out more or clarify something in relation to that character(s).

Forum theatre

This convention involves one group performing the words and actions of an improvisation. The rest of the class watch and then act as directors in order to rework it, taking account of what they have seen. Another way of using this is to enable the observers and directors to pause the action and add further ideas and suggestions, then the action continues.

Figure 9.5

Typical settings can be explored:

- woods
- palace
- castle

Story maps are a way of recording the geographical locations of the tale. Significant words can also be included and this can also be a helpful support when the children come to retell the tale. By focusing on the features of settings the children can engage in living inside the text. Pictures and descriptions can be used to create scenes and improvisations. Sounds and noises could be added, with percussion instruments or body percussion, to create atmosphere. For example, Little Red Riding Hood skipping through the woods, picking flowers on a sunny day, could be contrasted with a more threatening scene with the trees, goblins, fairies and the wolf whispering chilling words and phrases. A focus on the significance of setting in relation to the plot development can show key events such as transformation of character, as in *The Tunnel* and *Hansel and Gretel* by Anthony Browne.

Figure 9.6 Story map for *Little Red Riding Hood*

The clever use of intertextuality, or stories within stories, in alternative tales could be incorporated, such as *Once Upon a Time* and *Once Upon a Picnic* by John Prater or *The Jolly Postman* by the Alhbergs, where the children meet a range of characters while in the setting.

Investigating story structures can be a way of developing story memory. A range of activities can be used to support this, such as:

● story seeds – three seeds representing beginning, middle and end;

● story plates – a useful visual tool on a paper plate that is used to record the sequence of events in the tale (like the famous Willow Pattern Plate design);

● story maps – as mentioned previously;

- storyboard – a sequential development of the story using pictorial representation; this is very similar to a comic strip; words could also be added; and

- symbolic or key word summaries – another way of remembering the order of events.

This is also a way of noting key language features and memorable language from the story. This would include repetitive phrases, rich language, powerful words and the rhythms and rhymes of the text.

Immersion in the art of storytelling

Although all children will have some experience of listening to and telling stories, the children will need storytelling modelled. Storytellers employ a number of skills to assist the telling and create their style, including varying the voice, changing the pace, using pauses to build tension, use of gestures, facial expressions and props. A professional storyteller is an invaluable resource as their skills are finely honed. There are a wealth to choose from, from a variety of styles and traditions. They can model to and with the children, and together they can identify and share the features of good storytelling. For information about storytelling, storytellers and other resources, visit the Society for Storytelling (www.sfs.org.uk).

Alternatively, librarians, parents or teachers may be particularly skilled, energetic and enthusiastic. However, confidence as a storyteller comes with practice and support. A storyteller does not necessarily have to be a performer or extrovert as there are many ways to share a tale. 'Practice and experience enable the storyteller to bring out the full potential of a story' (Colwell 1991, cited in Grainger 1997 : 152).

A storyteller's chair or throne can be introduced, perhaps with some interesting fabric draped over it. Here the children can practise telling and retelling stories to themselves, a friend or a small group. The children can use props to prompt and aid their tellings such as a crown, gown or cloak, a spinning wheel, a single pea in a casket/box, royal stationary, maps or a mirror. Other storytelling aids might include masks, puppets, images, photographs, story quilts, sacks or boxes. As the children listen to tales being told they can be engaged in considering what makes a good storyteller?

The titles of the children's known traditional tales (prepared earlier) can also be used for a story buzz where the children choose a title, find a partner and share the story orally. Here different versions will emerge and a discussion in relation to differences and similarities can develop accordingly.

Further exploration
Altered traditional tales
As the children develop greater confidence with being tellers of tales, they will continuously add and embellish. A multitude of altered traditional tale texts exists

and is being added to constantly. These offer examples of exchanges, expansions and experimentations. The children, particularly at Key Stage 2, can be involved in the transformation and subversion of texts through telling, drawing and writing for different audiences and purposes. These activities could form a unit of work of their own. Ideas include:

- changing the main character(s), introducing new character(s) or developing existing character(s). *The Stinky Cheese Man and Other Fairly Stupid Tales* by Jon Scieszka and illustrator Lane Smith offers a wealth of examples such as *Goldilocks and the Three Elephants. Little Wolf's Book of Badness* by Ian Whybrow and Tony Ross offers an insight into the character of Little Wolf and other wolves;

- challenging gender stereotypes through the choice of character, such as those offered in *Princess Smartypants* and *Prince Cinders* by Babette Cole, *The PaperBag Princess* by Robert Munsch and *The Practical Princess and Other Liberating Fairy Tales* by Jay Williams and Rick Schreiter;

- changing the geographical setting or historical period, such as in *Snow White in New York* by Fiona French;

- changing task(s), such as knitting spaghetti into string vests and making bank notes out of old fish in *Rumply Crumply Stinky Pin* by Laurence Anholt and Arthur Robbins;

- changing the ending, like the example offered in *The Frog Prince Continued* by Jon Scieszka and Steve Johnson;

- modernising the tale, such as in the *Seriously Silly Stories* series by Laurence Anholt and Arthur Robbins;

- reversing roles, such as in *The Three Wolves and the Big Bad Pig* by Eugene Trivizas and Helen Oxenbury, *Mr Wolf and the Three Bears* by Jan Fearnley, or the Good Samaritan Jim, in *Jim and the Beanstalk* by Raymond Briggs.

Extension: Using the film Shrek (Dreamworks) to develop understanding of traditional tales and storytelling

Rather like using a novel, the construction of the activities here relies on showing the film in excerpts and working with each excerpt accordingly. By the end of the focus the children will have seen the whole film.

Shrek is a modern fairytale with the themes of good versus evil and beauty versus ugliness. There are stereotyped characters but also some unexpected twists and subversion. The structure is well known and begins with the introduction of the main character. There is a problem to solve leading to a quest and a rescue, a twist when there is a misunderstanding, another problem resolved and all ends happily ever after.

Excerpt 1 to when Shrek vows he is going to see Lord Faquaard and get his swamp back.
Introduction to plot:

- Use story seeds, board or summary for the read-aloud text at the very beginning of the story.
- Identify references to fairy tales and nursery rhymes and engage in story buzz.
- Create 'Wanted' posters for fairy tale creatures.

Character:

- Develop a profile for Shrek and donkey.
- Hot-seat Shrek – may need to use teacher-in-role strategy initially.
- Create a role on the wall for Shrek.

Settings:

- Describe the swamp and Shrek's house using talk partners.

Excerpt 2 to when Shrek and Donkey agree to go on quest to rescue Princess Fiona.
Character:

- Create a passport for Lord Faquaard.

Setting:

- Draw and label a map of the Fairytale Theme Park.

Development of plot:

- Consider when magic mirror shows Lord Faquaard his choices of bride. Recreate a *Blind Date* version of this or hot-seat each bachelorette.
- Develop a discussion considering what would make a perfect world.

Excerpt 3 to just after meeting Robin Hood and the merry men.
Character:

- Develop a profile and role on the wall for Princess Fiona.
- Write a diary entry from Princess Fiona's point of view stating her disappointment at the way she was rescued.

Setting:

- Draw a map of the castle and instructions for the best route to take in the rescue.

Development of action:

- Create a 6 o'clock news or a newspaper report recounting Princess Fiona's rescue.

Excerpt 4 to when Fiona meets Lord Faquaard and agrees to marry him.
Development of plot:

- Write recipes for Weed Rat Stew, Swamp Toad Soup or create own recipe.
- Play with the rhyme that Princess Fiona uses to share her secret and make up your own rhyme.

Character – development of relationship and tension:

- Role-play when Shrek overhears the conversation between Princess Fiona and Donkey.
- Write a letter to Shrek, either from the point of view of Donkey or Princess Fiona, explaining the conversation, misunderstanding and sharing the secret.

Excerpt 5 to celebration at the end.
Resolution:

- Retell the ending.
- Play with the ending and create a new one.
- Interview Donkey, Princess Fiona and Shrek about their adventure.
- Create a news report – 'Shrek the Hero'.
- Create a story plate, map or symbols of the structure and main events in the story.
- Tell the whole story from Lord Farquaad's point of view.

For further information on using film texts as a way of teaching literacy and language, visit the film education website (www.filmeducation.org).

Final product

The children could choose the story that they are most confident in telling from those studied and take part in a storytelling festival and celebration. The title of the event could be decided by the children and promotional posters created. Such an event could engage the children in telling their story or stories to a range of audiences, such as children from other classes, parents and teachers. Story tapes of the children telling their tales could be recorded for assessment purposes and, indeed, for use in the future as a resource in the listening area. Video recordings could also provide a helpful record and another way for the children to respond to and evaluate their own and other children's use of features of a good storyteller and skills of storytelling.

Concluding thoughts

The creative context and language art of storytelling engages children in develop-ing their understanding of the power and supremacy of story. Learning to tell

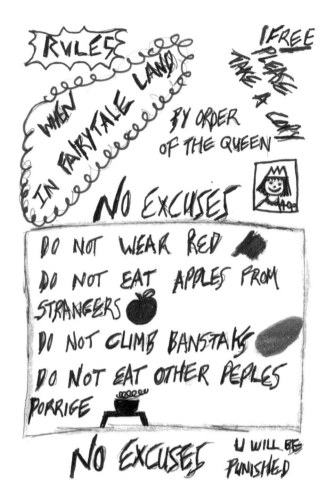

Figure 9.7

stories is satisfying and worthwhile and the children will grow in confidence and competence. By drawing on the wealth of high-quality traditional tales available, the children's commitment and response to text and writing for a variety of different audiences and purposes can be developed. This focus on traditional tales and storytelling will capture their imaginations and engage them in the joyful creation of their own tales for telling.

Children's literature used in this chapter and unit of work

Janet and Allen Ahlberg, *The Jolly Christmas Postman*, Heinemann.

Janet and Allen Ahlberg, *The Jolly Pocket Postman*, Heinemann.

Janet and Allen Ahlberg, *The Jolly Postman*, Heinemann.

Laurence Anholt and Arthur Robbins, *Seriously Silly Stories* series:

  Rumply Crumply Stinky Pin

  Cinderboy

Little Red Riding Wolf

The Emperor's Underwear

Snow White and the Seven Aliens

Daft Jack and the Bean Stack

Billy Beast

The Rather Small Turnip

Raymond Briggs, *Jim and the Beanstalk*, Puffin.

Anthony Browne, *Hansel and Gretel*, Walker Books.

Anthony Browne, *The Tunnel*, Walker Books.

Babette Cole, *Prince Cinders*, Puffin.

Babette Cole, *Princess Smartypants*, Puffin.

Dreamworks, *Shrek*.

Jan Fearnley, *Mr Wolf and the Three Bears*, Egmont Children's Books.

Fiona French, *Snow White in New York*, Oxford University Press.

Robert Munsch, *The PaperBag Princess*, Scholastic.

John Prater, *Once Upon a Picnic*, Walker Books.

John Prater, *Once Upon a Time*, Walker Books.

Jon Scieszka and Lane Smith, *The Stinky Cheese Man and Other Fairly Stupid Tales*, Puffin.

Jon Scieszka and Steve Johnson, *The Frog Prince Continued*, Viking.

Eugene Trivizas and Helen Oxenbury, *The Three Wolves and the Big Bad Pig*, Mammoth.

Ian Whybrow and Tony Ross, *Little Wolf's Book of Badness*, Collins.

Jay Williams and Rick Schreiter, *The Practical Princess and Other Liberating Fairy Tales*, Hippo.

References

Annarella, L. A. (1999) *Encouraging Creativity and Imagination in the Classroom*. Illinois: Viewpoints.

Barrs, M. and Cork, V. (2001) *The Reader in the Writer: The Influence of Literature upon Writing at KS2*. London: CLPE.

Bearne, E. (1994) 'Where do stories come from?', in Styles, M., Bearne, E. and Watson V. (eds) *The Prose and the Passion*. London: Cassell.

Bearne, E. (2003) Ways of Knowing; Ways of Showing – Towards an Integrated Theory of Text', in Styles, M. and Bearne, E. (eds) *Art, Narrative and Childhood*. Stoke-on-Trent: Trentham.

Bettelheim, B. (1991) *The Uses of Enchantment: The Meaning and Importance of Fairy Tales*. London: Penguin.

Bromley, H. (1999) 'Storytelling: having a go with the box (1)'. *The Primary English Magazine*, January/February.

Bromley, H. (1999) 'Storytelling: having a go with the box (2)'. *The Primary English Magazine*, March/April.

Bruner, J. (1962) *On Knowing: Essays for the Left Hand*. Cambridge, MA: Harvard University Press.

Browne, A. (1999) *Teaching Writing at Key Stage 1 and Before*. Cheltenham: Stanley Thornes.

Bruner, J. (1986) *Actual Minds, Possible Worlds*. Cambridge, MA: Harvard University Press.

Bryant, P. (1989) 'Nursery rhymes, phonological skills and reading'. *Journal of Child Language*, **16**, 407–28.

Chambers, A. (1993) *Tell Me: Children Reading and Talk*. Stroud: Thimble Press.

Colwell, E. (1980) (2nd edition, 1991) *Storytelling*. Stroud: Thimble Press.

Corden, R. (2000) *Literacy and Learning through Talk: Strategies for the Primary Classroom*. Milton Keynes: Open University Press.

Craft, A. (2000) *Creativity across the Primary Curriculum*. London: Routledge.

Dacey, J. and Lennon, K. (2000) *Understanding Creativity: The Interplay of Biological, Psychological and Social Factors*. Buffalo, New York: Creative Education Foundation.

Fox, C. (1990a) 'The genesis of argument in narrative discourse'. *English in Education*, **24**(1).

Fox, C. (1993) *At the Very Edge of the Forest: The Influence of Literature on Storytelling by Children*. London: Cassell.

Fox, C. (1997) 'Children's conceptions of imaginative play revealed in their oral stories', in Hall, N. and Martello, J. (eds) *Listening to Children Think: Exploring Talk in the Early Years*. London: Hodder and Stoughton.

Friere, P. (1972) *Cultural Action for Freedom*. London: Penguin.

Glastonbury, M. (1982) 'What books tell girls'. *The English Magazine*, 9.

Goodwin, P. (ed.) (2004) *Literacy through Creativity*. London: David Fulton.

Goswami, U. and Bryant, P. (1990) *Phonological skills and Learning to Read*. Hillsdale, NJ: Laurence Erlbaum.

Grainger, T. (1997) *Traditional Storytelling*. Rugby: Scholastic.

Grainger, T. (2001) 'Crick crack chin, my story's in – stories and storytelling', in Goodwin, P. (ed.) *The Articulate Classroom*. London: David Fulton.

Grainger, T. and Pickard, A. (2004) *Drama: Reading, Writing and Speaking Our Way Forwards*. Royston: UKLA.

Grugeon, E. and Gardner, P. (2000) *The Art of Storytelling for Teachers and Pupils*. London: David Fulton.

Grugeon, E. and Harding, L. (2004) 'Discovering creativity on the playground', in Goodwin, P. (ed.) *Literacy Through Creativity*. London: David Fulton.

Hardy, B. (1977) 'Narrative as a primary act of mind', in Meek, M., Warlow, A. and Barton, G. (eds) *The Cool Web: The Pattern of Children's Reading*. London: The Bodley Head.

Harrett, J. (2004) *Tell Me Another . . . Speaking, Listening and Learning through Storytelling*. Royston: UKLA.

Howe, A. and Johnson, J. (1992) *Common Bonds: Storytelling in the Classroom*. London: Hodder and Stoughton.

Kress, G. (1986) 'Interrelationships of reading and writing', in Wilkinson, A. (ed.) *The Writing of Writing*. Milton Keynes: Open University Press.

Lupton, H. (2000) 'Betsy Whyte and the dreaming', in Hodges, C., Drummond, M. and Styles, M. *Tales, Tellers and Texts*. London: Cassell.

Mallan, K. (1991) *Children as Storytellers*. Newtown, NSW: Primary English Teaching Association.

Marsh J. and Millard, E. (2000) *Literacy and Popular Culture using Children's Culture in the Classroom*. London: Paul Chapman.

Martin, T. and Leather, B. (1994) *Reading and Texts in the Primary Years*. Milton Keynes: Open University Press.

Martinez, M., Roser, N. and Dooley, C. (2003) 'Young children's literary meaning making', in Hall, N., Larson, J. and Marsh, J. (eds) *Handbook of Early Childhood Literacy*. London: Sage.

Medlicott, M. (ed.) (1989) *By Word of Mouth: The Revival of Storytelling*. London: Channel 4 Broadside Publications.

Meek, M. (1988) *How Texts Teach What Readers Learn*. Stroud: Thimble Press.

Meek, M. (1991) *On Being Literate*. London: The Bodley Head.

Moss, G. (1999) 'Boys and non-fiction: cause or effect?' *Literacy Today*, **21**, 19.

Paley, V. G. (1981) *Wally's Stories*. Cambridge, MA: Harvard University Press.

Rosen, H. (1984) *Stories and Meanings*. Sheffield: NATE.

Rosen, M. (1998) *Did I Hear You Write?* (2nd edn). Nottingham: Andre Deutsch.

Rosenblatt, L. (1978) *The Reader, the Text and the Poem: The Transactional Theory of Literacy at Work*. Carbondale, IL: South Illinois Press.

Taylor, M. (1994) 'What children's books tell us about teaching language', in Styles, M., Bearne, E. and Watson, V. *The Prose and the Passion*. London: Cassell.

Toye, N. and Prendiville, F. (2000) *Drama and Traditional Story in the Early Years*. London: RoutledgeFalmer.

Weaver, R.Y. (1999) 'Society, educational systems and entrepreneurship'. *Industry and Higher Education*, **13**, December, 376–81.

Wells, G. (1987) *The Meaning Makers*. London: Hodder and Stoughton.

Whitehead, M. (1997) *Language and Literacy in the Early Years* (2nd edn). London: Paul Chapman.

Wilkinson, A., Davies, A. and Berrill, D. (1990) *Spoken English Illuminated*. Buckingham: Open University Press.

Zipes, J. (1983) *Fairy Tales and the Art of Subversion*. London: Methuen.

Zipes, J. (1995) *Creative Storytelling: Building Community, Changing Lives*. London: Routledge.

Using picture-books with older readers

Justine Earl

Unlike some text-types, it is perhaps necessary to argue for the use of picture-books beyond Key Stage 1/lower Key Stage 2. In my experience, it is not uncommon to encounter the assertion from some teachers and parents that fiction books containing pictures as well as text are unsuitable for Year 5 or Year 6 boys. To dismiss picture-books out of hand in this way is to deny children the opportunity to explore rich, multi-layered, challenging texts. It also fails to recognise the importance of the picture-book in a world where the complex interweaving of image and words is both commonplace and powerful.

Of course, some authors clearly have an audience of younger, emerging readers in mind for their picture-books, such as Eric Hill's *Spot* books, and we are all familiar with simple word recognition books or alphabet texts. This chapter, however, concerns itself with picture-books that are aimed at more experienced readers, that repay close reading and re-reading, and can be appreciated on many levels. In short, they are challenging texts. The challenge may, among other things, be in terms of the subject matter or theme, the symbolic representation, the layout and design, or in the way the images and text 'interanimate' (Meek 1992:176) each other.

Judith Graham (2004:1) reminds us that 'The picture book is unforgettable mental nourishment, furnishing us with images and tunes for life.'

This chapter will argue for the value of using such texts with primary children in upper Key Stage 2 and will contend that quality picture fiction is not just valuable for older primary children but is also a necessity and a joy.

The uniqueness of each picture-book author and illustrator team provides a wealth of material to be explored with children. Discussion of how readers engage with such texts reveals exciting insights into how children approach reading. The close attention that children give to challenging picture-books can tell teachers more about children as readers than was previously known. Children still struggling with decoding in Key Stage 2 can demonstrate sophisticated understandings (Graham 1990). Suddenly, less-fluent decoders can take their place as good 'readers' – exploring complex relationships between images and words and utilising higher-order reading skills in order to contribute to discussions. This is especially important when it is considered how some children may be prevented from demonstrating such understandings because of the barrier presented to them by a text which they struggle to decode. In this context, meaning-making and reflective response inevitably take second place to cracking the code of the marks on the page.

> When children are given the time they need to look at visual texts and talk, listen, draw, reflect and think about them, the results can be outstanding. When opportunities are provided to privilege visual and verbal skills, instead of concentrating on reading and writing, many children can *fly* intellectually. (Arizpe and Styles 2003: 241)

However, the picture-book is not only helpful for less-fluent readers; more able, older primary children are ready to express both personal and literary responses too (Jordan 1992). The simple fact that the whole text can be read in a short amount of time means that a great range of textual features and their impact on each other can be explored.

It is also the case that children can be 'better' readers of picture-books than adults: identifying important aspects in both images and written text, and displaying a tenacious approach to repeated readings as deeper possibilities are explored and ideas expanded. This is even more likely in the context of a community of readers, where collaboration enables creative inter-thinking. Thus the guided reading group, or literature circle (see Chapter 8), is a useful and dynamic setting for the sharing of quality, multi-layered picture-books.

One benefit of using picture-book texts to facilitate sophisticated and challenging explorations of language and literature is that it does not matter if the children are already familiar with a particular book. In fact, it can mean a deeper discussion and richer response because the book is already known. It is exciting for children, as they mature, to find new insights and reach new meanings and understandings of texts they thought they already knew well. Teachers can guide these explorations and be partners in these new discoveries.

The wholeness of texts

Since the introduction of the National Literacy Strategy (DfEE 1998) I have noticed a disturbing growth in the use of extracts during literacy sessions, particularly for older primary pupils. This has partly derived from the praiseworthy desire to analyse in some detail the literary devices and language used by real writers. Thus children are often required to study some aspect of a piece of text, perhaps in a shared or guided context, without ever seeing that extract in the context of the story as a whole. This may be because of the challenge involved in fitting the class novel into an already packed timetable (see Chapter 8). At times, use of extracts is defended as it provides a flavour of a novel which would be too challenging for many children to read in its entirety. For example, the work of Charles Dickens often appears in commercially produced schemes that provide extracts for primary schools. This practice is, in my opinion, an aesthetically dangerous one, as fine literary works are reduced to vehicles for the teaching of tiny bites of language knowledge. However, picture-books for older children become a very useful resource to help teachers overcome the problem of how to use whole texts in their literacy lessons.

The way the National Literacy Strategy Framework for Teaching (DfEE 1998) is constructed inevitably communicates a sense of incoherence. Presenting the curriculum in terms of separate strands – text-level, sentence-level and word-level (unwisely divorced from speaking and listening) – only serves to emphasise what I call the 'bittiness' of language. It is this bittiness which makes planning for literacy more challenging than some other subjects in the primary curriculum. Within each strand, seemingly discrete objectives wait patiently for a creative teacher to select them and to fit them neatly into a coherent whole – a carefully constructed unit of work. Without such careful thought and a creative, unit-based approach, single objectives can become problematic and misleading. At times their importance grows out of all proportion until the troubled teacher finds him or herself attempting to base a whole literacy session on the 'use of the comma in marking grammatical boundaries within sentences' (NLS, Year 3, Term 3).

Such 'bittiness' is compounded by the use of extracts. It is also perpetuated by some of the text-level NLS objectives that deal with certain features of fiction. For example, if children are asked to explore character profiles through reading and discussion, and then to create their own, but are never given the opportunity to consider why the writer might create such a character, the original explorations serve little purpose. What does it matter if the character has certain traits if the importance of these is not exposed through the reading of the whole text? How can children reflect upon how character links with plot, setting, themes, motives and the use of language if they do not place their character profiles into the context of a whole story?

It is the picture-fiction text that comes to our aid. The careful crafting of a complete text must be discussed and explored. In Chapter 8, Yvonne Stewart argues for the use of the whole novel at Key Stage 2. In this chapter I am championing the importance of the picture-book for older primary children, used alongside the novel and the short story (see Chapter 4). Quality, multi-layered picture-books allow a large number of complete texts to be shared and explored in a relatively short space of time. If well chosen, such texts provide the complexity, the interest and the challenge necessary for older primary children. It may be possible to encounter only one novel in each term, whereas children may interact with a significant number of whole texts in the form of picture-books. This may be through shared, guided or group reading, paired work or independent reading.

Creative combinations of words and pictures

Quality picture fiction books combine words and images in an almost magical way. The interaction of these elements presents a reality closer to the present world of children's literacy experiences than other literary texts. The multimodal nature of such texts provides rich opportunities as children explore and respond to the various roles of the written text and the images before them.

In many picture-books authors and illustrators allow the text and pictures to work in parallel – the illustrations mirroring the written word, such as in *Cow* by Malachy Doyle and Angelo Rinaldi. In others the pictures might add more detail, as do Julie Vivas's illustrations in *Wilfrid Gordon McDonald Partridge* by Mem Fox. Some go beyond the addition of detail and lead to new dimensions to the text as in Colin McNaughton's *Have You Seen Who's Just Moved In Next Door to Us.*

At times the images may contradict the text or present the reader with a seemingly unconnected context or scene. Two wonderful examples of such texts are *Come Away from the Water, Shirley* and its sister book *Time to Get Out of the Bath, Shirley* by John Burningham. The written text consists of the words of the adults in the books and is very straightforward. This is accompanied by illustrations on the left-hand pages which depict the simple actions of the adults. In contrast, the rich, colourful pictures on the right-hand page place the child as the main actor. The two sets of pictures appear to tell very different stories. Thus there is a real sense of what David Lewis terms 'indeterminacy' (2001:96). This uncertainty makes the Shirley books ripe for intellectual creative exploration by young readers. They are full of possibilities, some of which are beyond the imagination of adult readers. This will lead to rich discussions and unexpected responses.

The complex interweaving of images and words, its multimodality – which is a key aspect of current literacies and is the dominant form of texts encountered by the children of today (see Chapter 5) (Marsh and Millard 2000) – is played out on every page of each quality picture-book. As teachers we will want to take every opportunity to examine the craft of skilled picture-book creators in order to support children as they develop their critical, visual and emotional literacy skills. Exploration with children of the role of images and of the written text, whether complementary or contradictory, allows this dynamic relationship to be understood, discussed, evaluated and emulated. No other fiction genre suggested by the NLS (DfEE 1998) lends itself so perfectly to this. This is another key reason why such texts should continue to be used beyond Key Stage 1 and lower Key Stage 2. As children become more mature and experienced readers and writers, they are able to gain much from examining these multimodal texts in detail. Opportunities can be facilitated for children in Years 5, 6 and beyond to engage in rich activities that allow them to demonstrate and develop their knowledge of and responses to such texts.

Reading picture-books

The way a reader tackles a picture-book is worthy of discussion. Because the images and the words work together, the reader will glide from one to the other and back again, scanning the page as meanings are extended, questioned, interpreted and transformed (Arizpe and Styles 2003). Of course, the overall text grammar of picture-books is formed by both words and images. The layout, choice of font, overlay of images and words, together with the style and medium of the illustrations, are all part of the author/illustrator team's careful orchestration (Lewis 2001). The resulting synthesis in quality picture fiction is always creative, often playful and challenging.

Consider, for example, the use of font and image in *The Witch's Children* by Ursula Jones and Russell Ayto. In this story, the witch's children (the Eldest One, the Middle One and the Little One) visit the park. The birds and animals in the park all know that this means trouble. In this text, the presentation of both words and pictures enhances the meaning as author and illustrator use almost every visual device possible. The reader is shown a real sense of the windy day by the way the words and the pictures seem to move across the page (Figure 10.1). Different font choices are used to show how loudly the characters are shouting at the children, and the pictures of the shouting characters somehow also manage to emphasise their desperation. Capitalisation is used to good effect. No two pages are the same in terms of text and image layout. The dynamics of the text are such that sometimes the words fly diagonally across the page, or segments of text are placed with their own image. Such a book is very different to picture-books from many reading schemes where each page is often laid out in exactly the same way. The potential sophistication of interaction between words and images are, sadly, not often the priority of the planned learning of most reading schemes. It is therefore vital that pupils continue to investigate quality picture fiction as they progress as readers through the primary school.

In some picture-books the illustrations are worthy of note purely because of their stunning aesthetic quality in a particular style. For example, the illustrations of Christian Birmingham in *The Magical Bicycle* by Berlie Doherty have a distinct style and consequent impact. Other illustrators deliberately choose to create images in a range of styles (the Clarice Bean books by Lauren Child are good examples). Children can be encouraged to speculate on why particular styles and combinations have been selected. What effect does this have on the text as a whole, on the words and on the reader? Why are such decisions important? If other choices were to be made, what differences would come about? Children who are encouraged to articulate their observations about the style of image, the media selected and how pictures and words combine, are more likely to become closer critical observers and deeper thinkers about multi-layered texts in other artistic and commercial contexts within society (Buckingham 2003).

Figure 10.1

Such proficient readers are able to add to their own writing repertoire. When composing, they can call on their knowledge of typeface and layout; how to combine words, images and symbols; the effective selection of media and style and how to provide a rich reading experience for their audience. Thus the production of their composed picture fiction need not be reductive or simplistic. On the contrary, the thoughtful production of a picture-book could be the most exciting, motivating, creative, challenging publication of the child's writing career to date.

Authors and illustrators at play

One important aspect of the picture-book is that it is often playful and at times subversive. The playfulness may be in evidence in the overall style, in the interaction between words and pictures, in the selection of characters, in the twist in the tale, in the plot or in the theme. Some texts worth exploring are *The Sad Story of Veronica Who Played the Violin* by David McKee, which provides a surprise ending; *Ethel and Ernest*, in which Raymond Briggs uses his familiar comic-strip style to describe his family life; Anthony Browne's *Voices in the Park*, where the same story is told from the point of view of each of the characters; and *The Story of the Little Mole Who Knew that is was None of His Business* by Werner Holzwarth and Wolf Erlbruch.

Of course, I am not suggesting that good picture-books have always to be humorous (explore some of those listed above and you will see that immediately). Playfulness does not preclude serious and challenging issues. As children approach the end of their primary schooling they are undoubtedly old enough to appreciate the sophisticated use of playfulness in literature. They are ready and willing to try their hand at text transformation: to play with stereotypes, to subvert, to surprise. They are also ready to tackle gritty, meaningful subjects. The picture-book often provides a vehicle for accessible, relatively safe exploration of difficult subjects. These include sibling rivalry, jealousy, bereavement, anger, violence, separation, racism and environmental issues, indeed 'The very fact that picture books often provide a powerful way into such important issues . . . confirms their place as reading material for the older child' (Jordan 1992:116).

The Rabbits by John Marsden tackles the complex and emotive subject of the white invasion of Australia through its simple text and effective illustrations. In *Way Home*, by Libby Hathorn and Gregory Rogers, the main character, the boy Shane, is homeless. The reader only discovers this right at the end, which results in an immediate need to revisit the text as this realisation changes everything. The dark setting (evoked perfectly by the powerful pictures), in which one assumes the child is making his journey back to his safe, welcoming home, becomes even more menacing with the realisation that home is not what is expected. One has to read the text again with this new perspective. Children will react to this text as empathetic young readers. The text is all the more powerful as the child at its heart could be a similar age as the young readers it aims to thrill.

So within the range of picture-books ready to be introduced to our oldest primary readers is a wealth of challenging subjects. They provide a way into aspects of real life with which many children are ready to engage. They allow the opportunity for the readers to step out into other worlds and to taste experiences that are part of being human. This is even more important as they reach the end of their primary schooling and attempt to figure out their place in their world.

Reading beyond decoding

As well as offering rich themes and subjects, picture-books provide many opportunities for developing the so-called higher-order reading skills. There is often no real struggle with the decoding involved and so children are able to engage quickly in deep thought about meanings. The way that quality picture fiction operates on many levels makes it perfect for inference, deduction, analysis of narrative viewpoint and other language features – questioning, response, prediction and so on. Simplicity of written text does not necessarily mean that the book as a whole does not offer significant challenge to the upper Key Stage 2 reader. Look, for example, at *The Tunnel* by Anthony Browne. The following extract from towards the end of the story is typical in terms of level of decoding difficulty:

Just when she knew she could run no further, she came to a clearing.
There was a figure, still as stone.
It was her brother.
'Oh no!' she sobbed. 'I'm too late.'

Yet this simplicity of language belies the sophisticated nature of the text as a whole. This is a wonderful picture-book, full of sibling rivalry and family issues with which a child reader may identify. It is also packed with inter-textual references (particularly to fairy tales). But it goes even further in challenging the reader as it resonates with connections to myth and legend, making the mundane brother–sister relationship somehow grow to cosmic proportions and connect with all relationships that have existed before.

As we might expect from Anthony Browne, the pictures he provides do much more than merely illustrate the words:

> The text and illustrations keep referring back to themselves and this leads to re-readings and moving back and forth between the pages, and between the words and the pictures in order to make yet more connection between the incoming visual messages.
> (Arizpe and Styles 2003:100)

At the centre of the book is a double-page picture of the sister running through a menacing fairy tale wood. And, as in all such woods, she is undergoing transformation. This is a powerful image in the text, and rightly so as it is a key theme of the book. The extract above is at the point when Rose sees that her brother has been turned to stone. Only she can save him, and, instinctively, she knows how. The characters are changed by their experiences. It was the Year 5 children with whom I explored this text who pointed out to me that the boy abandons his ball and his sister leaves her book before they journey separately through the tunnel. These young readers realised the significance of this and through discussion we explored the idea of the ball and book as symbols of the characters. Why did the author choose to have them leave these symbols behind as they progressed through the story? In his work, Browne is a frequent user of carefully chosen symbols. An exploration of these develops children's understanding of image and metaphor.

It was also a moment of real fascination when the children working with me in guided reading realised that the author only reveals the names of both the main characters right at the end of the story. Until this point – when the accompanying picture at last shows the two children face-to-face – they are referred to as simply sister and brother. Now they are Rose and Jack. This conscious decision of the writer is something that generated real, lively discussion among the children in a guided reading group. It seems so simple and yet means a great deal. There is so much to this book that it can easily be the basis of a coherent and rich unit of work – covering aspects such as characterisation, setting, narrative perspective, links with other texts, as well as demanding that the children utilise a whole host of higher-order reading skills. The straightforward plot makes it perfect for exploring narrative structure through story mapping. Story maps are literally maps drawn by the children that set out the path of the story. A combination of words and pictures used to construct the map makes them thought-provoking pieces of work that can be made collaboratively.

Clearly, Anthony Browne is a significant author worthy of exploration at Key Stage 2. A unit of work lasting at least three weeks, if not twice that, with his picture fiction at its heart would motivate, challenge, enthral and develop older primary readers and writers. (See suggestions at the end of this chapter for texts and ideas.) As with many other quality picture fiction writers and illustrators, Browne invites readers of his books to work hard. The formation of his texts is loose enough to let the reader co-construct meaning. For example, let us return to *The Tunnel*. How or why Jack becomes stone is not explained. So there is potential for exploring this gap in the text with children. The possibilities may be investigated through drama techniques such as hot-seating, improvised dialogue or freeze-frame (see Chapter 9). Browne's illustrations constantly invite close observation, and cause laughter, questions, assertions and protests.

Gaps in texts are perfect ways into children's own compositions. Once they have acted out the possible dialogue between Jack and Rose, after he is rescued, it would be a short step to writing this conversation down. We might wonder how Rose's diary entry would read for this remarkable day, or how their mother might respond to the changed relationship of her previously isolated children. Gaps in texts also demand that readers go beyond the literal and read between the lines. Gaps allow children to predict possibilities and to interrogate the text in order to address their puzzles. This is much less necessary when the text is so tightly constructed that there is little room for the reader to contribute to the meaning-making. This is particularly true for some children's novel writers, e.g. Enid Blyton and, to some extent, J.K. Rowling.

The words in picture fiction

The interaction between words and pictures is a crucial part of picture fiction, but this does not mean that the written language is not worthy of exploration. Picture fiction provides a wealth of different linguistic styles and examples of cleverly employed language features. There are texts full of figurative language, such as *The Little Boat* by Kathy Henderson and Patrick Benson, where the sea is personified: 'the sea greets the land', 'the sea grew uneasy'. Other texts are particularly poetic or evocative, such as *The Whales' Song* by Dyan Sheldon and Gary Blythe, or are actually in the form of a poem. Some use a more informal register, perhaps to communicate something about the character or simply to employ a different tone. Picture fiction provides clear examples of a range of sentence types, of conventional and more playful uses of punctuation. Dialogue is often in evidence as is reported speech. There may be examples of dialect use.

Of course, even if the choice were made to explore the written text without the illustrations (perhaps on an overhead or through a data projector or just written out for all to access on flipchart paper) it would be wrong not to reunite text and image. After all, the words do not exist in isolation.

At times it may be relevant to share just the words or just the image in order to make a particular teaching point. However, the whole text is so easy to share in the case of picture fiction that there is no danger that the children will miss experiencing the complete work. Ask the children to visualise the possible images that might accompany the written text before sharing with them the illustrations from the book. It is fascinating to compare the range of images that the children have created to accompany the same piece of text and then to return to the illustration in the book itself.

Drawing is a form of communicative composition (Vygotsky 1978; Kress 1997) and children can demonstrate quite sophisticated knowledge of effective illustration. If they have had the opportunity to discuss rich visual texts, they can then make choices as to whether their image mirrors, enhances, contradicts or significantly develops the written word. Activities like this ensure that the primary classroom is a place where visual literacy is valued and the reading of images is developed.

Some picture fiction books for older readers contain a great deal of written text. Books such as these are more like illustrated short stories, but where the illustrations are still very important. They are still picture-books, with all that this means for the interaction between the images and the written text. An example of this sort of text is the inspirational book *Fly, Eagle, Fly! An African Tale*, retold by Christopher Gregorowski with pictures by Niki Daly. Language analysis at word, sentence and text level is just as possible in such texts as in longer novels.

Of course children can also learn much about the effective use of language by engaging with books where there is not a great deal of written text. For example, the deceptively simple book *Next Please* by Ernst Jandl and Norman Junge is set in the toy doctor's waiting room, where five very different toys are waiting for a consultation. The written text is repetitive and minimal, with no more than two lines for each page. Yet it is effective; it is the right words for the context. This is the complete text:

Five are waiting.

Door opens.
One comes out.

'Next, please.'
One goes in.

Four waiting.

Door opens.
One comes out.

'Next, please.'
One goes in.

Three waiting.

Door opens.
One comes out.

'Next, please.'
One goes in.

Two waiting.

Door opens.
One comes out.

'Next, please.'
One goes in.

One waiting.
All alone.

Door opens.
One comes out.

'Next, please.'
Last one goes in.

'Hello, young fellow, are you the last one?'
'Yes, Doctor. None waiting.'

From this text it is possible to look at various language features, such as the use and punctuation of direct speech, simple versus complex sentences or the use of the comma. But much more importantly in my opinion is the use of the right style, register and construction of language for the context, together with the magical juxtaposition of words and images.

The parallel page of each pair presents images that are crying out for the addition of thought and speech bubbles. The longer the toy characters have to wait the more the suspense grows. What is going through each toy's mind as they wait their turn to see the doctor? What might they talk about? Will they tell each other the stories of their injuries? Then there is the missing plot-line happening behind the doctor's closed door. This text is perfect for discussion of simultaneous events – plot and sub-plot. It is so easy to examine this aspect of fiction writing within the context of such a simple book. What treatment is each toy receiving while the others wait? Are repairs possible? What is the conversation between doctor and toy? Perhaps we discover how the accident happened. This might be a very different version of events from the recounts in the waiting room! Children who are able to write their own longer version of this picture-book are demonstrating their level of engagement with and understanding of the text as a whole. They are reading beyond the literal written word and they are showing a real understanding of how quality picture-books work. *Next Please* works perfectly as a stimulus for the creation of a play.

It is the pictures that animate the toys and suggest their various characteristics to the reader. For this text, asking children to attempt character profiles for the toys would be a useful and meaningful activity. Successful completion of such a task would only really be possible after quality discussion of the text in a shared or guided group and after a range of talk-based as well as written activities. It would be helpful to precede the creation of the profiles with drama and role-play which would be so easy to set up for this text. Just a reconstruction of the front cover illustration, with added dialogue, would reveal the children's thoughts about this book.

Of course, an in-depth exploration of a simple text like *Next Please* also equips Key Stage 2 children to become effective reading buddies with younger children. They are then well prepared to scaffold younger readers as they tackle texts like this together. This is just one benefit of working with multi-layered picture fiction texts. Many appeal to a great range of ages and are perfect for this beneficial pairing of readers from different key stages.

Children as picture-book authors and illustrators

When constructing a unit of work for literacy, it is helpful to identify the possible end-product which the children will work towards. Of course, this can be in a range of forms: an oral presentation, a piece of drama, a poster or display, a written piece, a class anthology, an individual book and so on. The beauty of asking children to work towards the publication of a picture-book is that it is challenging yet achievable. The time available for the unit will dictate the type of picture

Figure 10.2

fiction text that it will be possible to complete, but other than that the choices will be all the children's.

The quality picture fiction that is available covers a great range of genres and subjects: real life, fantasy, humour, traditional tales, historical, biography, to list just a few. There are also beautiful and powerful texts from a range of cultures. So teachers have at their disposal a huge number of texts to act as models or stimuli for children's own compositions. An aspect of the book can be harnessed as a frame for children to use and to structure their own story around (as the child did who read *Snow White in New York* by Fiona French and wrote her own picture-book which re-invented Snow White as a 'surf chick' and began 'Once upon a surf time'). Or perhaps the interaction between the words and the pictures is the stimulus for the child's own composition. As this chapter has aimed to illustrate, tackled properly, the publication of a picture fiction text is so much more than merely writing the words and then drawing an accompanying picture.

It is possible to work closely with children as they develop their ability to read words and pictures together. They will begin to be able to comment on the narrative importance of the images as well as the words. Quality picture fiction allows them to discover the interpretative aspects of the genre and to spot references embedded in the pictures that have been carefully created to illustrate the written text. Young readers are able to understand that the words change the meaning of the pictures and the pictures impact on the meaning of the words (Nodelman 1988). Thus their own picture fiction texts will reflect their sophisticated knowledge of this wonderful genre. Of course, this is only possible if the planned units of work allow immersion in the texts; careful exploration of a range of quality texts; rich, talk-based experiences; shared and group activities; and time to develop their own thoughts, responses and preferences.

A real understanding of the way that picture fiction works leads to new possibilities in children's compositions. They are free to play with typeface, picture size, overall layout, page shape and loose construction of text. They can select the genre they wish to tackle as well as integrate a range of language features. They can think about inclusion of dialogue, lists, labels, instructions, use of non-standard English and exclamations. They will be creating truly mulitmodal texts. It is true that, as yet, it is unlikely that such texts will be part of the Standard Assessment Tests at the end of Key Stage 2 (although, promisingly, QCA has collaborated with the United Kingdom Literacy Association to produce the booklet *More than Words: Multimodal Texts in the Classroom*, 2004). The fact that children may not be required to produce such texts for SATs will not prevent teachers focusing on them. Teachers know that writing for SATs is not related at all to being a real writer.

It would be an interesting activity to pair children into author and illustrator teams. The collaboration would need to start at the very beginning of composition. It would not be a simple case of the author handing the finished product to the illustrator, but a creative partnership. The dynamic relationship between the words and pictures would need to be discussed and the team would agree on their approach – whether the two would mirror each other, enhance, extend or contradict. The style of the language and of the pictures needs consideration.

An author focus: Anthony Browne

Children in upper Key Stage 2 would benefit enormously from experiencing a literacy unit based on the picture-books of Anthony Browne. His books are always rich and multi-layered. He is a master of intertextuality, and readers of all ages delight in looking carefully at the images, returning to the words and back to the images again. Narrative is very important and both words and images drive the story. In an interview, Browne spoke about creating words and pictures simultaneously: 'at its best they go together. I don't write the story first. Some other illustrators do. But it's more like a film.' (From an interview with Anthony Browne in Arizpe and Styles 2003:206.)

Browne's illustrations have a surreal quality and children enjoy speculating on why he has chosen to include certain images. This is definitely the case in the texts *Through the Magic Mirror* and *The Visitors Who Came to Stay*. The latter book deals with changes to family life when Katy's father 'brought home a new friend. Katy and her dad weren't alone anymore.' The written text is very direct, telling the reader how Katy is feeling. The images are a mixture of the literal and the bizarre, reflecting the confusion that Katy, and no doubt the other characters, feels.

The theme of transformations continues in another of Browne's books, *Changes*. This deals directly with a boy's thoughts and fears as the arrival of a new baby in the family approaches. So the theme of the family would be a useful focus for exploration through his books. In *Piggybook*, Browne shows a mother who does all the work in the family until she can take no more. She writes a note to tell her husband and sons that they are pigs and leaves them to fend for themselves. As in *Changes*, Browne illustrates the transformations that occur in the story by creating images that are literally changing from one thing to another: the kettle which is becoming a cat, the armchair that looks like a gorilla, hands that are becoming pigs' trotters.

Another book, *Gorilla*, deals with the loneliness of an only child in a one-parent family (once again, a daughter with her father); and *Zoo*, although obviously examining the issue of animals in captivity, also looks at the family unit and the various interactions between family members. The acts of the humans are placed carefully next to the almost non-activity of the miserable animals.

Voices in the Park deals with two very different families. Two parents, two children and two dogs visit the park. Here Browne emphasises the contrasts between the families with very different illustrations of the same visit, even selecting a different font for each voice: the girl Smudge, the boy Charles, Charles's mother and Smudge's father. Each perspective is unique. So this text is perfect for exploring narrative viewpoint. Exploration of the symbols in the pictures enhances children's understanding of the characters and their lives. Each section of the book is a soliloquy. The children can be the characters, sharing their thoughts. It would be helpful to use the technique of 'role on the wall' to develop this sense of character. Draw round one of the children or an adult to represent a character and then fill the person-shaped space with possible dialogue or words that evoke that character. Acting in role, children can be hot-seated so that we can discover more about the characters. Children can unite the characters and replay the book in role, showing all the perspectives in one piece of drama. I would like to challenge the children to create a soundtrack or musical theme for each section of the text. How would they manage to communicate the characters through music?

Links with the National Literacy Strategy

Unfortunately, there is a distinct lack of explicit reference to the possibilities provided by using quality picture fiction with any age of readers in the National Literacy Srategy (DfEE 1998). As Graham points out, 'we see no great emphasis on picture books as the start of thinking, critical response and literacy understandings ... There are no suggestions for how we can work with a composite text' (Graham 2004: 2).

Despite the lack of clear focus on picture-books, there are many National Literacy Strategy objectives throughout Key Stage 2 that can be applied to picture fiction and addressed. Objectives concerning the features of fiction, like characterisation, plot, structure and setting, and those objectives concerned with reading skills and experiences can all be addressed perfectly with picture fiction.

Conclusion

This chapter has argued for the use of quality picture-books with older primary children. Teachers will want to consider which of the picture fiction texts in their collections really do support imaginative and creative responses. They will want to introduce children to texts that provide mental and emotional stimulation and can embed themselves in these young readers' literary memories.

Such texts are rich in so many ways; they are multi-layered, multimodal and they ooze intertextuality. They have a quality of satisfying 'wholeness', which means that readers not only engage quickly with a complete text but also that they begin to realise that every choice made by the author and illustrator matters.

Picture fiction texts of real quality provide a challenge to readers of all ages, including our oldest and our most able. Whether the challenge lies in the subject matter, the use of literary devices, the style, the interaction of words and images or the loose construction of the text as a whole, the older primary reader will gain much from experiencing these stories. Such texts provoke exciting responses, real interest and fascination in children. I would be incredulous if anyone would suggest that the superb picture-books like *The Day I Swapped My Dad for Two Goldfish* and *The Wolves in the Walls* by Neil Gaiman and David McKean do not provide sufficiently challenging material for Years 5 and 6. In fact, these texts would probably be best met in this part of Key Stage 2. They are unique in their approach to the genre and speak directly to the child reader.

Not only will experiences with quality picture fiction result in language development, deep thought and extended understanding of texts and life, but they will also be exciting and enjoyable for children and their teachers. Therefore, picture-books should be honoured, and not reduced to mere vehicles for the achievement of objectives. The books should not be seen as 'good for' 'shared reading', but rather as worthy of collaborative exploration. Teachers who are open to the possibilities of quality picture fiction books will welcome them into the classrooms, book corners and libraries of Upper Key Stage 2, and not leave them behind in Key Stage 1.

Children's books referred to in this chapter (in order of mention)

Malachy Doyle and Angelo Rinaldi, (2002). *Cow.* Simon and Schuster.

Mem Fox and Julie Vivas, (1987). *Wilfrid Gordon McDonald Partridge.* Puffin Books.

Colin McNaughton, (1991). *Have You Seen Who's Just Moved In Next Door to Us.* Walker Books.

John Burningham, (1977). *Come Away from the Water, Shirley.* Jonathan Cape.

John Burningham, (1978). *Time to Get Out of the Bath, Shirley.* Jonathan Cape.

Ursula Jones and Russell Ayto, (2001). *The Witch's Children.* Orchard Books.

Berlie Doherty and Christian Birmingham, (1996). *The Magical Bicycle.* Picture Lions.

David McKee, (1988). *The Sad Story of Veronica Who Played the Violin.* Red Fox.

Raymond Briggs, (1998). *Ethel and Ernest.* Jonathan Cape.

Werner Holzwarth and Wolf Erlbruch, (1994). *The Story of the Little Mole Who Knew that is was None of His Business.* David Bennett Books.

John Marsden, (1998). *Rabbits* (illustrated by Shaun Tann). Lothian Books.

Libby Hathorn and Gregory Rogers, (1994). *Way Home.* Andersen Press.

Anthony Browne, (1989). *The Tunnel.* MacRae.

Kathy Henderson and Patrick Benson, (1995). *The Little Boat.* Walker Books.

Dyan Sheldon and Gary Blythe, (1990). *The Whales' Song.* Hutchinson Children's Books.

Christopher Gregorowski and Niki Daly, (2000). *Fly, Eagle, Fly! An African Tale.* Tafelberg Publishers.

Ernst Jandl and Norman Junge, (2001). *Next Please.* Hutchinson Children's Books.

Fiona French, (1986). *Snow White in New York.* Hamilton.

Neil Gaiman and Dave McKean, (2004). *The Day I Swapped My Dad for Two Goldfish.* Bloomsbury.

Neil Gaiman and Dave McKean, (2004). *The Wolves in the Walls.* Bloomsbury.

Some recommended books by Anthony Browne

Changes, (1990). MacRae.

Gorilla, (1983). MacRae.

Piggybook, (1986). MacRae.

Through the Magic Mirror, (1976). Oxford University Press.

The Tunnel, (1989). MacRae.

The Visitors Who Came to Stay, (1984). Hamish Hamilton.

Voices in the Park, (1998). Doubleday.

Zoo, (1992). MacRae.

References

Arizpe, E. and Styles, M. (2003) *Children Reading Pictures: Interpreting Visual Texts*. London: RoutledgeFalmer.

Browne, A. (1996) *Voices in the Park*. London: Doubleday.

Buckingham, D. (2003) *Media Education: Literacy, Learning and Contemporary Culture*. Cambridge: Polity Press.

DfEE (1998) *National Literacy Strategy*. London: DfEE.

Graham, J. (1990) *Pictures on a Page*. Sheffield: National Association of the Teachers of English.

Graham, L (2003) *Writing Journals*. Royston: UKLA.

Graham, J (2004) *Cracking Good Picture Books*. Sheffield: National Association of the Teachers of English.

Jordan, B. (1992) 'Good for any age – picture books and the experienced reader', in Styles, M., Bearne, E. and Watson V. (eds) *After Alice*. London: Cassell.

Kress, G. (1997) *Before Writing: Rethinking the Paths to Literacy*. London: Routledge.

Lewis, D. (2001) *Reading Contemporary Picturebooks: Picturing Text*. London: RoutledgeFalmer.

Marsh, J. and Millard, E. (2000) *Literacy and Popular Culture: Using Children's Culture in the Classroom*. London: Paul Chapman Publishing.

Meek, M. (1992) 'Children reading – now', in Styles, M., Bearne, E. and Watson, V. (eds) *After Alice*. London: Cassell.

Nodelman, P. (1988) *Words about Pictures: The Narrative Art of Children's Picture Books*. Georgia: University of Georgia Press.

QCA and UKLA (2004) *More than Words: Multimodal Texts in the Classroom*. London: QCA.

Vygotsky, L. S. (1978) *Mind in Society: The Development of Higher Psychological Processes*. Cambridge, MA: Harvard University Press.

Long ago, in a galaxy far away . . .

Hazel Bryan

. . . there existed strange peoples, with curious customs and bizarre rituals. Yet, interestingly, the travellers aboard the *Millennium Falcon* had little trouble coexisting with their fellow galactic citizens. The socio-cultural, pluralist society in which our children and we exist presents us, frequently, with peoples, customs and rituals that are, perhaps, strange and new to us. How then are we, as teachers, to understand our role in relation to this complex society we inhabit? What are our moral duties with respect to the children in our classrooms? It has been argued that:

> Parents and society in general are surely right to expect teachers to try to foster and reinforce those basic moral and social rules and/or dispositions of honesty, fairness, courtesy, tolerance and respect for others presupposed to civilised interpersonal association – irrespective of the peculiarities of personal belief. (Carr 2003 : 134)

Carr reminds us that our classrooms are microcosms of society. As such, teachers have an obligation to understand their role in a holistic, organic sense with an emphasis on developing the whole child. What, then, does this mean for us, as teachers of English? It means, I believe, that we should embrace a broad view of the purpose of literacy, harnessing its power to provide stimulating, thought-provoking learning experiences. Historically, there have been shifts in emphasis upon the use of English, from the hierarchical, fixed tradition of English presented by Arnold, Newbolt and Leavis (where English was presented as the vehicle through which a national identity could be fostered) to Britton (who sought to promote the actual life experiences of pupils, placing them, rather than the text, at the heart of the learning experience). The visions of English within each of these paradigms are developed around a clear epistemology and embody a particular political perspective. Each version of English views the purpose of English differently; each version has a different approach to subject knowledge and each version places both the teacher and the learner differently in relation to the subject. As such, English, culture and identity are inextricably linked (Marshall 2000). But what of our culture and identity today? Within the colourful, pluralist context of British society, what might the role of the English teacher be? It has been suggested that 'Teachers and schools exercise influence not only upon the thoughts and minds of students, but also on their wider development as persons. In an important sense, education shapes persons and their lives' (McLaughlin 2000 : 112). No small undertaking then! But what of those inter-galactic travellers we considered earlier? How might an in-depth study of their experiences throughout the universe help us to shape the thoughts and minds of the children in our classrooms? This chapter argues that science fiction is the perfect vehicle through which young imaginations can be set alight, moral dilemmas can be explored and the question of what it is to be human can be perfectly contextualised. The chapter offers, initially, a definition of science fiction, exploring the essence of this genre. The chapter then moves to a brief history, from early fantasy stories, through American pulp fiction to the blockbusters of today's box-office hits. Key themes and icons of the genre are then explored in the context of children's texts. Finally, a suggested unit of work is offered. This unit has been written with the aim of exploring science fiction in the primary classroom with the theme of 'cross-curricular work' woven through it. We know that 'Children learn best when they are excited and engaged' (DfES 2003); this unit of work aims to embrace children's interests and to offer a rich, cross-curricular experience where 'curiosity, fascination and mobility of thought' (Brice Heath and Wolf, 2004 : 13) are foregrounded.

Towards a definition of science fiction

Science fiction as a genre is, traditionally, difficult to define. There are multiple interpretations, and children and adults alike will have reader expectations, probably including images of the future, encounters with previously unknown life forms – possibly featuring advanced technology, robots, spaceships and so on. Science fiction has always been closely interwoven with fantasy, and this, too, will necessarily inform reader expectations. By drawing upon other story elements and tropes at will, science fiction freely weaves mystery, romance and horror into one text. Take, for example, the film text of *Superman* – there is mystery surrounding the character of Clark Kent, romance between Superman and Lois Lane and tension in the menacing figure of Lex Luther. If science fiction borrows so freely from other genres, what is it that drives the narrative? What might we identify, along with the children in our classroom, that is somehow the essence of science fiction? It has been suggested that a *'sense of wonder* is the emotional heart of science fiction' (Mendlesohn 2003 : 3), and it is precisely this that is the impulse that drives the narrative. This notion of a sense of wonder is helpfully broken down by David Nye into two dimensions: a sense of wonder at the beauty of natural phenomena and at technological advances.

From the genesis of the genre (mid-1920s America), storylines were developed around two keystones – either the discovery of a new world, or a new invention.

These central elements necessarily drove the narrative, and as such, words that expressed a sense of wonder (amazing, fantastic, awe-inspiring) became synonymous with science fiction. This is where, from a child's point of view, the imagination can be allowed to run riot. The sheer pleasure of imagining and creating worlds or inventions lends itself to a descriptive utopia. As a writer, the child must provide the reader with enough information to inhabit the new world, or visualise the invention, and as such, 'the reading of a science fiction story is always an active process of translation' (Jones 2003 : 5). To counter the temptation to see the writing of science fiction as an 'info-dump', we might encourage children to think of the process as 'accompanying the characters on a voyage of discovery' (Attebery 2003 : 33), where 'info-dumps' can be reconceptualised as detective's clues. Immersion in the genre, then, in terms of the creation of a new world or invention, will fire the imagination and give rise to original ideas and, in particular, expressive vocabulary. Indeed, Broderick (2003 : 59) reminds us of the 'sheer luminosity of metaphor that had always worked at a dreamlike level in classic science fiction'. However, wonderful inventions and new worlds will necessarily have *consequences* for humankind. It is this 'What if?' question that is central to science fiction, transforming it into speculative fiction.

The discourse of science fiction is centred on humankind in relation to the world, or universe (Mendlesohn 2003). Great events, Mendlesohn argues (such as Moon landings or wars) and great ideas (such as immortality or alien contact) are central themes, 'for science fiction is perhaps the last real bastion of Romantic fiction: science fiction protagonists fall in love with the macrocosm' (p. 9). Think of the way Spiderman resists the relationship with Mary-Jane, putting the safety of the world and the struggle with the Green Goblin before personal happiness; or how Superman is constantly called from an encounter with Lois Lane to save the universe from the wicked deeds of Lex Luther. It is in the troubled person of Anakin Skywalker, in the *Star Wars* films, that these 'rules' are explored and challenged. Not content to follow strict Jedi codes, Anakin wants it all, and begins a forbidden relationship with Princess Amidala, resulting in the birth of Luke Skywalker and Princess Leia. Anakin, of course, doomed from birth, transforms into Darth Vader, and is ultimately, and ironically, brought down by his own children in an epic struggle of good versus evil.

As polysemic discourse, science fiction is invaluable in the rich canon of primary texts, speaking to children in different ways, valuable for exploring a range of relevant themes such as gender, equal opportunity and racism. The fluidity of science fiction is central to both its appeal and relevance in the classroom.

The genesis of science fiction

Offering children a range of science fiction texts (books, comics, films) and asking them to define key features is an excellent starting point for discussion. Children should be offered opportunities to consider what the term 'science fiction' means. The imaginary voyage, a fantastical journey, appears to contain the first seeds of science fiction, although technology is subservient in early texts to religious, social or political themes. Texts such as Swift's *Gulliver's Travels* (1726), embody this emergent genre. The work of Copernicus resulted in questions about the nature of the solar system, the place of man within it and speculation about life, in particular on the Moon. While children may not be familiar with scientific pioneers, the process of working through such a question is thought-provoking – what must it have been like in centuries past, with little knowledge about other planets. Of course, science fiction narrative devices were inhibited before the development of scientific invention and, as such, magical imagery was employed. The story of the Arabian Nights is one such example. Fantastical journeys around, and deep inside, an unknown Earth, of course, became more problematic as *terra incognita* disappeared as a result of man's discoveries. Thus, the combination of technological, scientific invention and, therefore, terminology and understanding, and an increasingly known Earth, caused humankind to look to the greater universe – how satisfying it is, then, for children to work this out in speculative discussion.

A variation on this theme was alien beings travelling to Earth and, eventually, humankind travelling into the future as a result of technology rather than in a dream. H.G. Wells's time machine (1895) generated boundless possibilities. It is often argued that British science fiction had its genesis in the Gothic text *Frankenstein*, by Mary Shelley, where the device used (a doomed central creation bringing about the demise of its creator) became well established (Stableford 2003). The moral implications within this tale are far-reaching, the 'so-whatness' or consequences having much relevance in our lives today. Moral fables developed within science fiction early on; again, one can look to Wells's *War of the Worlds* (1898) as a seminal text within which the reader is presented with realistic, moral dilemmas.

Early in the twentieth century, a very cheap and poor quality paper that was inexpensive to produce was used in large quantities; hence the development of pulp magazines or pulp fiction, which made zesty, colourful science fiction easily accessible to the public. I wonder how many of our children have ever considered the history of the comics they read? Although science fiction also appeared in books, cinema and radio, magazines were really the vehicles through which this distinctive style of fiction emerged. It has been argued that science fiction is not only a specific dimension of storytelling but also 'a niche for writers . . . a collection of visual images and a community of like-minded individuals' (Attebery 2003 : 32). How wonderful, then, for the writers and artists in our classrooms to feel they belong to a community exploring and contributing to science fiction.

The year 1977 saw the dynamic translation of science fiction, an often marginal mode of fiction, to an enormous stage, with the release of the films *Star Wars* and *Close Encounters of the Third Kind*. Female heroes, political issues, questions of morality and race are presented within these film texts. In this sense, science fiction holds a mirror to our values as humans and enables us to look in on ourselves from another perspective. What is it to be human in the bar on the planet where the *Millennium Falcon* lands, in *Star Wars*, where beings from other galaxies come together? What are the unwritten rules of etiquette, race or gender in such a place? Within this colourful, galactic context, children can begin to develop a sense of understanding around these issues. Since 1977, mainstream science fiction (or space opera as it is sometimes known) has become part of popular culture, particularly cinema and television texts, with children's favourites such as *Men in Black* and *Jurassic Park* becoming box-office hits. The appetite for science fiction among young people, it seems, is ever-increasing.

Themes and icons

Science fiction texts employ icons to signal to the reader that they are entering a new world, distinctly different from their own (Jones 2003). A sharing of traditional science fiction icons, perhaps during shared time, would be a good starting point in the classroom. Icons would include, for example, space vessels, clothing, equipment, robots, weapons and food. The children's familiarity with these icons can be discussed. As an introduction to the concept of science fiction icons, a shared reading of a film text, with discussion of the key icons, would enable children to familiarise themselves with the central features of this genre. As writers, children will then be in a position to embark upon their own writing journey with the tools of the trade at their fingertips.

A keystone of science fiction writing is the futuristic setting. This, too, would be a good starting point for imaginative, speculative classroom discussion, as it is within this setting that alien life forms' rituals and customs exist. It is here that a sense of wonder can be articulated – this futuristic setting might contain images of sleek technology or descriptions of other galaxies.

Another science fiction icon is *spectacle*. Spectacle within science fiction films is traditionally given a high profile. Consider the images of *King Kong*, where narrative is suspended in order to provide the viewer with opportunity to savour the scenes; *Jurassic Park*, where dynamic special effects inspire a sense of wonder; or *Star Wars*, where the bleak blandness of desert and space require the viewer to consider themselves in relation to the universe. Within the classroom, children should be given opportunities to consider and discuss spectacle within science fiction films: the effect, for example, of the images at the beginning of *Superman* (with Christopher Reeve), where the familiar, everyday bustle of the *Daily Planet* is set against stunning, futuristic scenes and awe-inspiring music. In contrast to this celebration of special effects and their impact, children should be introduced to critical reading of film text. Does, for example, the breathtaking spectacle in science fiction films detract from the development of characters or narrative? Take

Dr Who or *Men in Black* as examples: is the development of character or plot lost at the expense of breathtaking effects?

The rocket, 'an inevitable symbol of energy and escape' (Jones 2003 : 164), is an early icon which, while having the capacity to take mankind into space, is somewhat limited. The spaceship, on the other hand, has the capacity to function as a complete system, supporting hundreds of life forms. In this way, children can become the designers of a contained world within a spaceship, creating customs, jobs and social networks. Thus the spaceship with its socio-cultural pluralism becomes the 'norm' (take, for example, the starship *Enterprise* in *Star Trek*), and anything outside of the spaceship can be understood as 'alien'. (However, the film *Alien* famously employed a different device, where the threat came from *within* the spaceship. Although this film is unsuitable for use in the primary classroom, the device is one worth sharing with your writers.) When spaceships become safe havens, space 'stations' become colourful gathering places, vibrant bazaars where all life forms encounter each other. The bar scene in *Star Wars*, after Hans Solo has landed the *Millennium Falcon*, is one such example, which provides rich material for classroom discussion about the rules of etiquette that might govern such a place. How would one conduct oneself in this bar? What would the children do? Why do we need to know about codes of conduct anyway?

Robots, of course, are a favourite icon in children's science fiction. Who can fail to be amused by R2D2 and C3PO? Children may, of course, enjoy simply designing their own robots. On the other hand, the storm troopers within *Star Wars* are the enemy; the film *I, Robot* casts Will Smith against a destructive thinking machine, and the daleks are the last word in lethal contraptions. Robots, therefore, whether good or bad, often represent an underclass. When this underclass begins to think for itself, trouble lies ahead. It would be interesting to ask the children if *they* felt that R2D2 or C3PO were equals. If not, why not, and how should they be treated? What might be the galactic rights of the robot? Children could discuss and draw up a convention. This will, of course, give rise to disagreement and conflict. Setting up a 'Moral Maize' scenario – where children take on roles to question witnesses, stakeholders and experts to form conclusions – would provide children with a forum to question, present and explore issues of rights and equality.

Hero figures are key icons in science fiction texts, as indeed they are in other genres. Traditionally, the hero figure has been male, with a damsel somewhere in the background. However, it is often not the relationship between the hero and damsel that is foregrounded in science fiction but rather the 'idea', a dynamic couple battling together against the universe. This can be seen in *King Kong*, *Superman*, *Flash Gordon* and *Spiderman*, where a sense of wonder is created by the 'idea' (such as a giant ape), and the hero and damsel are merely the vehicles through which this 'idea' is presented and explored. Female heroines began to take centre-stage following Princess Leia's example in *Star Wars*. Since then, strong female characters, like Lara Croft, have become part of popular culture. The contrast to the hero figure is the alienated villain, usually a potential genius with a big ego, facing a hostile existence, such as Anakin Skywalker or the Green Goblin. With astounding powers, these characters have the potential to do great good, but a fatal flaw in their make-up drives them to the 'dark side'.

These are the key science fiction icons that can be explored in class. In addition to knowledge about icons, children will need to have a sense of science fiction *themes*. This will empower children to read texts in a more sophisticated fashion and to shape their own writing accordingly. It would be interesting to challenge the children to classify the science fiction texts they have encountered to date. By way of a start, Bould (2003) suggests the following possible themes:

Monster movies (*Jurassic Park, King Kong, Teenage Mutant Ninja Turtles, Planet of the Apes*);
Science fiction texts that celebrate the white heat of technology (*Stingray, Captain Scarlet and the Mysterons, Thunderbirds*);
Ethical dilemmas (*Aquilla, Dr Who, Star Trek, Star Wars*);
Surgical science fiction (*Frankenstein*);
Interplanetary adventures (*Flash Gordon*).

These, then, are the key icons and themes around which science fiction texts are built. We know that in story 'the world of struggle, conflict, doubt, ingenuity, desire and frustration is depicted' (Claxton 2001 : 137). Within science fiction, the evocative possibilities of space and the future add an exciting dimension, one that can fire the imagination. Children, we know, 'are engaged by learning that develops and stretches them and excites their imagination' (DfES 2003:9), and science fiction, I would argue, is the perfect vehicle through which this can be achieved.

Suggested unit of work (using a cross-curricular approach) for Key Stage 2

Science fiction, as explained above, can be classified into themes (ethical dilemmas, monster movies, a celebration of technology, interplanetary adventures). One approach to the selection of the text-type would be to spend a given period of time exploring chosen themes. This unit of work is developed over three weeks. The aim is to spend week 1 introducing children to the concept of science fiction, to embrace the images and icons of science fiction that are 'out there'. Week 2 is dedicated to using science fiction to explore ethical dilemmas. In this sense, week 2 becomes rather more inward-looking, using science fiction as the vehicle through which moral issues can be considered. Week 3 takes this self-reflection a step further, providing multisensory experiences which, it is hoped, will inspire personal responses to the idea of space.

Week 1: immersion in the genre

The classroom

This week involves the children being treated to an explosive immersion in the genre in general. You should aim to celebrate all things science fiction, thereby really whetting the children's appetites. It would be wise to saturate children in visual science fiction images from the beginning of the week. Thinking back to the icons introduced earlier in the chapter, you should aim to display classic images (spaceships, science fiction heroes and heroines, diagrams of the solar system and posters of *Jurassic Park*, *Men in Black* or other science fiction texts) around the classroom.

Watch *Superman* (original Christopher Reeve version). In particular, spend time watching the opening scenes of *Metropolis* and the futuristic images. Discuss the impact on the viewer of the style of *Metropolis* – what information is the viewer given? What is the impact of the way in which the camera takes the viewer into space? What is the use of time in these scenes? Try watching these scenes without the music. Discuss the impact of the amazingly evocative images. What are the science fiction icons in the opening scenes? Then listen to the music without the images. How does this music make you feel? What are the images that come into your head when you listen to this music? Does it sound like any other music you know? Can you suggest other music that might work with these opening scenes? After deconstructing these elements of the opening scenes, watch them again with the children to consider the way in which atmosphere is built using both sound and vision.

Read *Aquilla*, by Andrew Norris. This text should be read by the teacher to the class for sheer pleasure this week, perhaps before or after lunch and/or at the end of the day. It will be revisited in week 2.

Explore the icons of science fiction with your children. This might involve an initial discussion of what science fiction means to them. What, for example, do they feel is the difference between science fiction and fantasy?

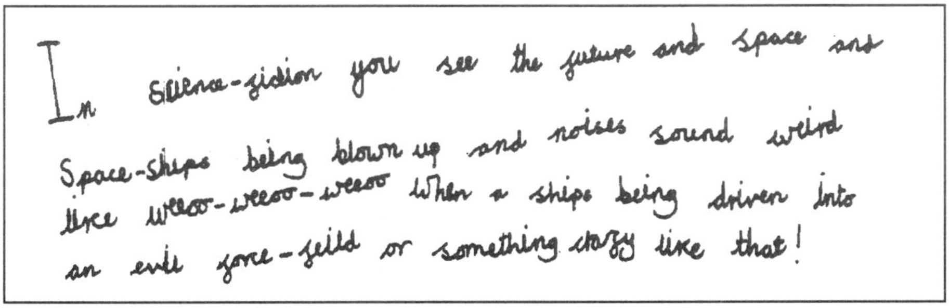

In science-fiction you see the future and space and space-ships being blown up and noises sound weird like weeo-weeoo-weeoo when a ships being driven into an evil force-feild or something crazy like that!

Figure 11.1

What do the children think are the classic icons of science fiction? This could be explored in either shared, guided or independent work, depending on the children. You may wish to simply ask children to write images they feel are important, as the child in Figure 11.2 has done. Alternatively, you could allow children to create a large, dynamic collage of science fiction images.

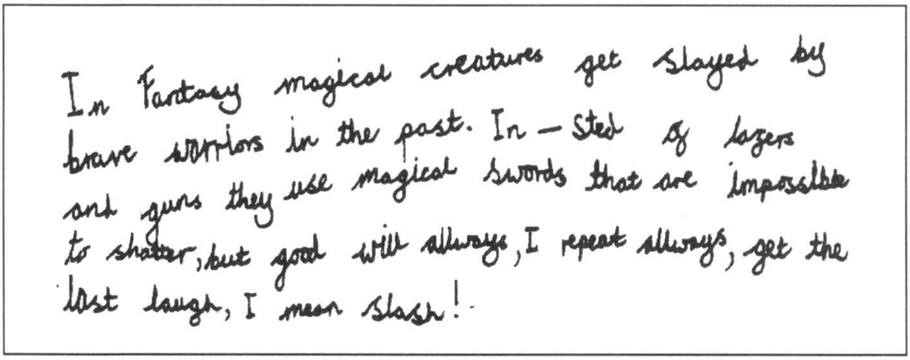
In Fantasy magical creatures get slayed by brave worriors in the past. In-sted of lazers and guns they use magical swords that are impossible to shatter, but good will allways, I repeat allways, get the last laugh, I mean slash!

Figure 11.2

You may wish to provide children with the opportunity to make papier-mâché planets that they paint and name, finally suspending them from the classroom ceiling and thereby creating a new solar system within which tales of epic adventure may be spun.

Your class may receive a strange letter one day, sent by an inhabitant of one of the planets hanging from your classroom ceiling. Aggressors, who have destroyed the homes of the friendly aliens have overcome the planet, and one of them has contacted your class to ask if the children will help rebuild their homes. If the children agree, they must become alien-home architects. There are rules that govern the design of alien dwellings. Each dwelling is constructed of four cubes. Only the faces are allowed to touch. Children may be given four multi-link cubes each, to start with, to design their alien home. They may design a tower block, a bungalow or something in between. Once this has been designed, children should draw up architect's plans showing all four perspectives and a bird's-eye view, using squared paper and coloured pencils. Children should then allow others to attempt to construct their alien home using their architect plan. When this has been achieved, nets may be drawn up and, eventually, larger alien homes may be built. These may be tiled (how much will it cost to tile a tower or a bungalow?). The tiles must be made from tessellating shapes. How much will it cost to put windows in the homes? Do the designs of the homes influence the cost? Children may wish to display the costings as bills to be sent to the aliens. If you have room in your classroom you may wish to actually create an alien town. Children could write to the aliens informing them of their progress. Aliens could write back, sending postcards of their home.

Week 2: ethical dilemmas in science fiction

Activity 1

Watch the *Star Wars* video during shared reading. This text shows Anakin Skywalker as a child being presented to the Jedi Council as a potential Jedi knight. Clearly, there are issues around Anakin's appointment as a Jedi. His application, while supported by one knight, is opposed by others on account of his 'test results'. Create a Jedi Council in your classroom. The aim, through role-play, is to emulate the council scenes from the film, but with original reasons for supporting or rejecting Anakin. You will need to give children plenty of time to consider their positions and statements. You may, in discussion before this activity, ask children to decide whether they are for or against Anakin's appointment. It would be possible to then create writing teams, to work on their case. Alternatively, this could be done during guided writing, where you are able to provide rather more support. Once the cases have been prepared, you should allow children time to practise in role. You may wish to make an event of this, and allow children time to compose suitable music (perhaps a fanfare or drum roll) to signify the opening of the Jedi Council. After the Council has presented all cases you could allow a small team of children to leave the room to consider a verdict. The verdict should then be read out. A follow-up activity, either through discussion or writing, could entail a consideration of the consequences of each action.

Activity 2

Using the same *Star Wars* video, watch the scene where Anakin attempts, in vain, to save his mother from death at the hands of her captors. Anakin's response to her death is extreme. Discuss with the children his actions. What are the ethical dimensions to his actions? Can one feel compassion for Anakin? Are there any grounds for his actions? Children should be allowed, in small groups, time to discuss their thoughts and feelings. This could take place in guided reading. From here, a guided writing session could provide children with an opportunity to write a statement each, depending on their opinion, about whether Anakin should feel ashamed of his actions, or justified in what he has done. This can then be followed up with a role-play session where, through a conscience alley (see Chapter 9), Anakin must walk through a line of children, each giving him the 'for and against' argument for his actions. Anakin, at the end of the line, must reflect on his actions and take a position.

Activity 3

Revisit *Aquilla*, by Andrew Norris. This text will have been read for pleasure last week. During a shared time you could revisit the text, stopping to consider the following questions: What would you do if your friend fell down a hole in such circumstances? What would you do if you fell down that hole? How would you get out? (no mobile phones!). What would you do if you discovered the Roman spaceship? What should the boys have done? Do you agree with their actions? Imagine you did have a mobile phone, but you could only use it to send a text message. Write out the message you would send.

Activity 4

In Design Technology, set children the challenge of creating a cockpit for the spaceship that has flashing lights. You might want to ask the children to draw their designs first, paying attention to previously unknown technology and terminology. Ask children to look carefully at adverts on television and in magazines for new cars, in preparation for this task. Some children might like to extend this work into designing adverts for this Roman spaceship when it was new.

Week 3

By now, children in your class will have been excited and inspired by many dynamic activities. They will have been well and truly immersed in the genre. It is now time to change the tempo, to develop a quieter, more reflective approach to science fiction. Ask the children to create lightscapes that reflect space. Light, we are told, 'is one of the great emotive components of our aesthetic perception' (Ceppi and Zini 2001 : 46). Provide the children with opportunities to explore the effect of shapes (plastic bottles, cotton reels, string) on the OHP. Colour will be a given dimension if the plastic bottles are coloured. If not, coloured transparencies will provide fascinating potential. Shadow, too, is evocative as it can be 'diaphanous, almost spectral, or very dense, perfectly ordered, or chaotic; fragmented or compact' (ibid.). Children should be encouraged to explore the effect of light and shadow around the school. This could give rise to art work or descriptive writing. You may wish to extend this work to consider prisms from a scientific perspective.

The next step in developing sensory awareness to enhance children's thoughts about space might be the consideration of texture. The aim here is to allow children to encounter the school environment, exploring the myriad textures around them. Encourage the children to record these textures using a digital camera which could then be used as a catalyst for other work, or using words with pictures to describe their findings. This work can all be displayed. The tactile qualities discovered around the school could be recorded under themes such as 'rough', 'soft' and so on, with wonderful vocabulary under each heading. The third step in sensitising pupils to the world around them, in order to help them imagine 'otherness', is to focus on the sense of smell. You may wish to provide things for children to smell in class (flowers, scented candles, coffee, polish), but also allow them to go on a 'scent trail' of the school and to reflect upon their favourite smells. Finally, the fourth step is 'conscious listening' (ibid.: 90) where children should be awakened to acoustic geography and different soundscapes in and around the school. We are in danger, we are warned, of losing the 'consciousness of listening' (ibid.: 91). The soundscape of space is an essential element in this work.

We are reminded that 'people learn through imagination, and as they do so, they cultivate imagination as a learning tool' (Claxton 2001:284). These deeply reflective and creative experiences will provide a basis for children to compose a piece of work that, for them, reflects their thoughts about space. This could be a coloured light composition using the OHP, a sketch of fascinating textures, with perhaps accompanying words, or a piece of music inspired by the sounds around the school. These compositions could be presented to other children. During this deeply reflective week you may want to read a contrasting science fiction text to your class. Terry Pratchett's *Diggers* is to be recommended. Magnificently light-hearted, this text can be read for sheer pleasure, or as a springboard into writing.

To sum up this unit of work, Week 1 opens with a dynamic saturation in the themes, icons and images of science fiction. The aim in this first week is to inspire children, to find out what science fiction means to them and to offer a range of learning experiences that are science fiction-related. Week 2 takes the theme of 'ethical dilemmas' in science fiction, providing children with complex moral issues to ponder. By Week 3 the aim is to focus still more closely, to use multisensory exploration to inform a personal 'space' composition. The design of this unit of work represents an attempt to, first, excite children, to locate them within a genre and equip them with tools to read and write science fiction texts. From there the aim has been, through science fiction, to challenge and provoke moral responses to complex issues. Finally, the aim has been to facilitate a deeply personal response to the nature of space and us in relation to it.

Science fiction, we are told 'is that set of stories . . . which *argues* the world; which argues the *case* of the world' (Clute 2003:78). The aim of this chapter has been to demystify science fiction, to reveal why science fiction texts are invaluable in the canon of primary literature. As readers and writers of science fiction texts, children encounter the big questions of the universe and ourselves in relation to that universe.

References

Attebery, B. (2003) 'The magazine era: 1926–1960', in James, E. and Mendlesohn, F. (eds) *The Cambridge Companion to Science Fiction*. Cambridge: Cambridge University Press.

Bould, M. (2003) 'Film and television', in James, E. and Mendlesohn, F. (eds) *The Cambridge Companion to Science Fiction*. Cambridge: Cambridge University Press.

Brice Heath, S. and Wolf, S. (2004) *Visual Learning in the Community School*. London: Creative Partnerships.

Broderick, D. (2003) 'New wave and backwash', in James, E. and Mendlesohn, F. (eds) *The Cambridge Companion to Science Fiction*. Cambridge: Cambridge University Press.

Carr, D. (2000) *Professionalism and Ethics in Teaching*. London: Routledge.

Ceppi, G. and Zini, M. (eds) (2001) *Children, Spaces, Relations*. Reggio Emilia, Italy: Reggio Children.

Claxton, G. (2001) *Wise Up*. Stafford: Network Educational Press.

Clute, J. (2003) 'Science fiction from 1980 to the present', in James, E. and Mendlesohn, F. (eds) *The Cambridge Companion to Science Fiction*. Cambridge: Cambridge University Press.

DfES (2003) *Excellence and Enjoyment*. Nottingham: DfES Publications.

Jones, G. (2003) 'The icons of science fiction', in James, E. and Mendlesohn, F. (eds) *The Cambridge Companion to Science Fiction*. Cambridge: Cambridge University Press.

Marshall, B. (2000) 'A rough guide to English teachers' *English in Education*, **34**(1), Spring. NATE

McLaughlin, T. (2000) 'Values in Education', in Beck, J. and Earl, M. (eds) *Key Issues in Secondary Education*. London: Cassell.

Mendlesohn, F. (2003) 'Introduction: reading science fiction', in James, E. and Mendlesohn, F. (eds) *Cambridge Guide to Science Fiction*. Cambridge: Cambridge University Press.

Stableford, B. (2003) 'Science fiction before the genre', in James, E. and Mendlesohn, F. (eds) *The Cambridge Companion to Science Fiction*. Cambridge: Cambridge University Press.

Index

After a page number, 'f.' indicates a figure, or figure and text.